HOKKAIDO

Misawa

Ishikari R.
Daisetsuzan N.P.
poro
nitose airport
aoi
etsu

JAPAN AIR LINES

Sendai

N

S

JAPAN ALPS

HONSHU

L. Chuzenji
Nikko

Gifu
Nagoya

Fuji-Hakone
N.P.
Mt. Fuji
Odawara
Atami

Izu
Peninsula

Tokyo

Yokohama
Kamakura

Tateyama

Pearl Is.
Kashikojima
o Bay

Oshima Is.

ALL THE BEST IN JAPAN
With Manila, Hong Kong
and Macao

Karl H. V. Berthold
2425 Tracy Place, N.W.
Washington, D. C.

All the Best in Japan
with Manila, Hong Kong and Macao

SYDNEY CLARK

All the Best in
Japan
with Manila, Hong Kong and Macao

With Illustrations and Maps

DODD, MEAD & COMPANY
NEW YORK   1959

Published April, 1958
Second Printing, May, 1958
Third Printing, June, 1959

LIBRARY OF CONGRESS CATALOG CARD NUMBER: 58-8290

PRINTED IN THE UNITED STATES OF AMERICA

LATE NOTES 1959/60

Please note the following important changes of address: The New York offices of the *Japan Tourist Association* and the *Japan Travel Bureau* (page 6), formerly at 10 and 9, respectively, Rockefeller Plaza, are now both at 45 Rockefeller Plaza, which is the International Building. The JTA is in a street-floor office of this building, with direct entrance at 11 West 50th Street, while the JTB is on an upper floor, in Suite 1961. The JTA office is no longer in the charge of "Kim" Kimura, who returned to Tokyo to take over important promotional work there, but is directed by an able successor, Yoji Enomoto. The *Hong Kong Tourist Association* (page 246) has changed its headquarters office from Victoria to: No. 1 East Wing, Peninsula Hotel, Kowloon, Hong Kong. An Information Office is open on the nearby Star Ferry Pier. The Association has been directed ever since its inception by Major H. F. Stanley.

Japan's current advance in all basic ways, certainly including the promotion of foreign tourism, is phenomenal, more or less matching that of West Germany, and in the field of tourism this is the more remarkable since Japan had virtually no prewar experience. Except for Tokyo's Imperial Hotel, a veteran now enjoying its second youth, and a handful of lesser Western-style hotels in such cities as Yokohama, Kyoto, Osaka and Kobe, there was nothing prior to World War II that could be called preparation for Western tourists. Today, there are 106 fully modern Western hotels in Japan, many of them very large, plus 172 ryokans, or Japanese inns (pages 52-56) that are specially registered with the government as being suitable for the use of foreign visitors.

Good hotels are only one facet, though assuredly the most important, of Japan's new tourist industry. Other facets, such as new thermal establishments, new restaurants and coffee houses in wide variety, new nightclubs in dazzling array, new theaters, from those that offer glittering girlie revues to traditional kabuki theaters—one of this type costing nearly 3 million dollars recently opened in Osaka—new and newer department stores, new luxury trains, new airports and air services and new tours and touring means are encountered everywhere, and in Tokyo, now undeniably the world's largest city, ambitious novelties are continually being unveiled. The most spectacular of these capital features, built in less than 18 months and completed as 1958 gave way to 1959, is the—

Tokyo Tower. This "unified TV and Radio Tower, with Modern Science Museum" is the world's tallest tower, though not the world's tallest building, which honor still goes to New York's Empire State Building. The Tokyo Tower, built by Japanese designers and engineers from Japanese materials, is 1092 feet high, surpassing the Eiffel Tower by about 90 feet. Its chief function is to serve as a multi-purpose broadcasting station for television and radio programs, but for the delectation of visitors, Japanese and foreign, there are two large observation platforms. The first, at a height of 390 feet and with a "deck space" of 16,000 square feet, is reached by means of three elevators, each carrying 23 passengers. The Tower is open daily from 9 A.M. to 9 P.M. and admission costs only 120 yen, hardly over a quarter of a dollar. The second observation platform, also reached, of course, by elevator, is at the 738-foot level and provides a comprehensive panoramic view not only of Greater Tokyo, numbering, with its immediate environs nearly 16 million inhabitants, but Tokyo Bay, Yokohama, Fujiyama, the long Izu Peninsula (page 155) and, on clear days, even the ranges of the North and South Japan Alps. At the Tower's base is a *Modern Science Museum* of four floors and basement. The basement contains much machinery and technical equipment, the first and second floors contain a restaurant, various offices and a shopping arcade, while the third and fourth floors constitute the museum itself, which is given over to the display of the latest electronic devices, with many working models. A primary purpose of these exhibits, as of up-to-date science museums in the Western world, is to show their practical relationship to everyday living in a "gadget world" such as ours and this must make Japanese beholders more eager than ever to stock their homes, especially the kitchens, with the services and appliances long familiar in American homes. The Tokyo Tower was financed, and is operated, by the Nippon Television City Corporation and some 20,000 to 50,000 persons pay admission each day to enter it. Big Tokyo does things in a big way.

* * *

Now for some details of "What's New" in the tourist world of Tokyo and the provinces.

Hotels in Tokyo

The *Imperial Hotel* (pages 45-49) opened its new building in the summer of 1958, adding 450 new rooms, including 50 suites, which brought its total to over 900 rooms, all with private bath. In the newest part, which looms behind and high above the original structure designed by Frank Lloyd Wright yet does not damage the artistic symmetry of that famous building, is a new main dining room called the *Phoenix Room* and another restaurant called the *Imperial Viking*, which specializes in smörgåsbord. (This name has replaced "Copenhagen Room," mentioned on page 48 as the name originally planned.) The Imperial "complex" includes, in all, six dining rooms, several bars, a café terrace, a grand banquet hall, a roof garden, a theater and a 350-car garage. It is unquestionably the most famous hotel in the Orient, as well as the largest.

Six other new Tokyo hotels and large annexes are now nearing completion or are already opened, as follows:

Aviation Hotel, now nearing completion, is an 11-story, 112-room structure at Ginza-Nishi, 8-chome built and owned by the Japan Air Lines Hotel Company. An announced special feature is a roof garden where barbecue dinners in Oriental style are to be served.

Dai-ichi Hotel Annex is nowhere near the parent Dai-ichi Hotel (page 50) but in Shiba Park, well to the southwest. It is to have 650 Western-style rooms.

Shiba Park Hotel Annex will be built adjacent to its parent hotel (page 51), but its opening is not scheduled for the immediate future.

Hotel New Japan is at Akasaka, southwest of the moated Imperial Castle. It is expected to open soon, but full statistics are not yet available.

Hotel Toshi Center, in the central Chiyoda Ward, opened in the spring of 1959. Of its 55 rooms, 41 are Western-style, 14 Japanese-style.

Ginza Tokyu Hotel, in the area of Tokyo's main stem, is a large one of over 400 rooms due for opening before the end of 1960.

New Hotels Not in Tokyo

Nine new hotels, all of them now open, call for mention, as follows:

Silk Hotel, completed in the spring of 1959, is an interesting 81-room specialty occupying the 6th, 7th and 8th floors of Yokohama's huge *Silk Center Building* in the former British area of the city, a structure which was six years building. The edifice houses a restaurant, a tearoom, a coffee shop, a silk exchange, silk exhibition rooms and, of special visitor-interest, a *Silk Museum* on the 3rd floor.

Osaka Grand Hotel (page 176) is one of Japan's newer big-city hotels, with 361 Western-style rooms, and 7 Japanese-style. This ultra-modern hostelry is centrally heated and air-conditioned and has its own underground garage.

Oiso Hotel, on Sagami Bay half way between Yokohama and the resort town of Atami (pages 153-55), is a charming seashore inn with 41 rooms, some Western, some Japanese, and 5 separate cottages. The inn has six fresh-water swimming pools; one of them 330 feet by 165, and near it is an 18-hole golf course.

Hotel Kowakien (53 Western rooms, 112 Japanese) is a resort hotel opened in 1959 in *Fuji-Hakone National Park*, near the famous Fujiya Hotel, described on pages 150-51. This is the newest addition to the holiday facilities of this lovely mountain-and-lake region.

Seizan Hotel (45 Western rooms, 27 Japanese) is at Karuizawa, a lovely summer resort over 3000 feet above sea level 88 miles by rail northwest of Tokyo. It is in a nest of older but good resort hotels and is near a popular golf course.

Kinugawa-onsen Hotel, accommodating nearly 600 guests, is a Japanese-type thermal hotel opened in 1958 at the Kinugawa Spa, near Nikko. It has 30 Western-style rooms but only three of them have private bath. I include it here because of its size and because it offers a good opportunity to Western visitors who would like to try "going Japanese" in a new hot-springs ryokan.

Hotel Toden Kaikan (15 Western rooms, 7 Japanese) is a city hotel in the heart of Kochi (page 183), a port on the southern shore of Shikoku Island. It is of considerable tourist importance in that it makes touring on this lovely island more practicable for Westerners than it has been.

Korura Station Hotel and *Kirishima Kogen Hotel* are two new hostelries in far-southwestern Kyushu Island, located respectively at Kokura, just across the Shimonoseki Strait and at Iino, on the Ebino Plateau in the south-central part of the island.

The hotels named above in Tokyo and the various prefectures of Japan are but forerunners of at least ten more new ones planned for the early future; and to stimulate "young travel"—U.S. students take notice—the Japanese government plans the erection of about a hundred *youth hostels* at appropriate points throughout the four main islands.

Among hotels that have notably enlarged their accommodations in the last year or two are Kyoto's hillside *Miyako Hotel* (page 166); Osaka's *International Fair Hotel* (neglected in the text but now richly worth mentioning for its 126 modern air-conditioned rooms and baths); Kashikojima's *Shima Kanko Hotel* (page 136), near Mikimoto's Pearl Farm; and the very high-grade *Kawana Hotel* (page 155), a resort inn on the Ito Peninsula, with two of the finest golf courses in the Orient close by.

* * *

Transportation

Air travel is of ever-increasing importance in the development of Oriental tourism, as is evidenced by the strenuous competition of leading systems of world-wide range to secure franchises for various routes and landing privileges at various airports, notably Tokyo's busy Haneda Airport. BOAC and Northwest Orient Airlines, for a single example, have been engaged in a long tug-of-war, the former to secure an extension to Tokyo of its San Francisco–Hong Kong route, the latter to prevent this new threat of competition. KLM and Air France, both of which I neglected to mention with other lines on page 6 of the text, are playing increasingly important roles in Pacific travel. As soon as the eight jet planes now on order are delivered KLM will reduce its polar route time, Amsterdam to Tokyo via Anchorage, to a mere 15 hours. Air France, in addition to its own services from Paris to Hong Kong and Tokyo by the southern route and to Tokyo by the fast polar route, has a major interest in the development of TAI (*Transports Aériens Intercontinentaux*), a new French luxury airline serving the South Pacific.

Pan American Airways (pages 4-6) continues to play its key role in the Oriental scheme of things and has emphasized its faith in the future of Japan tourism by opening a new office in Tokyo, conspicuously placed close to the Imperial Moat. With a ceiling-to-floor glass front and many eye-catching new features in its design, it is one of the most modern airline offices anywhere, and this is appropriate to the times, for its opening precedes by only a few months the coming into transpacific service of PAA's huge jet liners built to cruise at almost 600 miles per hour, bringing San Francisco within 10 or 11 hours of Tokyo.

Japan Air Lines (pages 6-7) continues to advance steadily both in its transpacific and Japanese services. In 1959, direct services Los Angeles–Tokyo and Seattle–Tokyo were added to the San Francisco–Tokyo route. JAL, like the other big systems, has jet planes on order, four of them at present, which will provide 25 seats in first class and 90 in tourist. Japanese designers are sitting up nights working on specialties of interior comfort and décor.

Sea travel for the leisurely will be enhanced by the construction of two giant luxury liners by and for NYK (Nippon Yusen Kaisha; pages 9-10). These will be 22,000-ton vessels with a speed of 25 knots and a passenger capacity of 150 in first class and 800 in tourist, tying Kobe and Yokohama to San Francisco and Los Angeles in a matter of 11 or 12 days. Their launching and their entrance into service will be events to watch for, probably in 1962.

Rail service in Japan is being advanced by the introduction of *additional* de luxe name trains traveling at high speed between major centers, as described on pages 138-39. The *Asakaze* (Morning Breeze), speeding between Tokyo and Kyushu Island, is an air-conditioned blue-and-cream-colored super-express of 13 coaches, with sleeping compartments in second class. The *Kodama* (Echo), which is the Blitz train between Tokyo and Osaka-Kobe mentioned on page 139, is a handsome 8-coach affair, streamlined and air-conditioned. All seats in the second-class coaches are equipped with ear-phone radios, which can be of real interest to the Western tourist as well as to Japanese travelers.

An ambitious plan was launched in the spring of 1959 to construct, over a period of six years, a new broad-gauge trunk line between Tokyo and Osaka, enabling luxury expresses, the world's fastest, to cover the distance, some 450 miles, in—they say—3 hours, meaning a maintained speed of 150 miles an hour! That speed is hard to believe, but we'll wait and see. The whole project is estimated to cost $340,000,000.

Highway construction is Japan's biggest challenge and, so far, her biggest transportation deficiency, but things are happening in this field too. A new national route connecting the Pacific Ocean and the Japan Sea was opened in 1959 through the completion of a short but difficult link called the Mikuni Highway in the Gumma Prefecture north of Tokyo. A 5-mile toll road has recently been opened in Kyoto leading up to the summit of Mt. Hiei (2782 feet), which is reached also by two cable lines ascending from different points. On the mountain's crest, in a cypress grove, is a structure of great historical and religious importance, the *Enryakuji Temple*, which should certainly have been included in the tabulation of Kyoto's temples given on pages 170-72. This temple was founded in 788; destroyed by Oda Nobunaga (page 33) in the 16th century; restored a few decades later by Hideyoshi Toyotomi (page 69) and greatly enlarged by Tokugawa Iemitsu (page 70) in the 17th century. If you have had your fill of Buddhist temples and Shinto shrines in the over-rich historic atmosphere of Kyoto you will, at any rate, revel in the wonderful prospect from the mountaintop, which includes not only the city and its environs but vast reaches of countryside and, at the mountain's very base, the blue waters of Japan's largest body of fresh water, *Lake Biwa*, whose area of 261 square miles makes it a little larger than Lake Geneva. Like its Swiss counterpart, Lake Biwa is served by good-sized steamers. Some of these make lake circuits in about 7 hours, while others make special scenic trips, in 5½ hours, to selected points called the "Eight Views."

In connection with the comment on Kyoto's mountaintop temple I should state that in the city's *Nijo Castle* (page 169) three rooms are now being interestingly restored as "stage settings." Life-size mannequins in the costumes of feudal times are conspicuous and one room is restored as a Reception Room of a shogun, with the shogun himself seated on a throne while feudal lords in ceremonial costumes surround him in deferential attitudes.

* * *

The *entertainment world* of Japan was given a big fillip by the recent opening of the great new kabuki theater, briefly mentioned above, in Osaka. Although this has a very satisfying Japanese look in its general exterior design, it is comfortably Western in its seating arrangements inside, with almost 2000 seats suited to Western derrières, these being supplemented by only 16 matted sections for any Japanese who find more comfort in sitting cross-legged on the floor. The mechanical workings of the stage for changes of scenery are quite as modern as any in America or Europe, featuring what is called a "slide-wagon system" of operating a large lift (50 feet by 12½) that can be easily subdivided into three smaller lifts. For the comfort of patrons there are two sets of escalators from the ground floor clear up to the third balcony and for the comfort of the inner man, and woman, there is a 400-guest dining room, plus a great array of special restaurants.

Perhaps the following item should not "properly" be included under the head of entertainment, or the lack of it, but I must mention that on April 1, 1958, as discussed on page 130, all of the so-called "gay quarters" in Japanese cities, meaning red light districts, including Tokyo's famous Yoshiwara area, were indeed closed down. Perhaps the red lights did not turn to blue, as many predicted, but the girls did go on the streets in great numbers, as virtually everyone predicted. To quote a dispatch printed in *The New York Times*, "Statistics show that commercial vice, previously restricted largely to licensed quarters, has spread to other neighborhoods in both large and small cities. Many girls who left the brothels to continue their profession on the streets regard the standard fine [often under $10] as a sort of business tax which they are reconciled to paying." But one excellent result has come of the law, as all agree, namely that impoverished parents now have no open marketplaces where they may sell their unwanted daughters to brothel owners, as was formerly the widespread custom.

*　　*　　*

Hong Kong shares the tourist surge of Japan and the whole Pacific area. Nearly 2000 new hotel rooms are to be added to the Colony's accommodations during the next couple of years, the most conspicuous newcomer being named, like Tokyo's leader, *Hotel Imperial*. New local touring ideas are also in operation, notably an aerial tour which takes its passengers over Hong Kong Island, Kowloon and parts of the New Territories. Still more glamorous is a "de luxe junk tour"—the term is not paradoxical in this case—that is announced for early inception. "A magnificent junk specially fitted with great comfort," to quote the announcement, will make cruises of several hours duration in the fascinating waters of Hong Kong, always replete with Oriental and Western shipping of just about every conceivable nature and origin. Supporting these fixed tours are extended opportunities for personal touring by car both on the island and in the New Territories. Two new roads of special scenic interest are almost ready to be opened.

A further evidence of Hong Kong's advance on all fronts is a magnificent new *City Hall* now to be built over a period of about two years. It will have concert halls, an art gallery, convention facilities and other big-city features.

Hong Kong's tourist importance in the PATA picture (pages 3-4) is emphasized by its forehandedness in preparing for the Jet Age. Well before the coming of the first jets the runways of its Kai Tak Airport were enlarged to permit the easy landing and take-off of the largest planes of this type fully loaded.

* * *

Macao, Portugal's tiny (6 square miles) colony on offshore islands of China, near Canton, shares, in a small way, the tourist prosperity of its big neighbor Hong Kong, but it wisely makes no great effort to compete with larger centers. A visit to Macao (pages 271-84) is the perfect "extra dividend" of a Hong Kong week or fortnight. Its Portuguese atmosphere and language, blended with the basic civilization of Old China, makes it "exotic-plus" and no one who reaches the British Crown Colony should fail to make the 4-hour steamer trip to it, staying, if possible, for at least one night. The hotel situation is still about the same as described in the text and H. Nolasco and Company is still the leading purveyor of local tours. Efforts are at present being made by the Nolasco firm and the Colony's very able governor to publicize Macao more widely as a "meeting place of East and West."

* * *

Manila and the Philippines in general are displaying a lot of tourist initiative and this is certainly warranted, for the republic's more than 7000 islands have, indeed, much to offer. In *festivals*, especially, it almost rivals Japan and you will notice that many travel agencies tend to sell Philippine travel on a fiesta basis. Of the major festival seasons—most of these popular outbreaks of emotion last several or many days—a few call for special emphasis and special consideration on the tourist's "planning board."

Holy Week and Easter celebrations are a reflection of those in Spain, from which the islanders draw much of their culture as well as their religion. Solemn processions in costume occur every day.

The *Month of May* is an almost continuous festival, two favorite themes inspiring it being *Flores de Mayo* (Flowers of May) and the *Santa Cruz de Mayo*, an elaborate month-long religious-secular pageant. This *Santacruzan*, as the latter is also called, is essentially a re-creation of the pilgrimage to the Holy Land by Empress Helena, the mother of Constantine, in search of the True Cross. It builds up from a simple start early in the month to a tremendous climax at the end, when the Empress, played by a beautiful Filipina dressed in jeweled gown and glittering crown, makes her journey accompanied by her imperial son and surrounded by many symbolic and mythological characters.

September sees *fluvial festivals* all over the Philippines, with the most elaborate "floating floats" competing in lavish displays as they drift gently or rapidly down the leading rivers.

Christmas festivities (pages 241-42) last 22 days, from December 16th to January 6th, which is Three Kings Day, or Epiphany.

This is the *gayest* of all the fiesta periods, sunlit by day, lantern-lit by night.

Hotels of Manila are still led, in a big and brilliant way, by the enlarged (700 rooms with the new addition) *Hotel Manila*, which is still directed by Cielito (Little Heaven) Zamora (pages 218-19). The newest hotel, however, is the first-class, air-conditioned, 104-room *Mabuhay*, the name being a Filipino word that corresponds to the Hawaiian Aloha. The Mabuhay is on a well-known shopping thoroughfare, Mabini Street, in the Ermita District, but its upper-floor rooms have a fine view of Manila Bay, including its famous sunsets.

An important tourist goal of Manila is the new *Manila Cathedral*, which was consecrated in December, 1958, replacing the one that was destroyed in World War II during the liberation of the city. This edifice is the fifth that has stood on the same exact site within the old Walled City (Intramuros). On special occasions the cathedral is illuminated with a "complete profile" of electric lights, from its portals to its lofty tower and the cross atop its dome.

The Philippine Travel and Tourist Association, long directed by Modesto Farolan, expects to receive up to 100,000 visitors annually when the Jet Age gets into its full sweep and it is doing its energetic best to provide new tourist attractions and conveniences. Four of the most important of these are: A gradual restoration of the *Intramuros* area; a cable car to join *Tagaytay Ridge* (pages 232-33) with the Taal Volcano in Taal Lake; a quick ferry service between Manila and *Corregidor* (pages 233-34); and a new short-cut road between *Baguio* (pages 234-36), the summer diplomatic capital, and the *Ifugao Rice Terraces*, a famous sight which has hitherto been rather difficult of access. For the less immediate future, meaning perhaps two or three years hence, a luxury inter-island passenger liner is promised and an extension of the Manila Railroad's lines, south to Sorsogan and north to Cazayan. More power, we say, to the planners for our pleasure!

A FOREWORD ON SELECTION

THIS book is chiefly on Japan but three other areas are added and the reader will likely ask, "Why those three? Why *only* those three?"

I have two specific answers. First, the Philippines, Hong Kong and Macao add three widely various touches of spice. The Philippine Republic has its Spanish background but American customs are prevalent and our "American" language, perhaps to your great surprise, is the Philippine national language, the language of education and business. Hong Kong, redolent of China but with a veneer of Britain, is, as everyone knows, one of the most fascinating places on earth. And Macao is China with a flavor of Portugal. Japan itself, the main subject of this book, has developed within me an affection I shall always cherish. One gradually becomes "addicted" to the Japanese people, diminutive in stature but great in personal charm and with a courtesy that is neither calculating nor obsequious.

My second specific answer to your question is simple and of very practical appeal. *You need no special inoculations for any of these places*, but only the usual smallpox vaccination certificate required by your own U.S. Health Department for re-entry into the United States from any direction. Now this, believe me, is of top importance. Anyone who has ever waded through the tedium, the delay, the personal inconvenience and the very considerable expense of typhus and typhoid and cholera and yellow fever shots, some of which must be repeated at intervals of a week or ten days, will heartily corroborate this.

You may go to the places covered in this book exactly as you would go to England or France, though some very cautious persons do take certain of the shots for extra protection. I don't.

I went on these entire journeys of research with only my passport and my familiar International Vaccination Certificate. Had I pushed this book's research farther, to Singapore, Bangkok, Indonesia, Burma, I would have run head-on into the stern and bothersome inoculation requirements.

CONTENTS

Illustrations follow page 70.

THE BACKGROUND OF THE PICTURE

YOURSELF IN THE PICTURE OF TOKYO

YOURSELF IN THE PICTURE OF MANILA

YOURSELF IN THE PICTURE OF HONG KONG

THE FOREGROUND OF THE PICTURE

CHAPTER 1

THE ORIENT BY AIR AND SEA

See PATA *First*

FOR all who travel to and in the Orient a big head start may be gained by taking off from San Francisco. Why? Because in that city, at 153 Kearny Street, is the *Pacific Travel Center*, with the head office of PATA, meaning *Pacific Area Travel Association*. There you may secure a lot of information and sound advice, along with a double handful of pamphlets and brochures about the areas you will visit, and with them the concise *Pacific Area Travel Handbook*, an illustrated annual about all the Pacific lands. This handbook costs only a dollar and can save you from many a costly false move and travel headache. Personally, I cannot imagine setting out for any part of the Pacific, whether to the areas covered by this book or to more distant places, from Thailand to New Zealand, without dropping in at the PATA headquarters to "chew it over."

PATA was first envisioned by Lorrin Thurston, publisher of the *Honolulu Advertiser*. When it was hardly more than a dream Bill Mullahey, Pan American Airways' director for the Central and South Pacific, put the impetus of his driving personality into it to make the dream a reality. Sam N. Mercer, now an executive of the American President Lines, became its director and nursed its infancy into robust youth and maturity. He was succeeded in 1957 by George M. Turner, who ably carries on PATA traditions as the director of its varied activities. The publicity chief is a spirited young woman named Miss Lee Tyler, whose title and gender I mention so that you won't address her, for advance in-

3

formation, as Mister Tyler. These people are your "accomplices before the fact" and can help you a lot.

A separate and equally helpful *Philippine Travel Information Office*, directed by Miss Cita Trinidad, is located in the same building, 153 Kearny Street.

Pacific Patterns of "Pan Am"

The various hop-skip-and-jump journeys necessary for researching the material for this volume were made by Pan American Airways and since the Pacific pioneering by this company, carried on over the past quarter century, constitutes one of America's typical business romances a few words of review seem in order.

Pan Am, as everyone knows, is Pan World in its scope, as in its full name, Pan American World Airways, with strands of its immense web reaching to almost every point on earth that is of interest to tourism or international business. Not the least intricate of its patterns is that which ties a dozen or more Pacific ports of call to our West Coast ports of Los Angeles, San Francisco, Portland and Seattle, with Honolulu as a Polynesian Half Way Halt, where a stopover may be made without formalities, Hawaii being part of America. By a new Great Circle Route across the Pacific PAA is now initiating a *direct, non-stop service* from the California cities to Tokyo and perhaps soon these flights will be made from Portland and Seattle as well. This shortens the transpacific flight by several hours.

The four areas covered in this book may be visited in a sort of trapezium pattern, in clockwise or counterclockwise order according to personal choice and seasons. Speaking generally, the clockwise order, visiting the Philippines first then working north, is recommendable if you go in the spring and the opposite order if you go in the fall. In summer, the weather is rather too hot in Japan, much too hot in Hong Kong and Macao and sizzling hot in the Philippines. June is a traditionally rainy month in Japan, but weather can be as quixotic there as in New England. Winter is to be avoided in Japan, especially if you plan, as certainly you should, to make some stays in Japanese inns. Central heating is a rarity in them and they'll be *cold*.

Pan American made its pioneer appearance in Pacific skies as a scheduled commercial carrier in 1935, when its flying boat service of the so-called China Clippers was inaugurated between Oakland and Pearl Harbor, generating intense popular excitement since this overseas leap was 540 miles greater than any that had previously been undertaken as a regular public service in any part of the world. A year or two later, the China Clippers justified their name by extending their service to China, then a free nation, the terminal being a lagoon just off Macao, the Portuguese enclave that is to be presented near the end of this book. Soon after World War II, long-range land planes were introduced into the transpacific service and the sea base in Macao was abandoned. In 1952, Pan Am's *westbound* flying time was sharply reduced by pioneering work in the introduction of very high-altitude flying (of course with cabins pressurized to low altitudes) to take advantage of the Pacific jet stream, a steady and powerful air current that flows from west to east in the air's upper reaches throughout the winter months. This novel development prepared the way for the longest scheduled non-stop flights in the history of aviation, between Tokyo and Honolulu.

All the above advances have been but steps toward greater speed, for the Age of the Jets lies immediately ahead, an era that will bring Japan within *nine hours* of California. The avalanche of jet-plane orders by the big air transport systems of the world commenced when Pan Am staked 269 million dollars on its faith in this newest advance by ordering a fleet of 45 Boeing and Douglas jets. I have gotten vicarious thrills by talking with persons who have enjoyed trial flights on these new craft and their excitement is contagious. The planes will carry over 100 passengers in first class or 125 to 130 in tourist class. Vibration is wholly eliminated and even sound is scarcely audible within the plane.

Competition in services to the Orient is strong, for in addition

to those of PAA, three other companies, Japan Air Lines (see
below), Northwest Orient Airlines (teaming with TWA for
round-the-world flights) and Canadian Pacific Airlines (teaming
with BOAC and Qantas), all operate first-rate services to Japan,
and almost every major European network now serves Tokyo.
Scandinavian Airlines System even has its vaunted and exciting
Polar Route from Copenhagen, but PAA remains the Giant of the
Pacific. Its growth has not brought callousness to its concern for
thrift, for it has strenuously promoted its budget-saving "Rainbow" services of tourist class along with its "President" services
of first, with choice of staterooms, berths or merely the full
stretch-out seats fancifully glamorized by the name Sleeperette.
The use of Rainbow services on the whole diagram of this book's
travel, if I may be personal, saved me *four hundred dollars* and
can save you the same. In tourist class you're somewhat more
crowded (*if* the plane happens to be full), you can't stretch out
so flat for sleep and your meals are merely adequate instead of
a series of banquets, with free drinks *ad libitum*, but maybe you'll
think twice before laying out an extra $400 for these comforts.
Of course the Go Now, Pay Later Plan, which PAA has long
promoted, is available for either first or tourist class payments
and it has proved immensely popular, though many vacationists
shudder at the idea of paying in deferred installments "after the
fun is over." In this, as in so many other problems of life, there
are two schools of thought.

Pan Am's world guide called *New Horizons* should certainly
be mentioned here, and not in parenthetical vein, for it has chapters on Japan, Hong Kong (with Macao) and the Philippines,
each of which may be had in separate pamphlet form.

The Wings of New Japan

The words of the above heading are boldly painted on all the
planes of Japan Air Lines' intercontinental services and they
tell their story of Japan's amazing postwar resurgence. The American take-off point for this company's long leap across the sea is

San Francisco, and, as with other lines, Honolulu is a halting point. The wings of Nippon then soar to Tokyo, with a halt at Wake, and continue deeper into the Orient, from Tokyo to Hong Kong and Bangkok.

Domestic services of JAL can be of prime importance to those who follow the program of this book, or any major part of it, for they cover Japan's three largest islands, Honshu, Kyushu and Hokkaido, with several daily flights, the ports of call, besides Tokyo, being respectively Osaka, Fukuoka and Sapporo. (There is also a regular service between Tokyo and Okinawa.) Japan, like Chile, is shaped something like a string bean or a pea pod, though it is not so tenuous as this sounds, being 170 miles wide at its widest point. Its length from northeast to southwest is 1300 miles, which is about the same as from Boston to Miami, so you will see how welcome a relief plane travel can be in breaking up long stretches by rail or road. Honshu and Kyushu, by the way, are connected by a railway tunnel under the Shimonoseki Straits and a parallel road tunnel is now under construction, but surface transportation for such distances takes a lot of time and to reach the capital of Hokkaido without taking to the air one must make a long railway journey to Aomori, followed by a ferry trip of 4½ hours to the port of Hakodate, followed by another long rail journey to the said capital, Sapporo.

Later, when this book rolls through the provinces of Japan, I shall have specific recommendations for use of JAL services, but it may be said now that a round-trip flight is essential in visiting Hokkaido and you will almost certainly wish to fly at least one way between Tokyo and Osaka or Fukuoka. DC-4's are now being used for domestic flights and they are operated with dependable punctuality and with the axiomatic courtesy of Japan.

The American Presidents and NYK

The *American President Lines*, serving Hawaii, Japan, Hong Kong, the Philippines and various areas of Southeast Asia while operating its popular round-the-world cruises, has built up, over the years, a commanding position in Pacific sea transportation comparable to that of Pan American in the Pacific air. In briefest form I will list some of APL's important services as they concern readers of this book, taking them up "President by President."

The *President Cleveland*, APL flagship, and the *President Wilson*, a sister ship, provide a luxurious and glamorous service once every three weeks from San Francisco and Los Angeles to Honolulu, Yokohama, Manila, Hong Kong and Kobe, with a repeat halt at Honolulu homeward bound. These sumptuous twin liners, each carrying 330 passengers in first class and 464 in tourist, are 610 feet long, have a displacement of 23,500 tons and a speed of 20 knots. You'll not think their advertising punch line "Your Country Club Afloat" too exuberant when you experience their various lounges, smoking rooms, bars, marine verandas, deck swimming pools and other floating counterparts of a country club.

The *President Hoover*, of about 14,200 tons displacement, sails once a month from San Francisco to all the ports of the Orient named above but does not include a halt at Honolulu in either direction.

The *President Polk* and the *President Monroe*, with 16,000 tons displacement, are APL's round-the-world cruise ships. Starting from New York, then passing through the Panama Canal and up to San Francisco they proceed to Honolulu, Yokohama, Kobe, Hong Kong, Singapore and on around the world.

The *Presidents Adams, Coolidge, Hayes* and *Jackson* are 12-passenger mariner-class cargoliners providing staterooms and suites of impressive luxury, with small but handsomely appointed public rooms and with service that is first-class in every way.

These ships, starting also from our East Coast, sail the same general round-the-world route as the *Presidents Polk* and *Monroe*, but their precise course may vary in accordance with cargo requirements. The APL also operates about twenty-five lesser freighters bearing the names of other U.S. presidents, so all in all the floating Presidents are a varied and very considerable fleet.

While on the subject of cargoliners and freighters I should mention also the "Three Bears" of the *Pacific Far East Line,* namely the *Golden Bear,* the *Korean Bear* and the *Japan Bear.* These new ships, each carrying 12 passengers, are of the same mariner class as the four Presidents named just above. Starting from San Francisco, they serve several Japanese ports as well as Hong Kong, Manila and other ports in the Philippines. The home offices of both APL and PFEL are at 311 California Street, San Francisco.

Nippon Yusen Kaisha is a trio of words long familiar to those travelers who have "gone down to the sea in ships." They stand for Japanese Steamship Company, whose ramifying operations have carried the Japanese flag to most of the world's ports. I have not yet crossed the Pacific in an NYK steamer but once I did take a ship of this line from Gibraltar, of all places, to Marseille and found its service very Japanese, which is to say very smiling and courteous.

NYK was hard hit by the war but it is gradually getting back into its stride. It has only one passenger liner now on the Pacific run, but its cargo vessels, each with accommodations for the usual 12 passengers in outside staterooms, seem to go everywhere, one of these services that may be of prime interest to planners being the semi-monthly run between New York and several Japanese ports, with halts at Panama, Los Angeles and San Francisco. Those who know, or can envision, the folksy delights of freighter travel in well-operated ships do not need to be told of the relaxation of travel by this means all the way from New York to Japan, whether by APL or NYK.

NYK's transpacific liner, which runs from Vancouver and Seattle to Kobe and Yokohama, with a halt at Honolulu, is the M.S. *Hikawa Maru,* of 11,600 gross tons. It carries 80 passengers in first class, 60 in 3rd A, which may be considered "Tourist Class," and 127 in 3rd B, which will hardly concern you. The accommodations in first class are of considerable luxury. For further information on sailings the prospective traveler will find

NYK branch offices in New York (24 State Street) and San Francisco (311 California Street) and special agencies in several other cities. (The word *Maru*, which is applied to every Japanese ship, has an interesting derivation. It means literally "round," the Japanese symbol of perfection, and was applied in feudal times to lordly castles in order to glorify them in popular estimation. So ships came to be thought of as floating castles. By this devious exercise in semantics you may realize that whenever you board a Maru you are embarking on a floating castle.)

Making an Entrance

Since May 15, 1957, Japan has enabled foreigners to enter the country easily and with a minimum of red tape, for on that date the requirement that each incomer acquire a Foreign Exchange Record Book was abandoned. Now you need declare only foreign notes (which will be entered in your passport), not travelers checks or letters of credit, and you need not produce a Record Book or anything else when you wish to exchange dollars or any other foreign currency into Japanese yen. When you leave Japan you may take out no more foreign notes than the amounts you have declared on entering. But if, at the last minute, you have some Japanese money left you may reconvert it, up to $100, into American money. Such reconversion is a liberal provision matched by few European or Latin-American countries that still require currency declarations.

Upon arrival in Japan, you will be given a *Specified Stores Tax Exemption Card* and this card, be advised, is decidedly for *your* benefit, since it exempts, in the specified stores, various important purchases, such as cameras, binoculars, cultured pearls and cloisonné, from the big Japanese Commodity Tax of 16 per cent. And an especially cheering thing about this is that the store *deducts* the 16 per cent from the price marked on the price tag, so it isn't merely a matter of not adding the tax but actually of deducting it. If, for instance, you should see a nice string of cultured pearls in the Mikimoto window or some other marked 60,000 yen, which is $166.66, you'll actually pay only 50,400 yen, which is $140. Your Specified Stores Tax Exemption Card has saved you $26.66.

I have reported this good news first, but to go back to the beginning of your planning, I have to state that in the matter of securing a temporary visa in your passport the requirements have not yet been fully eased. You must wade through the business in some Japanese consulate, filling in a long form and producing a ticket (or other proof of your plans) indicating that your travels will take you out of Japan (after a stay of less than 60 days) as well as taking you in.

On the other hand, you do not need passport photos in order to secure the Japanese visa, as you definitely do for certain other visas, such as that for Hong Kong. To avoid the "gyp photographers" that infest port areas in large U.S. cities you may wish the name of one in New York whom I know from experience to be honest and fair, as well as expert, so I will mention Anthony J. Babian, owner of the *Columbia Photo Studio* at 74 West 50th Street.

The customs formalities for tourists entering Japan on the standard temporary visa are simple enough, I'm happy to report, and you will be treated with the usual Japanese courtesy here as everywhere in the country.

One strenuous warning about money seems in order here. *Don't try to buy black market yen* in Hong Kong or elsewhere before entering Japan. You may have visited countries where the currency black market, or gray market, flourishes almost openly, with little or no effort made to curb it, but Japan is very strict in this matter and it is no part of Japanese politeness to let you off easy if you have offended. Punishment for evasion is severe, sometimes even involving a jail term. And anyway, the spread between the legal rate of 360 yen to the dollar and the black market rate of maybe 380 or 385 is so slight as to make it scarcely worth while to tamper with the rules even if they were not strictly enforced. Currency rates and rules have a way of changing from time to time and you would do well to get the latest information from some reliable exchange house. One that I have used for years with satisfaction is *Lionel Perera, Manfra and Brookes,* on the street-floor corridor of the big RCA Building at 30 Rockefeller Plaza, New York, another door of the office opening from 48 West 50th Street.

Introducing JTA and JTB

Foreign tourism in Japan was organized within a decade of the war's conclusion on a basis of thoroughness and efficiency seldom matched by countries in Europe and hardly ever, I would say, in Latin America, for the Japanese give priority in the Roster of Virtues to promptness and dependability.

I take great pleasure, in the manner of an after-dinner speaker, in introducing two organizations which . . .

To come to the point with the promptness I've just been praising, the JTA, for *Japan Tourist Association,* is an official government organization, opened in 1955 for the direct purpose of promoting and fostering foreign tourism—which is where you and I come in. The JTB, for *Japan Travel Bureau,* is a commercial organization, though also semi-official, somewhat in the manner of Italy's well-known CIT, which offers detailed travel information, arranges tourist itineraries, sets up guided tours, sells tickets of all kinds, makes hotel, plane and train bookings, handles your baggage problems and concerns itself with the multitudes of minutiae that can make your tour a prime success instead of a chain of worries and travel troubles.

Now let's take a closer look at each of these organizations in turn.

The JTA has its head office on the 8th floor of Tokyo's prominent *Kokusai Kanko Kaikan,* which is to say International Tourist Building—and those are three good words to know. This fine, modern building houses also one of the capital's first-rate, modern hotels of Western style called Hotel Kokusai Kanko, which you now readily translate. The JTA main office is in the hands of an experienced director named Iwao Yokota, powerfully seconded by Frank H. Agui. Branches are maintained in New York (10 Rockefeller Plaza), San Francisco (651 Market Street), Toronto (48 Front Street, West) and Honolulu (109 Princess Kaiulani Avenue). The New York office, which I happen to know best, is headed by S. W. ("Kim") Kimura, one of the most respected and best-liked travel representatives in the Big City. The JTA can be of inestimable help in steering your course and helping you to get started. If you are engaged in any special form of research or photography it can be your expert counselor, and the Tokyo office will even set up a suggested itinerary for you, though this work belongs more specifically to the other organization.

The JTB, to look now at this wellspring of practical aid, is a really vast and complex organization with head office close to the Tokyo Central Station in a building at the corner of W Avenue and R Avenue (more later on Tokyo's street names), several other offices in Tokyo, including a convenient one in the Imperial Hotel, and some *two hundred and fifty* branch offices all over Japan. More recently the JTB has opened overseas offices in Los Angeles (530 West 6th Street) and New York (9 Rockefeller Plaza). The opening of this last-named office in the spring of 1957 made New York the only foreign city to have *both* JTA and JTB branches. One of the JTB's very practical accomplishments is the publication of guidebooks to Japan. Its most comprehensive effort in this line is a 1000-page Baedeker-type volume (which is fairly small and easy to carry despite all its pages) called *Japan, The Official Guide.* For those who wish a smaller book containing most of the essentials but no detailed listing of hotels and other such practicalia, it publishes *Japan, The Pocket Guide;* and the Bureau supplements this with an interesting little book called *Quiz,* with the sub-heading *700 Answers to Questions on Things Japanese.*

In emphasizing the services of the JTB I would not by any means suggest neglecting to see *your own American travel agent.* If he's worth his salt he keeps his finger on the pulse of tourism everywhere and can help you immeasurably in planning your Orient tour and starting you on your way. My agent, to be personal again in this personal book, is *Metropolitan Travel Service,* 200 Berkeley Street, Boston, whose president, Ernest W. Ruegg, looks at travel in a modern and imaginative way.

On this current visit to Japan I have been to almost every nook and corner of the islands, so far as these have special tourist interest, and having used JTB services everywhere I can report from personal experience that its men don't let you down. If they promise to get you a ticket or booking by such-and-such an hour they come through with it. If they agree to have a guide at your hotel at nine o'clock to take you sightseeing or shopping, the guide will show up at nine o'clock, not five or ten minutes past nine. You'll like this meticulous care and when you leave for other lands, including your own, which incline to be less prone to such solicitude, you'll miss it.

CHAPTER 2

JAPAN ON BALANCE

Beware of First Impressions

To the average visitor arriving in Tokyo's Haneda Airport for the first time, Japan manages to put its "worst foot forward" and distressing as this is perhaps there's sound psychology in it, for the bleakness of these initial impressions is soon offset by a multitude of happier ones. For myself I can say that I survived the approach and soon came to love Japan and its people in no uncertain measure, so what I have to report now is written with an affection equal to its candor.

To come right out with it, Tokyo sprawls out from its center for miles and miles—and miles—in all directions, including that of Haneda Airport, where all overseas planes touch down, its outer reaches extending further, or so it seems to me, than do even those of London. The city boasts 8,345,404 inhabitants, or it did a very little while ago, but a net increase of over 10,000 occurs every month so this mammoth metropolis is having a neck-and-neck race with London and New York for first place in the world as the most populated city. Because of earthquake hazards most buildings except in the solid center and some scattered secondary centers, where impressive American-type reinforced concrete structures exist in large numbers, are of one or two or three stories and thousands of them are unpainted and undeniably ramshackle. This sight greets the eager traveler.

And then the streets! Tokyo has terrible growing pains. New construction is everywhere, especially all through the center, and a new subway, Tokyo's third, is causing added and drastic upheavals. The streets just haven't been able to keep pace with the phenomenal growth of the city and many of them are frankly awful, as are their so-called sidewalks, with bumps, holes, stretches of dirt or mud, and vast obstructions of building materials. They're bad in sunny weather, dreadful when it rains. Yes they are, and I can't honestly soften the picture.

And what about the traffic on these streets? There we have Pelion on Ossa. It is the maddest, shrillest, craziest city traffic I've ever seen and in the center it gets tied up in knots that a supreme scoutmaster of traffic could hardly undo. Private cars are not unduly numerous but the city fairly swarms with taxis of three types, all seemingly so unconcerned with human life that they are popularly called "kamikaze cabs." The smallest ones, mere road bugs but wonderfully agile, have 70 painted on the front or side and this means that they will carry you 2 kilometers, which is a mile and a quarter, for a modest 70 yen, which is 19 cents, and the tariff for longer hauls is also the lowest. A somewhat larger type of vehicle is marked 80 and an American-type car 100. Whatever their bracket these taxis race like four-wheeled devils for openings that are obviously as impossible to penetrate as is the needle's eye of Scripture for a camel. If they can't *quite* make it the driver jams on his brakes at the last second and you pitch forward against the front seat. To accent his urgency the driver keeps his hand on the horn at least half the time. All day and half the night the Tokyo air is filled with an unceasing symphony of motor horns, and these, I might add, are supplemented by the shrill wailing of the noodle venders' whistles, sounding rather like perambulating piccolos. Far into the night one hears this weird whistling, intended to attract late trade.

The authorities are trying, somewhat timidly, to curb the motorists' horn madness and the papers are full of warnings about fines for "needless sounding of horns," but that adjective is a wobbly one, hard to define, and the kamikazes, at least, seem to be little deterred by such gentle threats.

I said I'd come right out with it and certainly I have, but now

I ask you: "Kindly turn the page" and see what my second and third and nth impressions are.

These Things You'll Love

Japan has certain features of attraction that have been far too little publicized in the tourist world and I shall try to do my bit toward evening the balance. Geisha girls and Fujiyama have been unceasingly and overpoweringly publicized for decades but alluring as these are they're but the smallest fraction of that impalpable radiance of Nippon that we so lamely call "atmosphere." With luck you may have an evening or two of geisha entertainment and with luck you may see glorious snow-crested Fuji, though its summit is said to be clouded two days out of three in the spring months, but *Japan* is ever with you and all about you.

Your first shocks of pleasure, following your initially grim impressions of Tokyo street traffic, occur when your taxi reaches your hotel. To your amazement you'll find that when you pay the taxi driver—who hasn't, after all, killed you or anybody else in his mad dash—he will promptly pass you your change, all of it, and *drive swiftly away* in search of his next fare. He expects no tip and you should offer him none unless he has done some very special service for you. Where else but in Japan could this phenomenon occur?

At the door of your hotel, whether it is the celebrated Imperial, the eagerly desired goal of most American tourists, or some lesser hostelry, bellboys or bellgirls, bowing from the waist, will welcome you and relieve you of your luggage. After you've registered they'll take you to your room, install you politely, bow again *and disappear*. "Wait a minute," you'll say, calling down the corridor. "Here. This is for you," as you offer a gratuity. Again he or she will bow and politely *decline it*. That, at least, has been my experience over and over again, or it was until I learned not to offer tips. Even in the Imperial Hotel, the very nucleus of U.S. tourism, exactly this happened to me on three early occasions. Like all other hotels of any standing in Japan the Imperial adds to your bill a 10 per cent service charge "to replace individual tipping," as numerous notices state it, and the astonishing thing is that this notice *means exactly what it says.* Again I ask, "Where else in the tourist world could this phenomenon occur?" Service charges "in lieu of gratuities" exist in many countries of Europe, but can you recall your proffered "little extra" being *ever* declined? This could happen, conceivably, in Germany or Scandinavia, but it would be most exceptional. In Japan it is run of the mill, standard practice, and I earnestly hope that American tourists will recognize it and not attempt to break down servant morale.

Let me say again, and shout it out loud, the *smiling tiplessness of Japan* is one of Nippon's pervasive elements of charm. You don't tip in restaurants that have the service charge, as most places of quality do, nor in coffee houses and tearooms. You don't tip in theaters. Only for some *special* service do you tip, as, for instance, when on tour your driver convoys you for half a day over tortuous mountain highways. Japanese travel propaganda seems unduly modest in failing to emphasize this unique feature as a talking point. The *Official Guide* barely mentions, in its smallest print, that usually in hotels a service charge "obviates the necessity for tips to the help." The JTB's *Pocket Guide* doesn't mention the crucial subject at all and even Pan American's excellent and very knowledgeable handbook *New Horizons* dismisses the subject casually with the words: "Tipping. A bit less than with us."

You'll love *the pint-sized girls of Japan,* by which I don't mean merely the elaborately made up geisha girls but ordinary working girls, including department store clerks, travel office girls, elevator girls, waitresses and chambermaids, for they are another Nipponese charm of the very first caliber. They are lovely and dainty miniatures, almost without exception, and they seem equally appealing whether they wear Western clothes, trim uniforms or the traditional kimono and obi, with wooden getas or slippers as footwear. Their average height I would estimate at 4 feet 10 to 5 feet, their average weight at 85 to 105 pounds. Their skin, fresh and *always* hairless, is like peaches without the fuzz. Their hair, invariably jet black, is worn in ways more various than in America. You see it straight as strings. You see it waved. You see it brushed up, brushed back, parted, or hanging loose to the waist, and not infrequently you see it in a pert ponytail.

The girls of Japan bow, often from the waist, as naturally as they breathe. They bow when they serve you in any way. They bow when you enter an elevator that they are operating. In the big department stores uniformed girls stand beside the lower and upper level of each escalator, bowing and murmuring a greeting to each ascending or descending shopper.

They smile, and *how* they smile! Again, it is as natural as breathing, not calculated, or "prepared." They smile at you and they laugh among themselves, though not, you may be sure, at, or about you. The youngsters of Japan must all have their funny-bones in very exposed positions for they seem to be laughing half the time at something, or nothing. Watch any crowd walking along to or from or in a railway station or subway and I'll guarantee that at any given moment half of the young ones, at least, will be laughing or giggling. I've sometimes made a game of this, keeping an exact tally of smiling and sober faces, so my estimate is not based on guesswork.

I've been discussing Japanese girls clothed and duly draped, but if you would like to see their marvelously dainty bodies as nature made them, without any concealing fig leaf or bikini, you have but to go to one of Japan's popular hotspring spas. (For convenience this book will consider "hotspring" an unhyphenated adjective.) In Honshu and Kyushu, the custom of mixed nude bathing has somewhat diminished, though it has by no means been abandoned, but in Hokkaido it flourishes in all its glory. In Noboribetsu, for instance, in the huge indoor bath hall of the Dai-ichi Takimoto Inn, where abundant hot mineral waters gush constantly into a dozen or more pools, you will find families,

honeymoon couples, schoolboys and schoolgirls literally by the
score and all as naked as Adam and Eve before their fall, though
the bodies are faintly shrouded by a generous fog of steam and
each bather does carry a wash cloth which may be used, by the
sensitive ones, as a sort of portable fig leaf. It will be a thin afternoon or evening if the hall is not invaded by an excursion group
of fifty to a hundred 'teen-age schoolgirls squealing with joy as
they race about from one pool to another. I think you will find
them—interesting.

You'll love *the schoolchildren as tourists*. At every Buddhist
temple, Shinto shrine or other tourist sight you'll see them being
herded along by their teachers, for sightseeing is a very definite
part of every child's schooling. They all wear uniforms, in deference to democracy, so that there shall be no obvious difference
between rich and poor. The boys, even when very small, wear
black jackets and long black trousers and black caps. The girls
wear navy blue blouses, with white-trimmed sailor collars and
pleated skirts to match. If the group is from a school in a country
village most of the girls will be wearing their shiny jet-black
hair in a sharply barbered Dutch cut and many of them, with
eyes like slanted slits that seem quite to disappear when they
laugh, look like exact replicas of the porcelain dolls that Western
kiddies play with. Most of the children, both boys and girls, will
be laughing and all are consumed with curiosity about us, you
and me. The bolder ones will be itching to try their school English on us, for *all* must study English. You'll hear pert youngsters
here and there in the flock call out "Haró. Good morning. Thank
you very much," and then giggle in vast appreciation of their
own sallies. Haró, as you have readily guessed, is Japanese for
"Hello," there being no *l* in Japanese speech.

The *multitudes* of these children-in-uniform, encountered
everywhere you go, will constantly amaze you, even when you
grow accustomed to the spectacle. They flow around you like a
human river. Often you have literally to *plow* your way through
them. To us these giggling kids are a delight, but to the Japanese

government they are a constant source of worry, for the country, with some 90 million inhabitants, is already overpopulated and the national tally has been increasing by a million or more a year. Last year, however, there was a ray of hope, for the net increase was only 937,000, the first time since the war that it has been under a million. You and I will leave population worries to whom they may concern and will selfishly enjoy these swarming, scurrying, buoyant youngsters.

You'll love *the built-in courtesy* of all Japanese, young or old, rich or poor, for nothing quite like it exists anywhere else in the world. I'll grant that among the Japanese themselves the *formalities* of politeness reach heights, or depths, that seem to Westerners absurd. A young person meeting a distinguished older person on the sidewalk will sometimes bow deeply from the waist five or six times in succession, actually blocking pedestrian traffic with his or her protruding rump, for the more times one bows the greater is the deference shown. Self-depreciation is also a part of this traditional formality. A hostess offering a superb dinner, impeccably served, will apologize for the poor and meager quality of her hospitality. A person giving a costly and elegant present will ask forgiveness for venturing to proffer so small and worthless a gift. But you and I won't be often exposed to these traditional customs. Instead, we will revel in the dependable courtesy of *all* with whom we come in contact, from wealthy leaders of business or social life to the humblest drudge who serves us.

And finally—for I must abridge this catalog of virtues—you'll love *the Japanese instinct for beauty*. It is an instinct that you'll see, and cannot fail to see, in parks, in works of art, in the widespread passion for flower arrangement—a Japanese can spend an entire morning lovingly perfecting a single arrangement—and in the art of *bonsai*, the dwarfing of trees, many of which, only a foot high though a hundred years old, are flawless miniatures. You'll see it, perhaps above all, in Japanese inns and homes. We of the West tend always to put comforts first and beauty second.

With the Japanese it's quite the other way around. In Japanese inns, for instance, which are very rarely blessed with central heating, the rooms will be cruelly cold in winter and bleakly chilly in early spring and late fall, but to the Japanese customer this doesn't much matter. What does matter very much is that the room shall be decorated with restrained and faultless taste, that there shall be one or two exquisite *objets d'art* in the elevated alcove (*tokonoma*), which is an essential of every room, perhaps with one lovely scroll on the wall above it, a scroll having a 17-syllable poem of tradition or an inspirational message painted on it. And it matters very much that the room's windows shall look out upon a bit of a garden, perhaps with *one* tenderly groomed pine tree visible, and a mossy stone lantern under it.

Foreigners whose business is interior decorating or landscape gardening seem always to grow lyrical about what they like to call Japanese "understatement" in arts and decoration and gardening but one need not be an expert to sense this sure instinct for a type of beauty that is the very opposite of showy exuberance. The utterest layman notices and feels it like a sort of balm. Philistinism shrinks before its quiet assurance.

But There Are Things to Cope with Too

In the interest of balanced reporting I have to state that motor touring in Japan, while perfectly practicable almost everywhere— I have enjoyed a lot of it—leaves much to be desired. From the tourist's angle poor roads are Japan's most noticeable fault and the fact that a vigorous ten-year reconstruction plan has just got under way does not lend much comfort to those who plan to come now or soon. Great stretches of the roads you'll want to use are narrow and bumpy and many portions are thick with dust in dry weather, gooey with mud in wet. A further hazard is trucks and tourist busses, especially the excursion busses that carry schoolchildren on trips to see great national sights. It is a common experience to encounter six to ten of these lumbering behemoths in a row, each filled to the gunwales with excited children. You usually have to pull up at the side of the road while the procession slowly toils past, or if it is toiling in the same direction as you the problem of passing it is severe.

Statistics before me reveal that of Japan's vehicles officially tallied in a recent year, busses totaled a surprising 10 per cent. The figure for trucks (but the majority of these are in and near the big cities, *not* on the open highways) is a whopping 60 per cent, while that for passenger cars is only 25 per cent, the remaining 5 per cent being scored as "Special."

Another lack in the motoring picture is the absence of self-drive cars on hire. If you want to tour by car the thing to do, assuming that you're a visitor with limited time, is to hire a car with driver, but probably you'll want to do this anyway, for the job of navigating the roads is a wearying one, especially since you must accustom yourself to *left driving*, as in England, and at times you'll be puzzled by Japanese road signs.

This brings me to a problem of *language coping*, but that's a subject in itself, which I'll take up presently. Before doing so I must insert a sweetener about touring. If highway travel is bad, railway travel is quite wonderful, for Japan is perhaps the most railway-minded great country in the world. Rail service is excellent in quality and the punctuality of trains, *all* trains, is nothing less than spectacular. I think Japan comes the nearest of any country in the world to keeping its trains so precisely on time that "you can set your watch by them." Enthusiasts sometimes make similar claims for certain countries of Europe but only Japan, in my experience, succeeds in making the claim an actual fact of travel.

The Language of Japan, Take It Easy

The Japanese *spoken* language is considered by polyglots to be one of the easier languages of the world but unfortunately the *written* language is so utterly forbidding to Western eyes that it deters most visitors from attempting to learn even to speak it, except for a half dozen words or phrases. In this I'm inclined to think the visitors are wise, since their chances of making themselves understood by using their own language, supplemented by signs and gestures, are quite as good as if they were toilsomely to enunciate the heavy phrases that one finds in phrase books. Such books have a very real value, in my opinion, if they are not taken too literally and too seriously. The best one I know is *Say It in Japanese*, an easygoing, pocket-sized, well-indexed book by Mima Kai, of Columbia University, published by Dover Publications of New York. By perusing the phrases of such a book from time to time a good many words manage to take lodging in one's brain cells, but one should not flip over the pages nervously trying to find the golden phrase that fits the immediate need.

Let's take a few examples. If you want your bill at a hotel desk or a hotel dining room just ask for "The bill, please" or "The check, please" and make motions as of signing your name, but *don't* struggle with the phrase *"Kanjo-gaki o motte kite kudasai."* If you want to find the toilet just say, with rising inflection, the word "Toilet?" (which is now universally understood) and *don't* ask *"Otearai wa doko desuka?"* If you're sending a telegram and want to know the cost just ask "How much?" or maybe, in this case, try out the golden word *"Ikura?"* which means the same thing, but don't, for heaven's sake, follow the phrase-book counsel and ask the clerk *"Kono dempo no ryokin wa ikura desuka?"*

A few elementary phrases, very few, practically "learn themselves" and are worth acquiring if only for the fun of having them in your language arsenal. I'll venture to set down a dozen of them in their most bare-bones form, and of course in Roman letters, which don't exist in ordinary Japanese usage but are generously provided to help out foreigners. The circumflex accent, or merely a straight line, often appearing over â, ê, î, ô and û in word lists, is merely a convenience to the foreigner, indicating that the vowel has a longer, fuller sound than it would have without the mark. The diphthongs ai and ei are pronounced

respectively like eye and like ay in ray. This book will not bother
with circumflex accents or long marks, though I admit that these
are important for anyone making a serious study of the language,
and it will not attempt to indicate which syllable, in long words,
is stressed. I may say in general, however, that, as in French,
there is seldom a very pronounced stress on any syllable. As in
French, also, there is a virtual elision of certain vowels, usually
the one in the penult. Two typical examples of this are the names
Takarazuka, which is pronounced roughly Takaráz[u]ka, and
Asakusa, which is pronounced Asák[u]sa. And now for our
twelve good phrases and true.

Please	*Kudasai*, or *Dozo*
Thank you	*Arigato*
I'm sorry	*Sumi Masen*
Good morning	*Ohayo* (pronounced Ohio)
Good day (How do you do?)	*Konnichiwa*
Good-by	*Sayonara* (This is the title of a haunting song, as well as of a famous Michener novel.)
Take it easy (To the taxi man)	*Yukkuri*
How much (does it cost)?	*Ikura* (desuka)?
Your health (as a toast)	*Kampai!*
Chambermaid	*Jochu-san*
As quickly as possible	*Naru take hayaku*
When?; Where?	*Itsu?; Doko?*

These twelve phrases can be of real use to you, especially in
Japanese inns, where the staff, including the girl who answers
when you use the 'phone in your room, may not know a single
word of English. The word for soap (*sekken*) is a good one to
know, as is the word for bath (*ofuro*), and also the word for
water (*mizu*). I have asked for drinking water, pointing to my
empty glass, even in a smart Western-type hotel restaurant and
have been brought beer. The flustered little waitress-in-kimono,
not quite understanding my gesture, had been too timid to pursue
the conversation with me.

The words for yes (*hai* or *sodesu*) and no (*iie* or *chigaimasu*) are quite unnecessary to learn, since gestures will serve, but the common hai, for yes, is a word you will hear, or overhear, with delight, a thousand times. It sounds exactly like "high" and is uttered in quick staccato, "Hai! Hai hai!" over and over again, for Japanese people say yes far more eagerly and naturally than no.

The cardinals from one to ten and the words for hundred and thousand are simple and well worth knowing, so here they are:

one	*ichi*
two	*ni*
three	*san*
four	*shi*
five	*go*
six	*roku*
seven	*shichi*
eight	*hachi*
nine	*ku*
ten	*ju*
hundred	*hyaku*
thousand	*sen*

The humbler folk of Tokyo and all Japan, especially those who had their schooling before the war when English was not so universally taught, know very few words, if any at all, in our language and sometimes you'll find that your taxi man doesn't even understand your clearly spoken "Hotel Imperial," so it is well to know that this works out simply as *"Tei Koku Hoteru."* (As we've seen there is no *l* sound in Japanese; also, no word ever ends in a consonant, except *n*.) If you want to find a subway entrance—the subways of Tokyo are *easy* to learn—merely accost the nearest passer-by and murmur, with rising inflection, *"Chi ka tetsu?"*

Certain special "Japanisms" are pleasing to all visitors. One is the custom of adding the syllable san to one's surname. In a sense the san is in lieu of Mister—when I overhear Japanese people mentioning my name it seems always to be Clark-san—but this is far warmer and friendlier than our Mr., Mrs. or Miss. It can be added to a first name, masculine or feminine, when first-name intimacy is warranted.

Another charming custom is the concluding syllable *ko* of almost every feminine given name. It is a sort of diminutive, a bit like the German *chen* or *lein*, yet an integral part of the name, which, by the way, is nearly always translatable into a common noun or adjective. One hears, for instance, such names as Ranko (Little Orchid), Fusako (Little Luxury), Kimiko (Little Dear), Kinuko (Little Silk), Fumiko (Little Letter), Mariko (Little Ball) and Takako (Little Faithful). In Japanese inns it is quite in order for the guest to ask the maid who serves him, "Anata no o-namae wa?" ("What is your name?") and almost invariably the smiling girl will reply with a name ending in the pleasant syllable ko. It is a charming thing, the ko-ness of Japanese womanhood. Even some of the members of the Imperial Family, including the Empress herself, have the same diminutive as a part of their established name, that of Her Imperial Highness being Nagako.

Literally *hundreds* of words have been borrowed by the Japanese directly from English, though *r* must always be substituted for *l* and every word must end in a vowel (or *n*). Here are some examples, which I offer more for your amusement than for any practical value in travel:

station	*steshon*	beer	*biru*
radio	*rajio*	whisky	*uisuki*
television	*terebijon*	ice cream	*aisukurimu*
elevator	*erebeta*	building	*birujingu*
escalator	*esukareita*	door	*doa*
typewriter	*taipuraita*	number	*namba*
raincoat	*reinkoto*	baseball	*besuboru*

It is plain to see from the above list of samples, which could be spun out almost indefinitely, that a multitude of words that are as familiar, though a bit twisted, to the Japanese as to us make communication a lot easier than it would otherwise be.

The Japanese *written language* in standard use can be dismissed with two words, "Skip it," unless you are making a long or even permanent stay in the country. Chinese characters, or ideographs, are used, though these admittedly are a poor fit for Japanese speech. To make them fit better two supplementary syllabaries were long ago devised, in the 8th and 9th centuries, namely *kata-kana* and *hira-gana*. In an effort to confuse you as much as possible I will quote one passage from *Japan, The Official Guide*, under the heading "Language."

"Almost all books are written in a mixture of Chinese characters and kana [gana] of one kind or the other, the Chinese characters being employed to convey ideas in nouns and the stems of words, while the *kana* serve to transcribe particles and terminations. *Kana* is also often printed at the side of Chinese characters, especially difficult ones, as a sort of running comment, which usually indicates the pronunciation, sometimes the meaning."

And now that we've mastered the syllabaries let's perfect ourselves in the Chinese ideographs. If we know three thousand of them we are pretty well educated, but five or six thousand puts us in a stronger position and if we aspire to real scholarship we should be familiar with ten or twelve thousand. To make these ideographs capable of being handled by a typewriter somewhat smaller in size than a wardrobe trunk the Japanese government has sifted the ideographs to a basic seven hundred, knowledge of which makes humble citizens officially "literate." And speaking of the typewriter, by which I mean *taipuraita*, do, I urge you, find or make the opportunity to watch one at work in a Japanese office. About two or three times as large as an ordinary adding machine and with a platen maybe four times as large as that of an American office typewriter, the thing is absolutely fascinating in action. It has two "manuals," one for the ideographs and one, if I understand rightly, for the "kana of one kind or the other." For the former a "magic arm" or punching gadget reaches among the seven hundred keys to pick out the needed ideograph, then holds it in a firm grip and stamps it on the paper. Then it selects another, and another, at the typist's command, and if this seems slow and laborious work, which it is, remember that each ideograph is a *word*, or most of a word. That helps.

In all this matter of language you should hold a sympathetic thought for Japanese children, those laughing youngsters whom you encounter in their thousands at every turn. These kiddies must really *learn* the ideographs, along with the syllabaries, and it takes a substantial chunk of their young lives to achieve this. For a long time an earnest organization in Japan has been preaching the necessity of a change-over to Romanization of the written language, but this gets about as far as do earnest efforts for Esperanto in our land. The change would involve vast difficulties and expense. And besides, there is Red China, just across the way, with its 700 million people and Nationalist China down to the south, on Formosa. For contact with Japan's immediate neighbors the ancient ideographs are of some practical use.

The Religions of Japan—in Eclipse

In presenting the religions of Japan I shall be even more sketchy —though I trust never flippant—than in presenting the language, for I simply do not think it necessary for any except purposeful scholars or Christian missionaries to concern themselves deeply with the subject.

Almost all Japanese, over 99 per cent still, are tinctured, to some slight extent, with the nation's traditional religions, ritualistic Shinto and contemplative Buddhism, while about eight-tenths of 1 per cent are professing Christians.

"Shinto (The Way of the Gods)—[I feel safer to quote the official verbiage of *The Guide*]—is the native cult of Japan, combining nature worship and ancestor worship, the chief deity in its pantheon of so-called 'eight million gods' being Amaterasu-Omikami (Great-Heaven-Shining-Goddess). . . . This pantheon embraces many nature gods and goddesses of the sea, rivers, winds, fire and mountains—[Fujiyama is still a god to many old-timers]—and many deified persons."

The supreme deified person, until he was ingloriously defeated in World War II, was Emperor Hirohito, the 124th in the succession of god-emperors in the direct line of descent from the Great-Heaven-Shining-Goddess, Amaterasu-Omikami, and one of the phenomena of modern times is that a great nation, able to make war in a way that terribly threatened the world, actually accepted and believed, or seemed to, this elaborate fiction, so obviously fostered for purposes of militaristic nationalism. In prewar schools every schoolbook contained, at the very beginning, a proclamation to the effect that "Japan is ruled by the Emperor, who is a descendant of the Great-Heaven-Shining-Goddess, etc., etc." Every pupil was required to learn the names, letter-perfect, of the 124 god emperors. Every class in Japanese history opened with the recitation, in unison, of this long list, and also of a letter-to-the-nation concerning education, promulgated by the revered Emperor Meiji, and millions of Japanese adults can still reel off the whole thing at top speed.

In homes there was always a little Shinto shrine and emperor worship was a part of daily life. When the Emperor's name was mentioned good children rose and stood stiffly at attention. The children, and their parents too, believed, with varying degrees of sincerity and devotion, that Emperor Hirohito controlled the world, including even its weather. He could make it rain if rain was needed for the nation and he could ensure sunshine when a bright day was needed, particularly on April 29, his birthday. Many millions believed that it would not, could not, rain, in Tokyo at least, on April 29, unless by some divine whimsy, the Emperor wished it to rain. In war, the Emperor could, of course, influence the direction of falling enemy bombs and it was a prime article of national faith that no bomb could possibly fall on the

Imperial Palace nor on the sacred Meiji Shrine in Tokyo. When American bombs did indeed fall on both of these structures and utterly destroy them they sounded, for many, the death knell of sincere belief in the emperor's divinity. Orthodox, ritualistic Shinto, as a spiritual force, was given the final *coup de grâce* after the war when Emperor Hirohito, at General MacArthur's behest, publicly proclaimed, with a grace and humility that should command our respect, that he was, after all, no descendant of the Sun Goddess but a mere human being, even as his 90 million subjects.

So ritualistic Shinto died *as a religion,* but it lives on as a tradition, aiding the revival of nationalistic feeling. I have seen a Japanese woman of perhaps thirty openly mocking the forms of worship before a Shinto shrine, while a group of male admirers around her roared with laughter at her funny antics, yet the marvelous shrines of Nikko and Kyoto and Nara still command respect and Shinto priests, in their tall black hats, still go through their old maneuvers, sometimes while throngs of tourists, foreign and Japanese, eagerly photograph their colorful performances with stills and movies. In general, so far as I've been able to learn and observe, young Japan simply couldn't care less about Shinto or any other variety of formal religion. Militant atheism, à la Russe, seems to play no part in this but rather a grand indifference to the whole subject. I should state, however, that there is a reformed sect of Shinto called Tenrikyo that has a spiritual basis and is said to have some hold on some of the more earnest young people; and it is well known that the highest forms of Buddhism are based on pure and lofty idealism.

Buddhism, which came from China (and originally from India) in the 6th century, is hospitable to all religions, including Shinto, and most Japanese, however indifferent inwardly, go through the motions, to some small extent, of being both Buddhists and Shintoists. "The principle on which the Buddhist religion is founded" —[again I take refuge in an official statement]—"is faith in the Three Treasures, which mean the oneness of the Perfect Person

(Buddha), the Truth (Dharma) and the Community (Sangha). The Buddhism brought over to Japan was a developed form of this religion, demonstrated artistically in ceremonies and supported by a system of idealistic philosophy."

Over the centuries many sects and sub-sects developed in Japan and most of them have now deteriorated to the point of being saturated with superstitions. The priests sell charms and fortunetelling papers to gullible worshipers and in front of many temples, as, for instance, the Asakusa Kannon Temple (to Kannon, the Goddess of Mercy), adjoining the raucous Asakusa Amusement Quarter, one finds a large brazier of smoking incense. If anything ails the worshipper he simply puts his hand in the incense fumes and then rubs it on the part affected. This will tend to cure him of his affliction. For a long time, one afternoon, I watched worshipers applying this cure. Some of the old people were tearily, pathetically, in earnest about it, while most of the young ones did it perfunctorily, furtively or as an outright joke, giggling all the while as their buddies looked on.

It should not, as I've said, be thought that all Buddhism is but a web of such silly fripperies. It is, in essence, a religion, or philosophy, of calmness and toleration, even, in its highest form, a dedicated striving for perfection. A small number of deeply spiritual Americans are dedicated Buddhists of this serene and lofty type. At least one sub-sect in Japan, called Jodo-Shinshu which is a branch of the Amida Sect, with its 22 million followers, casts a baleful eye at all the false incrustations and superstitions that have grown up like rank weeds. The famous Nishi Honganji Temple of Kyoto, for one, belongs to this sect and sternly forbids all traffic in charms and fortunetelling. It has courageously combated superstitition, even to the point of sponsoring anti-Shinto tracts before the war, and this boldness brought a heap of troubles to it. The Secret Police, on at least one occasion, descended angrily upon the Nishi Honganji Temple and compelled it to burn all copies of various pamphlets which the government branded as seditious, though a few copies of one of them, I believe, escaped destruction and are still treasured as mementos of those days so dangerous to free thought.

Christianity has had a checkered career in Japan, sometimes welcomed, oftener persecuted, but nowadays again welcomed, respected and scot-free to promulgate its tenets. The minuscule percentage of Christians noted in statistics is misleading since many of those who have embraced this faith are leaders in business, education and national life. Christianity is gaining strongly, though not impressively in statistical tables. Many feel that it lost a golden chance in not marshaling its forces immediately after the war to fill the vacuum created by the debacle of Shinto.

The history of Christianity in Japan is, as I've said, an up-and-down story of success, failure, disaster and again success. Francis Xavier, the great Roman Catholic missionary of Spain, first introduced Catholicism to Japan in 1549 and for a while it flourished mightily. Civil and military leaders and court society took it up, at least in superficial form, and at one time in the middle of the 16th century its adherents numbered 200,000, most of them living on Kyushu Island. The Shogun Nobunaga looked with favor on them but later they came under suspicion and the great Hideyoshi Toyotomi finally drove them underground. Ieyasu Tokugawa, who established Edo (Tokyo) as the national capital, and who was the deified shogun destined to be honored by the fabulous Toshogu Shrine in Nikko, "chastised them with scorpions," to use the figure attributed to Rehoboam, especially after a famous rebellion in Shimabara, a town lying to the east of Nagasaki, when the Christians came out from underground and led a valiant war of several months' duration, attracting to their side many non-Christians who were disgruntled over heavy taxes.

The "Affair Shimabara" brought drastic retaliation that drove out all the missionaries and harshly banned the holding of Christian services. This seemed to finish Christianity in Japan but in due course a remarkable phenomenon occurred. The faith was down but not out. For over 200 years it was kept alive in strict secrecy, especially in Urakami, a section of what is now Nagasaki.

When a Roman Catholic church was finally permitted to be built in Urakami many thousands of Christians appeared, as if by magic, to support and join it. The faith had been secretly nurtured through some ten generations, each one passing it on to the next, and now the Urakami church building was enabled to develop as a very large one, capable of seating 6000 persons. It became a major sight of Kyushu.

On August 9, 1945, the second atomic bomb ever dropped on a city—and one fervently hopes the last one ever to be dropped on any city—destroyed this greatest Christian edifice in the entire Orient. It is still a stark ruin, purposely left by Nagasaki as a memorial and a reminder to the world.

CHAPTER 3

SOME THINGS TO KNOW RIGHT OFF

THIS book will strive to be as useful as possible, especially to the first-timer, so perhaps a brief catalog of things to know should be drawn up here, including the *little* things often omitted or glossed over by the veteran traveler because they seem to him so obvious. But before presenting this catalog I will mention some sources of more detailed factual information, in addition to the PAA, PATA and JTB handbooks referred to in Chapter 1.

I think, first of all, of the JTA's semi-monthly illustrated paper called *Japan Travel News*, and next, perhaps, of a large volume called *We Japanese*, by K. Yamaguchi, proprietor of the famous Fujiya Hotel in Fuji-Hakone National Park, a book published in Japan. This is a veritable encyclopedia, but its style is lively and the author has taken delight in presenting, along with standard information, a lot of curious and little-known facts. In our country there is a volume on Japan in the *World in Color Series*, edited by Doré Ogrizek and published by McGraw-Hill. This book, written by French authors and translated into English by Paddy O'Hanlon, is lavishly illustrated in color, and although it contains little about the practicalia of tourist travel it is rich in its discussion of all facets of Japanese life. A standard short history of the Japanese nation is Professor Edwin O. Reischauer's *Japan Past and Present*, published by Alfred A. Knopf. On special features of Japanese life the JTB publishes a score or so of small books, the subjects ranging from *Floral Art* to *Japanese Postage Stamps* and from *Kabuki* to *The Tea Cult*.

And now I will present my own suggested catalog of things to know right off, listing them in alphabetical order:

Cigarettes of American and British make, though by no means all brands, are to be found in the leading hotel bars, supplementing the allowance of one carton which each visitor is allowed to bring in duty free. Japanese cigarettes are "not bad," the best and most expensive brand being named *Fuji* and a very popular brand being named *Peace*. I have seen *no* filtered cigarettes in Japan, either American or Japanese, but scuttlebut has it that a filtered brand called *Hope* is soon to be launched, so we may nourish—hope.

*   *   *

Climate. Japan is 1300 miles long, as I've said, which is about the same distance as that from Massachusetts to Miami, so the country naturally has about as many climates as our eastern seaboard. In northernmost Hokkaido it is just plain *cold*, with lots of snow during six months of the year and chill winds and drizzles even in May and September. Tokyo's temperature is called by Japanese about like that of Washington, D. C., but in my experience it has seemed much less subject than Washington to extremes of steamy heat and biting cold. The southern island of Kyushu is considerably warmer than the Tokyo area and in Nagasaki little snow falls.

"The rainy season," says the *Official Guide*, "sets in about the middle of June and lasts three or four weeks," but I have been subjected to copious rains from late April all through May. "Very unusual indeed," said my Japanese friends, laughing at their own use of chamber-of-commerce lingo.

The cherry-blossom season is usually at its height in Tokyo during the first two weeks of April, when some of its famous avenues seem lined with delicate pink clouds, but at higher altitudes, such as Lake Chuzenji, above Nikko, and in northern areas, especially Hokkaido, I have enjoyed these cherry clouds as late as mid-May.

Your clothing should depend, as with us, on the season when you make your tour and on what parts of Japan you expect chiefly to visit. Since most tourists devote most or all of their time to Honshu, the core island of the country, though they're

missing a lot if they fail to visit the other islands, clothing for a
temperate climate should be brought, with emphasis on stout
walking shoes and a raincoat. Except in winter, a light overcoat
normally gives warmth enough, or even a raincoat, supplemented
by a sweater for the higher altitudes.

*   *   *

Drinking water is good to excellent in almost every city and
resort of Japan, which is lucky, because mineral water, as we
know it, seems not to be had anywhere. If you order it, and if
the waitress understands your odd whimsy, you'll receive a bottle
of sparkling soda water.

*   *   *

Electrical appliances. The voltage in Japanese cities and towns
is 110, so your American razor can be used without a transformer,
in hotels and inns. Virtually all of the hostelries you will use have
American-style outlets, into which you can plug your appliances,
a fact that will delight those frustrated travelers who have tried
in vain to plug in their appliances in European hotels.

*   *   *

English-language newspapers, all of them full of world news
and American sports as well as Japanese and local news and sports,
are a godsend to the visitor and in many large hotels compli-
mentary copies are shoved under bedroom doors each morning,
or brought to the room with the breakfast order. The *Mainichi,*
the *Nippon Times* and the *Japan News* are standard papers, as is
the *Asahi Evening News,* whose main plant is in Osaka. The
Mainichi carries unblushing advertisements of "Nude Photo Stu-
dios" boasting "many lovely models for your choice, also young
ladies to guide you anywhere," and of "Sex Drug Stores" and of
"Turkish Bath and Massage," administered "by pretty young
girls; also bar service."

*   *   *

An *English-Japanese telephone directory of foreign residents and business firms* is published annually in Tokyo by the *Nippon Times* and is often found in hotel rooms, at least in such major hotels as the Imperial. This can be a lifesaver, since the visitor can make exactly nothing out of the regular Japanese phone book.

*   *   *

Festivals are of great importance in any traveler's planning for a visit to Japan and the chief ones, with their dates, shall be listed here.

New Year's Day is a gay national holiday, though more for family observance than for public celebrations. Houses are decorated with branches of pine, plum tree and bamboo, enhanced by fern leaves at the door.

March 3 (the third day of the third month) is the *Dolls' Festival,* called also the *Girls' Festival* and sometimes, too, the *Peach Blossom Festival* because of the peach blossoms used for decoration. On this day, which is celebrated nationally, all cities have ambitious displays of dolls dressed in the regalia of the ancient Imperial Court. Even the Emperor and Empress are represented.

April 8 is *Buddha's Birthday,* celebrated with a *Flower Festival.* In hundreds of temples images of the Infant Buddha are lavishly decorated.

May 5 (the fifth day of the fifth month) is the *Boys' Festival.* Dolls symbolizing manly valor are displayed and many thousands of huge hollow "fishes," always in the form of a carp (with his open mouth catching the wind to fill him out) flutter from bamboo poles. The carp is supposed to be swimming valiantly up a swift stream and so the Japanese boy must fight his way against all obstacles and pressures to manhood.

May 17 (but in some years May 18) marks a very great festival at the Toshogu Shrine in *Nikko,* with one of the most colorful processions to be seen in all Japan, a "repeat performance" occurring on October 17.

July 7 (the seventh day—and night—of the seventh month) marks the *Star Festival,* called *Tanabata* in Japanese. Myriads of poems to the stars are written on strips of colored paper and fastened to bamboo branches. Some streets become veritable starbursts of color.

July 17 to 20 is the core of a nine-day celebration, in *Kyoto,* of the *Gion Festival* of the Yasaka Shrine. Gorgeously decorated floats, some mounted with 100-foot towers, parade through the city's chief streets.

July 21 is celebrated in *Tokyo* with a brilliant display of fireworks on the Sumida River.

Late in *August* (check date with the JTB), on the concluding day of the *Bon Season,* which starts in mid-July with the *Feast of Lanterns* honoring the dead, a weirdly wonderful illumination takes place on a mountainside above *Kyoto.* A colossal bonfire is lighted in the shape of the Chinese ideograph 大, for *dai,* meaning BIG. The two curved strokes are respectively about 500 and 400 feet long and the cross stroke 228 feet long.

November 15 marks the *Shichi-go-san Festival,* meaning Seven- -five-three. It is a special, nationwide Shinto festival for children aged seven (shichi), five (go) or three (san) years.

Christmas Day is of small importance in Japan as a whole, though Christian families do, of course, celebrate it in more or less traditional Western style and some of the large stores, with an eye to business, put gaily decorated Christmas trees in their windows.

*   *   *

Japanese beer is excellent and very widely enjoyed. Some of the good standard brands are *Asahi; Kirin; Gold; Nippon; Sapporo.* I am solemnly assured—by Sapporo residents—that the last-named is the best.

*   *   *

Japanese manners and customs are of extraordinary interest and some of them need to be known and understood "right off." The ceremonious bowing-from-the-waist which one sees everywhere, sometimes even on crowded sidewalks, is a fascinating thing to behold and American residents sometimes manage to achieve the habit, or a reasonable facsimile thereof. The deeper you bow, and the more times, the more you indicate respect and, as I have mentioned earlier, I have sometimes seen theater aisles or sidewalks quite blocked while four or five or six very deep bows take place.

One sees women bowing to each other, men bowing to each other, women bowing to men, but I don't recall seeing men bow deeply to women, for the roles of the sexes are quite reversed in Japan and our Western sense of chivalry to women is *not* in flower. The women wait on their men, defer to them, obey them and never think of so uncivil a thing as offering any hint of criticism. A husband addresses his wife by her first name, Takako, Ranko or whatnot, but she would never presume to address *him* by *his* first name. She uses the more respectful word "Anata," meaning simply "You." She never sits with him when he has guests, but she kneels to serve him and his friends with the viands she has prepared. They, of course, are sitting on their heels on the floor, around the low table, so if she *walked* in she would tower above them. In crowded subway trains or busses one doesn't offer one's seat to a woman. Said a Japanese friend who caught me doing just that, "I *like* that Western custom and really wish I could do it, but if I offered my seat to a woman it would be misunderstood. She would think I was making advances to her."

I'll have more to say about the position of women in Japan, but other manners and customs call for attention here, and first of all about *shoes.* You take them off every time when you enter a Japanese inn or restaurant or teahouse or temple or shrine and leave them at the door. This becomes, at times, a real nuisance, for you can't just kick them off (unless you're wearing loafers or "slipper-y" shoes) as old-time Japanese kick off their wooden getas, but must unlace them and later lace them up again. You put on heelless slippers if the floor is of wood, and perhaps you have then to climb a flight or two of stairs. If you can keep the heelless slippers on while climbing or descending stairs you're a better man than I am—Gunga Din! On entering your inn room, with its fine tatami matting floor, you kick off even the slippers and pad about in your stocking feet, but when you go to the bathroom you put on another pair of slippers, of heavier type, that you'll invariably find inside the bathroom door.

The subject of Japanese inns is a big and fascinating one, which shall be discussed in a later chapter, but *green tea* calls for an introduction here, for it is proffered not only upon one's arrival at any Japanese inn but at every turn where hospitality plays a part. It is brought, very hot, in a dainty porcelain cup without handle and is to be drunk without milk or lemon or sugar. Green tea is as much a part of Japanese life and hospitality as is black tea in England or coffee in Brazil.

* * *

Laundry is done with amazing quickness in Japan's tourist hotels. Tokyo's Hotel Imperial, for instance, has a notice in all the rooms to the effect that "Laundry left before 9:30 A.M. will be returned the same evening. If left before 3 P.M. it will be returned next day." And this is *regular* service, not extra with an extra charge. (On Sundays, laundry is neither accepted nor delivered.)

* * *

Light luggage is "of the essence" to all who travel long distances by air, for excess weight charges (above 44 pounds in tourist class and above 66 pounds in first class) can mount up fantastically. A brand I have liked of light but strong zippered luggage for men and women, including a special two-suiter for men, is manufactured by Daisy Products, Inc., of 140 West 22nd Street, New York, and marketed through luggage and department stores in most cities.

* * *

Mail, received and sent, is a subject of absorbing interest even to those who think they are visiting foreign parts to get away from it all. Air mail, both ways, is used almost exclusively by American travelers. Postage for an air mail letter from the States to Japan (or other lands of the Orient) is 25 cents for each half ounce and for an air mail postcard 10 cents, but of course our post office *Air Letters* will go anywhere in the world for 10 cents provided nothing is enclosed. From Japan an air mail letter up to 10 grams in weight (a little bit under half an ounce) calls for 70 yen and an air mail postcard 40 yen; but Japan too has *Aérogrammes* (Air Letters) priced at only 45 yen, that will carry your message anywhere in the world. You may conveniently buy them, along with regular postage stamps, in the branch post office in the Imperial Hotel.

For your *mail address* in Japan, I think the simplest thing is to pick out some leading hotel in Tokyo and have everything sent there. The hotel, if my experience is a fair sample, will follow your forwarding instructions with meticulous care. Two other simple addresses are, of course, the U.S. Embassy in Tokyo and the American Express Company, whose Tokyo office is in the Marunouchi Building opposite the Central Railway Station, but whose easy address is Box 115, Central Post Office.

*   *   *

Money is always a subject of prime and axiomatic interest to travelers, but in Japan it is not a thorny subject, for the Japanese yen is fixed at 360 to the dollar and everywhere, in shops and travel offices, you find conversion cards that quickly translate any sum of yen into dollars and vice versa. U.S. currency and travelers checks can be exchanged in many leading hotels, including the Imperial. Paper bills are now in denominations of 100 yen, 500 yen and 1000 yen, but it is probable that bills of 10,000 yen will soon be printed. Subsidiary coins are of 50 yen (silver-ish), 10 yen (copper), 5 yen (brass) and 1 yen (aluminum), the latter being suitable only as playthings for children.

The paper bills offer an interesting and painless lesson in Japanese history which some visitors enjoy. The 100-yen bill carries a picture of a 19th-century statesman named Count Taisuke Itagaki, who was a powerful supporter of Emperor Meiji and who is therefore well loved by all Japanese. His passion was personal liberty and when he was wounded by an assassin his famous last words were: "I may die, but liberty will live!" The 500-yen note pictures another progressive supporter of Emperor Meiji named Iwakura, who worked consistently for peace and who was effective in preventing a war with Korea. He visited the United States as Japan's first representative of the Meiji Restoration. The 1000-yen note pictures a personage of very ancient times, Crown Prince Shotoku, who revolutionized the government of his time (early 6th century) and promoted the cult of Buddhism, then a recent import from China.

The coins of Japan also display interesting art work, the 50-yen piece bearing the imperial symbol of the chrysanthemum, the 10-yen piece depicting the Heian Shrine of Kyoto and the 5-yen brassie showing a rice plant, the very symbol of life to all Japanese.

*   *   *

Motoring in Japan cannot yet be done on a U-Drive basis, but Japan is now mass-producing very good small cars (Nissan Motor Company, Toyota Motor Company, etc.) suitable for the country's narrow roads and you may wish to buy one and ultimately bring it home as a second car. *Japanese traffic keeps to the left*, a fact which I emphasize here quite as much for the pedestrian as for the motorist. Japanese politeness seems to break down in city traffic, so do not expect thoughtful care for pedestrians, as evidenced in Honolulu. *Look out for yourself!*

*   *   *

Photography is a basic passion of millions of Japanese. Excellent Japanese cameras are purchasable (with the 16 per cent commodity tax exempted in the Specified Stores) and of course also good Japanese black-and-white and color film. Black-and-white film processing is done in thousands of shops in one day. When you see the letters DPE outside a shop it is merely the shop-keeper's way of telling you that he handles developing, printing and enlarging.

*   *   *

Picture postcards are purchasable in Japan only in *sets* of ten or a dozen, which seems to me unfortunate. If you want to send one or two lovely cards from Nikko, Nara or Kobe you have to buy a whole set for each city. However, the sets are very inexpensive and most of them are really lovely color shots.

*   *   *

Sake is too well known to traveling Americans and even to city Americans who have sampled Japanese fare in their home town to need any introduction, but "just in case," I'll say that this national beverage of Japan is a very pleasant, transparent alcoholic drink brewed from rice and drunk warm from tiny porcelain cups. Its alcoholic content is more like that of sherry than of hard liquor but ten or a dozen miniature cupfuls of it can give you a cheerful glow. Japanese youths not infrequently down it in quantity, chiefly when on holiday sprees, and you'll note that their glow has grown to downright inebriety, but taken in halfway reasonable amounts it's a delightful accompaniment to a good sukiyaki or tempura meal. Sake used to be mellowed in casks of cryptomeria wood (Japanese cedar) to give it extra fragrance and sometimes it is still thus mellowed, but much more often, in this commercial age, it is simply bottled and shipped to its various markets.

CHAPTER 4

HOTELS, WESTERN AND JAPANESE

The Imperial Hotel, Temple of Tourism

TOKYO's *Imperial Hotel* was built in its earliest form as a place quite literally for visiting "vips" and especially for invited guests of the Imperial Household and the court, so it bore, as such, a sort of resemblance to Washington's Blair House in our day, where guests of the White House are entertained. It is one of the world's elite caravansaries, with immense traditions, matched in glamour and historic importance by no more than half a dozen hotels in the whole world of travel, and even that small company was reduced by one when Shepheard's of Cairo was burned to the ground by Communist-led rioters in 1952.

Once when I was talking with the proprietress of the bookshop in the lobby of the Imperial she said, with real earnestness, "I wish you'd tell your readers, at least in outline, the *history* of this hotel, for half the people who come to my shop, even for a magazine, ask me about it." I thought this request significant of the widespread interest in the hotel, so I'll gladly comply, though only in briefest synopsis, since a whole book could easily be written about it.

In 1887, three Japanese noblemen, Marquis Inouye, Viscount Shibusawa and Baron Okura, all close to the Imperial Family, decided that Japan's capital city should have a hotel suitable for Westerners, for until that time there had been nothing but unheated Japanese inns, where every guest sat on the floor, slept on the floor and invariably had his meals brought by a maidservant to his low table on the floor. No such thing as running

45

water had been thought of, nor had a hotel dining room or restaurant been imaginable, but this was the period of the Meiji Restoration when Japan's more progressive leaders were becoming fascinated by Western ways. A long-term lease of land was secured in the heart of the city and the three pioneers raised the money for a three-story wooden hotel, the Imperial Household being the chief shareholder and itself investing heavily. The first Imperial was completed in 1890 and guests averaged hardly more than ten a day.

In 1910, with the completion of the Trans-Siberian Railway, venturesome round-the-world travelers were beginning to pour into Japan and that year even saw the advent of the first big planned tour, no less than 500 persons descending upon the hotel at one time.

In 1919, the hotel being then in its thirtieth year, Frank Lloyd Wright and an engineer named Miller were engaged to design a new building and the capital was increased to $3,000,000, a vast sum for a hotel in those days. This new Imperial was opened on July 4, 1922, for a reception for Admiral Edwin Denby, then our Secretary of the Navy. Frank Lloyd Wright has always been a controversial figure and has thrived on criticism, so it is no shock to learn that he has had critics in plenty of this great structure. Its design was boldly original, both in general and in detail, and perhaps he sacrificed daylight in some parts of the building for the sake of beauty, but after all, this building is in *Japan*, where a sense of artistry should always be paramount. The "house that Wright built" has been supplemented by a new building whose bedrooms contain every conceivable comfort, including air-conditioning and sound-proof double windows, which are a mighty good thing in Tokyo-of-the-noisy-night, and a still newer and far larger annex, with 450 rooms and baths, including 50 sumptuous suites, to cost $8,000,000, is under construction and should be ready for occupancy by the latter half of 1958. The present hotel complex has 488 guest rooms with accommodations for 750 persons, and when the newer and larger addition is completed there will be a total of 938 guest rooms, with accommodations for 1616 persons. So much for statistics, but I am outrunning history.

On September 1, 1923, only fourteen months after the hotel's opening, came the terrible earthquake and fire, which devastated Tokyo in one of the most frightful disasters any great city has known and caused fantastic loss of life. By heroic efforts of the staff the whole hotel was saved, though the heat from adjoining buildings on fire melted the window glass and started several incipient fires on the roof. On the following day the embassies of the United States, Great Britain, France and Italy, along with various foreign legations, burned out from their own quarters, moved into the Imperial. On and from that day the Imperial experienced its "finest hour." I wish I could record the whole story for it is thrilling all the way, but a few excerpts must suffice from an account written by Mr. T. Inumaru, then as now the hotel's manager, and published in the Japan Advertiser on January 24, 1924.

"As we had kept our building, we had to do everything we could for all the refugees. Of course we took in anyone who came. No matter what kind of dress people had on, if they came in we thought they must be our old customers or acquaintances from the neighborhood. Every meal time we gave rice balls to more than 2500 Japanese. Refugees could come in from the park [Hibiya Park, across the way] and get their rice boxes filled. If there was not enough rice to give we made rice soup and kept it ready for more than a thousand.

"In the hotel we had no water supply, no lights, no stoves to use, no telephone. No cars or trains were running; no telegrams could be sent. As for water, luckily an outside hydrant right by the kitchen never stopped running, so we made our campfire there for cooking. As we could not bake bread, without the use of our ranges, we made a kind of Irish stew, with plenty of onions and dumplings. So we got along. For the first four days from the earthquake we didn't make any charge for meals or room to anyone, even the former guests. We let anyone come into the dining room without charge.

"And so the emergency passed. Reconstruction will come more quickly if all of us who did not lose in the disaster can enter into the feelings of those who lost everything."

*   *   *

Hotel Imperial is today the mecca of all who visit Japan. It is crowded to the gunwales all the time and thousands have to be turned away. In some periods of overcrowding, stays of only three days can be granted but this situation will be greatly eased when the new project is completed. That will have ten stories above ground and five below ground, with parking space, in all, for 350 cars. Among its various new dining and banquet facilities Mr. Inumaru plans a "Copenhagen Room" in tribute to the polar air route from Copenhagen to Tokyo initiated in 1957 by Scandinavian Airlines System.

The Wright-built structure, though in its fourth decade of existence, is a glamorous landmark of tourism. Almost always there is some magnificent decoration in the center of the lobby. Once I admired a big cherry tree, pink-clouded with blossoms. On another visit a floodlighted five-story pagoda filled the same space. It was an exact replica, one-tenth the actual size, of the famous pagoda of the Toshogu Shrine in Nikko made in a labor of 22 years by Kijuro Hasegawa, architect of the Imperial Household Agency.

Directly beyond these changing displays lies the hotel's main dining room, with an orchestra ensconced in the balcony. In other parts of the same building are the grillroom (steaks, chops, etc.); the Prunier Room (seafood); the Sukiyaki Room; the Garden Bar; the Banquet Hall; two beautiful courtyard gardens, in one of which, the South Court Garden, tea is served on summer days; a Peacock Alley of Japanese design; and a good-sized theater, in which I once laughed till I wept at a first-rate performance of Noel Coward's *Blithe Spirit* presented by the Tokyo Amateur Dramatic Club.

In the aisles leading from the main lobby are ticket offices of the dozen or so air lines serving Tokyo and in the building's basement is an arcade with a post office, a telegraph office, a JTB office, a barber shop and beauty parlor, a drug store and about a score of fine gift shops selling everything, from woodblock prints to fine brocades to Mikimoto's cultured pearls.

The Imperial is one of those desired havens which eager travelers cross oceans to enjoy. And remember this: Its tariffs, which I know to have been criticized by American hotel men as "too low for such a place," now $6.00 and up for a single room and bath, $9.00 and up for a double room and bath, are subject to a 10 per cent service charge and above that *you do not tip*, except for extra special service.

Other Tokyo Hotels, Western Style

Tokyo is setting its sights for the Jet Age, when it expects to welcome two and a half times as many visitors as now crowd the air lanes and sea lanes. Among projected new hotels, the most important, if and when it becomes a fact rather than a project, will be a new unit, the first in the Orient, of the Intercontinental Hotels Corporation, a subsidiary of Pan American Airways, which already operates a chain of superior modern hotels in many foreign lands and in the Caribbean Islands. It is too early, as yet, to make any firm prediction about this development, now under earnest discussion, but I mention it merely as something to watch for with interest.

But today's hotels, the ones you can use now, are of more urgent interest, so I will introduce briefly some of the most desirable of them which I have explored, listing first a rather arbitrary Big Six (some listers would make it seven or eight) and then three lesser places of special nature.

Hotel Nikkatsu, in a very central location at the corner of A and Z Avenues (MacArthur nomenclature), is the most modern of them and actually the most expensive, its tariffs being substantially higher than those of the Imperial. It is an extremely bright and cheerful hotel occupying the four top floors of the ultra-modern Nikkatsu Building and with its own modern, well-ventilated garage in the same building's sub-basement. Its main dining room, called the Silver Room, sparkles with good cheer to enhance its good food, and there is also a grillroom called the Green Room, where service is à la carte. On a broad balcony above the lobby is a bar lounge where one may watch TV. Nearly all of this hotel's 133 rooms are twin-bed doubles and its most luxurious suites, each with a grand crescent of windows on the corner of the building, seem worth their lofty tariff, which is $30 a day. In the first basement of the Nikkatsu Building is an arcade of fine shops rivaling those in the Imperial's arcade.

Hotel Kokusai Kanko means International Tourist Hotel and this Tokyo hostelry fits its name. Very modern and very Western in character, with accommodations for 144 guests, it occupies a considerable part of the International Tourist Building, rising immediately to the east of the Tokyo Central Station. On the 8th floor of this imposing building you'll find the headquarters of the Japan Tourist Association.

Hotel Dai-ichi, meaning "Number One" (General MacArthur's headquarters were in another building similarly named Dai-ichi), is indeed a very large hotel, with 626 guest rooms, many of them singles, occupying the whole of an 8-story building near the Shimbashi Railway Station, three or four blocks south of the Imperial. It was formerly used by the U.S. Armed Forces but after it was derequisitioned it was thoroughly done over in modern style. It advertises its facilities in panting English as "enjoyable to the depth of the charm in an atmosphere of elegancy and joyfulness," but I found it rather too much like a compactly designed office building to warrant such glowing prose. However, it is very comfortable, though the private baths are small.

Hotel Tokyo is a good modern hotel on 4th Street, a stone's throw southwest of Tokyo Central Station. It has 80 rooms, all with bath and radio.

Hotel Teito, also with 80 rooms, looms up on A Avenue, just outside the Imperial Palace moat, in a way to suggest a national bank and its sign seems almost as big as itself. It is now, I understand, about to add a substantial annex. The Teito is usually classed as one of Tokyo's Big Six.

Prince Hotel, my sixth of the Big Six, is not big at all in size or capacity, having only 37 rooms, but it is a quality place in a lovely park setting near the junction of A and B Avenues, some 15 minutes south of the center by car.

And now for the three lesser places, though many would include the first of these in the big-league.

Hotel Marunouchi, located on W Avenue and 4th Street, close to the Tokyo Central Station and hence to Hotel Tokyo, is a good-sized place with 139 rooms, well patronized by Americans. Handily situated on the opposite side of the avenue is the Supper Club Marunouchi, with a dance orchestra and elaborate floor shows. On Thursday evenings the hotel puts on an entertainment of its own, in its own premises.

Tokyo Station Hotel, with 60 rooms, is *in* the Tokyo Central Station, which structure, by the way, is closely modeled after the Central Station of Amsterdam. It's as handy as any place could be, especially for those who arrive by train from Yokohama. It is definitely a humbler place, and cheaper, than any of those listed above, but it is entirely suitable for thrift-budget travel.

Shiba Park Hotel, to conclude this list, is unique in Tokyo and indeed in all Japan. Briefly, it is the brain child of the same Mr. Inumaru who directs Hotel Imperial and who is also president of the Japan Hotel Association. He felt that a thoroughly good and extremely inexpensive hotel would meet a felt need in Tokyo, so he built this hotel in Shiba Park and opened it in the summer of 1956. "Now hear this": The uniform charge is an amazingly modest $5 a day per person, *with all three meals in-*

cluded. The hotel is a modern and pleasant one of four stories (no elevator), each room has a toilet and shower, and of course it has central heating, like all Western hotels (but no Japanese inns) of good standing. Always it is fully patronized, especially by Americans who like to save as much of their travel money as possible for things other than mere luxury of living.

Japanese Inns, Their Perils and Perfections

There are several very good Japanese inns in Tokyo, two of which I shall presently identify, but first let's consider the subject in general. I have already mentioned some basic features, but let's look at the Japanese inn—*ryokan* is the word—in close-up detail, for there is nothing remotely like it anywhere else in the world.

A Japanese woman, and she will *invariably* be petite and pleasant, bows deeply in welcome and if the place is fully and solely Japanese she will probably be kneeling and will bow her head till it touches her knees. To repeat some earlier mentioned facts, you unlace your shoes and leave them at the door, putting on the usual heelless slippers to shuffle along the corridors and perhaps up a flight of stairs. At the door of your room you kick off the slippers and step upon the tatami-matted floor in your stocking feet, and if the room has a private bathroom, as some of the best rooms in the more pretentious inns do, you find inside the bathroom door a heavier pair of slippers, still and always heelless, which you are supposed to put on for use while there. The matting of your bedroom floor is surely the world's finest such material, being made of two-inch filler of rice straw surfaced with an exquisitely fine woven reed covering. It is yielding and comforting to tired feet.

At one side of your room will be an elevated alcove (toko-noma), which was in very early times the sleeping couch, when floors were of chilly earth, but is now merely a place for one or two lovely bibelots, backed perhaps by an artistic scroll. If the room is large and pretentious it may have a sort of belvedere alcove, with a table and two chairs, these last items being generous concessions to Western ideas of comfort, for to all-Japanese guests *the floor's the thing.* You sit on the floor on a *zabuton* (cushion) and eat from a foot-high table. You sleep on the floor on one or two or three padded quilts (*futon*) and are covered, for warmth, with more padded quilts. Such items as you remove from your luggage you lay directly on the floor or in flat baskets provided for the purpose, except that your suits may (usually) be placed on hangers on a rack with pole, or even, sometimes, in a closet.

Floor living seems to first-time visitors odd, puzzling, awkward, even downright uncomfortable, but you soon accustom yourself to it and even get to like it *except for your legs,* which, if they're anything like mine, simply refuse to fold under you neatly and be sat upon. You try sticking them out one side, then the other, then out in front. Nothing helps very much, though a foot-high elbow rest that is sometimes provided does lend some comfort. The only trouble with it is that it tends to slip on the smooth matting and you have to hike it up, and your reposing body with it, from time to time.

When you first enter your room, your chambermaid (*jochu-san*), who will be as petite, dainty and smiling as was the greeter at the outer door, will come with you, or immediately after you, to bring your cup of very hot green tea. If you are a man she will indicate by words or motions that you are to remove your coat and trousers and when you've done so she will drape a light kimono, more properly called a *yukata,* around you and tie it with a sash. If the room is cold, as it probably will be in spring and fall, and wickedly cold in winter, for the charcoal brazier or toaster-size electric heater provides only token warmth, she'll put a heavy kimono around you, over the yukata, and tie you in snugly. Then she'll sit opposite you at the low table, as you sip your tea, so she'll be ready to give you any further needed service. You probably can't chat with her because you can't speak Japanese and she'll have only a phrase or two of English, but she'll be "lovely to look at."

Late in the afternoon, usually between 5 and 6 o'clock, guests take their hot baths and this institution, believe me, is something to conjure with in Japanese inns. Yes, it's quite true, all bathe in the same big tank-like tub, men and women, boys and girls, and the only covering is a *tenugui*, or large washcloth, which each uses before entering the tub. In other words, mixed nude bathing is still done, though rather less than formerly and considerably less in the smart, tourist-conscious inns than in the simpler, strictly Japanese inns.

But there's a special feature about bathing in Japan that every visitor should know and recognize. You never actually wash yourself in the tub, since that is for a long hot soak, and the water will be HOT. As I've said rather incidentally above, you soap, scrub and rinse yourself *outside the tub* before jumping in, and this is important for it would be a grievous *faux pas* to jump into the tub before washing yourself with meticulous thoroughness. To achieve this you use a basin and your washcloth and have a small wooden stool or a strip of planking to sit on or to put each foot on in turn. When you've finished just jump right into the tub, unless it's too full of other men and women, in which case sit by and let the earlier comers have a good soak before your turn comes.

In most cases, especially in the higher class inns, you may arrange, at certain hours, for private use of the bath if modesty has you in its clutches, but this brings us to another pleasant hazard. Your chambermaid, and again I say that this is less feasible in semi-tourist, partly Westernized inns than in the old-line, simon-pure Japanese variety, will help you to take your private bath. She will at least scrub your back patiently and cheerily if you request this service. If you are a man she will likely hesitate to wash your chest, stomach and legs and will smilingly pass the soap, washcloth and basin to you for this purpose, though such balking, in my experience, has not been universal. If you are a young man she'll probably be more skittish than if you are—my age. If you are a boldly experimental type of male you'll enjoy trying out the co-operation of your jochu-san. I got a Japanese friend to give me three golden phrases, the first one being for use over the phone, if your room has one, the second and third being addressed to the maid. Here they are.

Please send the maid: *Jochu-san o yonde kudasai.*

Please prepare the bath: *Ofuro negai masu.*

Will you please wash my back?: *Senaka o nagashite kudasai?*

Before leaving the sizzling subject of Japanese hot baths I'll mention again that in many hotspring resorts, some of which I'll introduce as they enter the pattern of this book, each leading inn has its own large pool of natural hot water where twenty to a hundred, or even two hundred, persons "mix-bathe" together, and here too the men and women soap and rinse themselves outside the pool, along its steaming periphery, and when thoroughly clean they enter the pool. Usually, but not always, the sexes undress in separate rooms located at either end of the pool, or they may undress in their rooms and come to the edge of the pool wearing their yukata. Atami Hotel, at Atami, not far south of Tokyo, is one popular spa-inn with its own pool but this isn't a patch on such outsized pools as that of the Dai-ichi Takimoto of Noboribetsu, which seems like a veritable nudist colony, though if this sounds gross and fleshy please withhold judgment until you've witnessed the grace and smooth daintiness of the undraped Japanese form. The fashionable Fujiya Hotel, in Fuji-Hakone Park, by way of contrast to the inns just mentioned, is so primly Westernized, though gloriously Japanese in its structure and decoration, that it actually requires the patrons who use its "Dream Pool" to wear bathing suits! Yes, you're quite right. This deplorable trend toward pussyfoot Westernism should be halted. Maybe you'll do your part to encourage the natural Nipponism of tradition.

"As I was saying"—your maid, in a genuine ryokan (you now know this word for Japanese inn) will bring all of your meals to your room, though if you would rather have a comfortable chair to sit on, suitable for your Western legs, instead of Japanese atmosphere, you will find, in many of the top inns, a dining room where you may sit, perhaps quite alone, eating, in the way to which you are accustomed, the food to which you are accustomed. But when I go Japanese I usually like to go all the way, letting my legs sprawl where they may.

Tokyo is not the best city for your initiation to the perils and perfections of the Japanese ryokan, but if you should decide to try one in the capital you'll find the *Fukuda Inn* very well appointed. It has 20 bedrooms, each named for a different flower, as are its public rooms, and the artistry of the whole place is impeccably Japanese. Another good inn, some of whose rooms are semi-Western in style and appointments, is the *Shinkomatsu*, located centrally, within a few steps of the Ginza, the celebrated central artery of Tokyo.

THE BACKGROUND OF THE PICTURE

CHAPTER 5

THE STORY OF JAPAN, A WORLD PUZZLE

Nineteen Centuries from Then to Now

PROBABLY no nation in history has been such a puzzle to its fellow-nations as has the Japanese Empire, crowded into its four major islands and some minor ones totaling an area less than that of California. How, "by the beard of Enigma," did a nation that was hermetically sealed for centuries in self-imposed isolation, only to be opened in 1853 by the bold challenge of American Commodore Matthew C. Perry, become a world power in just half a century and soon thereafter one of the Big Five and then a dire threat to our own great nation?

I'm afraid I don't know all the answers but I do know some of them from fascinated study of several competent histories, including the authoritative one called *Japan, Past and Present* by Harvard Professor Edwin O. Reischauer, who was born in Tokyo and studied for years in the Imperial Universities of Tokyo and Kyoto.

Rather than drag you through the intricacies of Japan's pre-Perry centuries, about eighteen of them that are reasonably well known to earnest historians, I will dispose of that long period in syllabus brevity, following this with a glossary of important Japanese terms, and will then present modern Japan, the nation that emereged from its hard shell in the middle of the 19th century.

To oversimplify the beginnings, Japan was born of China, in a cultural sense, as Europe was born of the Mediterranean cultures, and even in ethnic ways she must certainly trace her family tree

59

to Chinese roots, though a primitive Mongoloid stock that had
seeped in from the Asian mainland, mostly by way of Korea, had
long existed and this was mixed with some Malayan and Polynesian stock and, to a very slight extent, with the rude aboriginal
Ainu stock, faint traces of which still survive in Hokkaido Island.

For some eighteen centuries, roughly contemporaneous with
the Christian era, Japan was overshadowed and awed by the
culture of her great mother, for China was old when Japan was
young and Chinese culture was a wonder of the world. It first
came in waves of invasion by way of Korea. Warriors on horse-
back brought the Bronze and Iron Ages to Japan at about the
time of the birth of Christ, an era when the Roman Empire was
already beginning to show the first symptoms of decay. More
specifically, these warriors brought with them (though insistent
legend makes the Sun Goddess the giver) three cherished Chinese
symbols which became Japan's Three Sacred Treasures, consti-
tuting the Imperial Regalia, and which are even now the symbols
of the Emperor's authority. They were, and are, the sword, the
semi-precious stone, which always took the curved shape of an
outsize comma, and the round bronze mirror.

Over the centuries, China was an inspiration, a challenge and
a problem to Japan, the older nation reaching its peak of influence over the newer in the period from the 6th to the 9th
century. Then, gradually and increasingly, Japan developed and
asserted her own way of life and built up some admirable skills
in architecture, in various arts and crafts, in a superb technique
of wood-block printing and, most typically of all, in truly marvelous landscape gardening, tree culture and flower arrangement.
Says René Sieffert in his history monograph in *Japan*, in "The
World in Color" series, writing of the Japanese gift of imitat-
ing, "Whilst the Japanese first copies in order to get his hand in,
he then interprets his imitations and devises them anew in his
own particular style." With the growth of her own culture,
Japan also built up a feudal society whose great families were
all-powerful and which eventually (in the 17th century) brought
on an extreme national isolation made of such stern stuff that

our modern isolationists seem world-minded by comparison. For more than two full centuries it cut the nation off from the outer world as no other highly developed nation has ever been cut off.

All this time there was an unbroken line of Emperors, a fact of which the average Japanese must often have been forgetful, for deification of the monarch did not set in with any force until *after* the opening of Japan by Commodore Perry. It was a political ruse invented, or at least strongly fostered, by a set of ambitious nationalist leaders who came to the fore in 1868 determined to overthrow feudalism and restore, outwardly, the regal power of the throne while retaining the actual power themselves. They loved the phrase "access to the throne" and sometimes they "interpreted" the Imperial will to suit themselves. This is called the *Meiji Restoration*, but the story of its build-up belongs in a later section of this chapter.

The Emperor's long involvement in the tangled web of feudalism reached the depths of absurdity yet the *fiction* that he ruled as well as reigned was never quite abandoned. In the late 9th century a powerful court family named Fujiwara won, by guile and strategy, complete domination over the Imperial family and for almost a thousand years this clan *and its offshoots*, in near or distant branches of the prolific family, monopolized all high court posts, with hardly a break, but this does not mean that the Fujiwara ran Japan. The facts of the case, at one typical period, are revealed in this rich passage from Professor Reischauer's book: "One finds in 13th-century Japan an Emperor who was a mere puppet in the hands of a retired Emperor and of . . . the Fujiwara, who together controlled a government which was in fact merely a sham government, completely dominated by the private government of the shogun [a sort of generalissimo]—who in turn was a puppet in the hands of a Hojo regent. The man behind the throne had become a series of men, each one in turn controlled by the man behind himself."

History and nationalistic legend are far apart in their findings on the origin of the Imperial Family. History says that a clan of priest-chiefs called Yamato, which won supremacy over other priest-chiefs in central and western Japan in the 2nd or 3rd century developed into the Japanese Imperial Family. The Yamato clan, however, fostered a fanciful legend to the effect that the Sun Goddess was its progenitress and to support the legend it developed the cult of sun-worshipping Shinto, which became the dominant religion of Japan. The Emperor was thus the descendant of the Sun, and in the 19th and 20th centuries, when nationalist jingoes needed a definite genealogy for their Emperors, they proclaimed with unflagging insistence that the first Emperor, one Jimmu Tenno, who came to the throne in 660 B.C., was the son of a son of Ameratsu, the Sun Goddess, who had sent her child to earth to propagate the Imperial Family. All subsequent Emperors thus became his heirs and thus indubitably divine. The word jingo, by the way, is a Japanese word, or name. The forceful Empress Jingo, apparently an actual person, not a legend, invaded Korea at a very early (and shadowy) date, and although she didn't quite win Korea her hot-headed chauvinism gave a new word to modern dictionaries.

Shinto is so intimately bound up with the whole structure of Japanese life that an elementary knowledge of it is essential to an understanding of even "tourist Japan." Shinto means "the way of the gods" and first developed as a naive form of nature worship. Says Professor Reischauer: "Shinto was based on a simple feeling of awe in the presence of any surprising or awesome phenomenon of nature—a waterfall, a mountain crag, a large tree, a peculiarly shaped stone, or even some lowly thing awesome only in its capacity for irritation, such as an insect. Anything awe-inspiring was called *kami*, a word usually translated as 'god' but basically meaning 'above,' and by extension 'superior.' This simple concept of deity should be borne in mind in trying to understand the deification in modern Japan of living Emperors *and of all Japanese soldiers who have died for their country.*" (The italics are mine.)

In an interesting summary by a scholar named J. Takabu, quoted in an article by James A. Michener, we are told that "Shintoism is not to be considered a religion and its spirits are by no means gods. Shinto is a composite body of old beliefs, customs, good-luck omens and national ritual. Its only purpose is to develop loyalty to one's land, one's long-established way of life." The Michener article, by the way, a double-length one rich in details, may be found in an old issue of *Holiday* (August, 1952). Subsequent events may have invalidated some of the author's comments but it remains a fascinating study, fascinatingly illustrated.

Modern Shinto developed into three strata, namely: (1) *State Shinto* at the top, including (before the defeat in World War II) stress on the deification of the Emperor, this whole stratum being a device of those with "access to the throne" to ensure a docile and devoted citizenry; (2) the *Shinto Sects*, thirteen in number, with their temples, robed priests and formal worship; and (3) *Popular Shinto*. This last, which directly affected the humbler folk, came to center chiefly around prayers for good crops and for a good crop of sons to till the fields. Correct, punctilious ceremonial performance was important to ensure satisfactory results, but, as stated in Chapter 2, Shinto now has very scant hold on young Japan, though a reformed sect called Tenrikyo does possess some spiritual quality and influence.

Summing up the effects of this three-ply religion in terms of military power, as of 1941, the Japanese fanaticism which amazed and challenged our American forces is seen to be quite natural. Beginning with the *Meiji Period*, 1868-1912, youngsters had it drilled incessantly into their minds, hearts and souls that the greatest joy they could hope for was to die in battle for their Emperor-god. By this act they would themselves become, in a small way, divine and could aid friends or vent their wrath on enemies. That helps to explain their Spartan courage, their wild willingness to rush into certain death with exultant cries of "Banzai!" It explains also the cheerful participation of airmen in the *kamikaze* plane squadrons. What easier way could there be to win immediate divinity!

The dramatic surrender of Japan to General MacArthur on board the "Mighty Mo" (September 2, 1945), the mild but drastically effective rule of MacArthur (1945-51), the establishment of a new and democratic constitution (May 3, 1947), the dismissal of MacArthur by President Truman (April 11, 1951), to be replaced by General Ridgway, and the final ratification of the peace treaty and administrative pact (March 20, 1952), restoring full sovereignty to Japan, are the stepping stones of recent history that have led to the building of the New Japan. This New Japan, the one you will see, is far more concerned with the present and the future than with elaborate fictions about the past.

A Little Glossary of Terms

Many intending visitors to Japan have hazy ideas of the actual meaning of certain Japanese terms that may have long been familiar enough as words, so to clear up such haziness on the more important points is the mission of this thumbnail glossary, arranged alphabetically.

Bushido, the "Way of the Warrior," is a modern term for an ancient ethical code observed by Japanese warrior-knights (samurai) of the feudal period. This code stressed bravery as a matter of course, but even more importantly, unswerving loyalty and obedience to the warrior's feudal lord. In the 20th century its meanings became, for modern soldiers, far more rugged and demanding. Before Japan's fateful attack on Pearl Harbor and all during the resulting war bushido, as we've seen, was dinned eternally, relentlessly, into every conscript's ears. It exalted the glory of loyalty to Emperor and to commanding officer. It made poverty, self-sacrifice, service without pay, shining goals of conduct, and death for the Emperor the shiniest goal of all. Suffering from jungle heat, mountain cold, hunger and thirst were strands of bushido. Toughening by being marched for exhausting hours without rest or nourishment or water, such methods were a part of bushido. The futility of such rigors, in view of the crushing defeat Japan suffered, must have cooled the fires of bushido and it seems unlikely that such total fanaticism will ever again infuse the common man of Nippon.

Daimyo, or *Daimio,* is the term for provincial feudal lord, more or less corresponding to the feudal lords of France and England. For a few centuries, especially the 14th and 15th, the Daimyos were dominant all over Japan, though the shogun and the Emperor were "also present."

Genro was a term for "elder statesman," especially during the Meiji Period of modern times (1868-1912).

Harakiri means literally "belly-cut," being a rude term for the more polite *seppuku.* This ghastly method of ceremonial suicide, if literally followed out, meant the slashing open of one's belly with a knife, in a low, then upward and circular motion, following this by emptying the entrails on the floor before the family shrine. It has always been thought of as an *honorable* end, not so much for the common man as for persons of rank who thus atoned for offending the Emperor or shogun or as a means of "squaring" some personal indignity or frustration.

The most famous case of harakiri in Japanese history was that of the "Forty-Seven Ronin," which occurred in 1703. The Forty-Seven were grievously incensed at an intolerable insult that had been inflicted upon their personal lord by a higher lord, an insult that had inflamed the lower lord and led him to draw his sword within the castle grounds of Edo (Tokyo), an unforgivable offense. For this offense he had been ordered to commit harakiri, which he did, thus condemning his forty-seven faithful followers to become Ronin, which term designated feudal knights (samurai) without a lord. The injustice of it rankled so fiercely in the collective breast that the Ronin plotted for two years to gain revenge. This they finally achieved by boldly breaking into the higher lord's home on a winter night and beheading him and his surrounding samurai, after which they took the head of the higher lord to the tomb of their own lord, and then announced their deed to the authorities and awaited the penalty. This show of self-sacrificing loyalty to their personal lord made them national heroes and in recognition of this the authorities graciously permitted all forty-seven of them to commit harakiri in the most approved style. Today, the Forty-Seven Ronin lie side by side in graves in the court of the Sengakuji Temple in Tokyo and the graves are a tourist sight. A forty-eighth grave is also there, this one marking the resting place of a friend of the Ronin. This man had shown open contempt for what he had wrongly judged to be their cowardice, whereas the Ronin had actually feigned cowardice to throw off suspicion. He expiated his sin in the only way he knew, by committing harakiri as his friends had done.

Over the centuries, harakiri, which has been a subject of gory fiction by the long ton, lost some of its horror. The victim usually made a minor cut in his belly and then had a loyal friend finish him off by a gunshot or by chopping off his head. Nowadays, harakiri is strictly prohibited and suicide, when it occurs, is quite "Westernized." It should not be thought that suicide, whether by noble or "humdrum" means, such as jumping off a bridge or a cliff, is common in Japan. It is probably not any commoner today than in most Western lands.

Kamikaze means "Divine Wind" and it has basic reference to the typhoon, especially one famous typhoon of 1281 which destroyed an attacking fleet of ships sent against Japan by no less a personage than the great Kublai Khan. In World War II, as everyone knows, the word designated those planes, singly or in squadrons, which attacked enemy ships in suicide raids.

Kuge were the court nobles of feudal times.

Metsuke were the secret police of the Tokugawa Period (1603-1867), which was the concluding era of feudalism. This was perhaps the world's first extensive and efficient secret police system and from it developed Japan's modern prewar system, including the dreaded "thought control" of 1925 et seq. Before and during World War II, Japan's secret police, with a long record of background and experience, made a formidable bulwark against freedom.

Mikado is a term for the Emperor *not* used in Japan but frequently used by foreigners past and present, including Messrs. Gilbert and Sullivan. Responsible historians rarely use this term, but Noah Webster does, telling us that it is derived from *mi*, a term of honor or respect, plus *kado*, meaning door. He does not tell us why anyone should refer to His Imperial Majesty as "Honorable Door," but other authorities explain that kado refers to the Gate of the Imperial Palace, which came to symbolize The Presence itself.

Samurai were men-at-arms in the service of their feudal lords or daimyos. Their fanatical loyalty to their lord is typified by the incident of the Forty-Seven Ronin recounted above under Harakiri.

Shimpa is a nickname for self-declared Communist fellow-travelers and sympathizers (the first two syllables are slightly distorted to make the nickname!) in today's Japan. Some Shimpa are found among Japan's university students and young intellectuals. Communism, rather dangerously strong during the first few years after the war, seems not to be any serious present menace, for it has greatly declined in political strength and prestige. Its adherents now have little power at the polls and its leadership is limited to a very few seats in the Diet.

Shogun is sometimes translated as Generalissimo and doubtless the successive shoguns thought of themselves in such grandiose vein. The first shogun, founder of the system, was Yoritomo Minamoto, who came to power in 1185. In a fashion typical of Japan throughout its long feudal history he let the Emperors and their Fujiwara courtiers carry on unmolested with their "government," which became more and more of a sham. He set up his own capital, usurped all actual power and developed his own personal army, permitting the generous fiction that he commanded it in the name of the Emperor. The shogun didn't need "access to the throne." Rather did the throne need access to him, but the Japanese are a polite nation and the Imperial court tried not to notice what was happening. The last shogunate came to an end, at least as an actual force, in 1867. Then began the Meiji Restoration of modern times.

Tycoon is a colloquial American version of the Japanese term *taikun*, meaning "great prince." Ambitious shoguns were wont to assume this essentially incorrect title in order to bolster their importance in political parleys. Americans first heard of it when the Tokugawa shogun of the time entered into negotiations with Commodore Perry in 1853.

Zaibatsu were the great business empires or cartels built up largely in the first four decades of this century, the two most famous ones, Mitsui and Mitsubishi, being known all over the world. Somewhat as in the case of the German cartels in Hitler's Reich the zaibatsu, though cannily fearful of the risks of a major war, were increasingly involved with the ambitious militarists who gained political ascendancy in Japan. General MacArthur, during the period of the American occupation, determined to break up these colossal and undemocratic business combines and he succeeded in doing so. The business empires, as such, were demolished, though the units of these empires remained and still remain as a great force in Japan. Big business, as in America, is still big business but the overpowering trusts are, at least in theory, things of the past.

Great Periods and Persons

Without torturing the complex subject, or the reader, this section aims to present some, not all, of the leading periods of Japanese history and the personages who dominated them.

Buddhism came to Japan in 552, under Emperor Kimmei, and was Japanized and greatly advanced by Prince-Regent Shotoku, the gentleman who now graces Japan's 1000-yen bills. (See *Money*—in Chapter 3.) It was a major influence, even *the* major influence, in shaping Japanese cultural history. In the words of René Seiffert, "Art, literature, ethics and thought all owe their stimulus and development to Buddhism."

The Nara Period (710-93) signifies the era when the Japanese capital, formerly subject to a sort of nomadism, shifting with each Emperor, took firm root, to the great benefit of Japan, in the lovely setting of *Nara*. Eight successive Emperors strengthened and beautified Nara as their proud capital.

The Heian Period (794-1185) marks the era when Heian-Kyo, alias *Kyoto*, lying some 25 miles north of Nara, was the national capital. The *Fujiwara Family*, acting as regents for Emperor Kammu and his successors, dominated the period and built up a sort of aristocratic dictator-dynasty whose yoke even the powerful and forward-looking ministry of Sugawara could not shake off. But in 1160, a military leader named *Kiyomori Taira*, related in a shadowy way to the Fujiwara, overthrew the direct dynasty and ruled as Prime Minister, still in Kyoto. In 1185, he and his family clique bowed, in turn, to another clique, led by *Yoritomo Minamoto* and this debacle ended the Heian, or Kyoto, Period.

The Kamakura Period (1185-1336) saw still another center, the coastal village of *Kamakura*, just a little south of Yokohama, emerge as a sort of *de facto* capital, though the Emperor and his court remained in Kyoto. *This was the beginning of shogunate government*, in essence a military dictatorship, which was initiated by Yoritomo and was destined to last nearly seven centuries until the Meiji Restoration of 1868. The Hojo family soon conquered the Minamoto family and other clans and cliques succeeded the Hojos, but the *system* of generalissimo, or shogunate, rule showed remarkable strength and durability.

The Edo, or *Tokugawa*, *Period* (1615-1868) was the culmination of the shogunate system, developing when an able and ambitious leader established a brand-new center around the citadel of Edo, making this the nucleus of what we now know as Tokyo. This leader will be named and briefly discussed below.

A few great figures of these feudal centuries of the shoguns emerge with such insistence and clarity that their names become familiar to all who interest themselves in Japanese history and two of them are of such towering importance that they should be known to everybody who visits Japan, however hastily. Here they are:

Hideyoshi Toyotomi, in supreme power as shogun from 1590 till his death in 1598, was a brilliant, ambitious, self-made man who climbed from lowly birth and station to the heights of power by sheer ability. Eliminating all rivals, he held absolute sway and two imposing memorials to his shogunate are the castle in Osaka, which fairly overpowers tourist senses today, and the Imperial Palace in Kyoto. Blots on his regime were his harsh persecution of Christianity on Kyushu and his conqueror's complex, which led him to undertake a senseless expedition against Korea that quickly collapsed with his death.

Ieyasu Tokugawa was the leader who established Edo (Tokyo) at his capital and founded the Edo Period, often called the Tokugawa Period. In a brilliant military campaign in and around Osaka (1615) he destroyed the remaining power of the Toyotomi family and thereafter ruled supreme.

At first he was tolerant of Christianity and lifted the ban on it, although he personally was far more interested in Confucianism. Later, however, he reimposed the ban, feeling that Christianity was a divisive factor threatening his regime, and in crushing the Shimabara Rebellion of the Christians near Nagasaki (see Chapter 2) he acted with such ferocity that his name was stained worse than that of his predecessor. His was a "strong" government, to use today's phrase for dictatorships, but it was beneficial to the country as a whole and brought relief from the confusions and family wars that had long rocked Japan.

Under Ieyasu's successors in the Tokugawa Shogunate, Japan reached the ultimate in isolationism but the country prospered, or at least the merchant class did, building, in some cases, immense fortunes which were the precursors of the zaibatsu fortunes of a later era. Such extreme isolationism, however, was bound to sow the seeds of its own destruction and this occurred with the coming of Commodore Perry (1853) and the rise of the Emperor-statesman named Meiji, mentioned in the historical review at the beginning of this chapter.

The Meiji Period (1868-1912) opened Japan widely to Western influences and modernism but it led to militarism and then disaster.

Fuji, proud symbol of Japan to all peoples, is seen here from one of the lakes of Fuji-Hakone National Park.

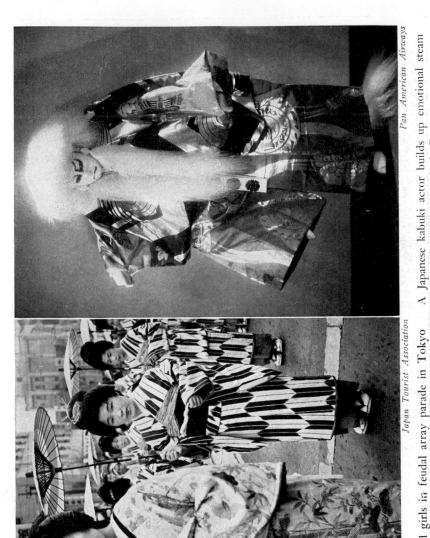

Solemn-faced girls in feudal array parade in Tokyo   A Japanese kabuki actor builds up emotional steam
in celebration of the city's 500th anniversary.   for the Lion's Dance.

Japan's girlie shows rival in spectacular effect anything that New York or Paris can offer. This is a scene from a show by the "Takarazuka Girls' Opera Troupe."

The Yomeimon (Sunshine) Gate of Nikko's Toshogu Shrine is the most elaborate such entrance in Japan. Every 20 years the whole shrine is redecorated with
two and a half million sheets of gold leaf, each about four square inches, and
vast quantities of flame-red cinnabar paint.

Nishina Harbor is one of the approaches to the Izu Peninsula, whose 30 thermal resorts make it a popular holiday goal.

Trained cormorants, held on leashes, fish every summer night in the Nagara River for small trout-like ayu, but rings around their necks prevent the birds from swallowing the fish, which are squeezed from their throats by the fishermen. A fisherman can manipulate as many as a dozen cormorants on separate leashes as they plunge for ayu. Fire in an iron bucket lures fish near the surface.

Japan Tourist Association

Pearl divers of Ago Bay, center of the cultured pearl industry pioneered more than 60 years ago by Kokichi Mikimoto.

The Heian Shrine of Kyoto was built as recently as 1894/95 to celebrate the 1100th anniversary of the founding of the city as the then national capital.

The midsummer Gion Festival in Kyoto is one of the most popular in Japan's whole crowded calendar. Floats like these parade through the main streets on July 17 and 24.

In romantic Nara the pagoda of the Kofukuji Temple is reflected in the waters of Sarusawa Pond.

(*Upper*) The night views of Nagasaki from the hills that surround that historic port city are among the most exciting of their kind.

(*Lower*) More than 400 tame deer, eager to be fed by tourists, roam the wooded acres of a park in Nara, which city was the first fixed capital of Japan (710-793).

(*Upper*) The celebrated bronze Daibutsu, or Great Buddha of Infinite Light, was erected in 1252 in Kamakura, south of Tokyo, and still sits in serene contemplation on the same spot. Its height and weight (42′ 6″; 103 tons) are matched by its genuine artistry, universally praised by critics.

(*Lower*) This hillside house in Nagasaki is always called the "Home of Madame Butterfly." Here, say those who can forgo fact in favor of romance, dwelt poor Butterfly, waiting in vain for the return of Lieutenant Pinkerton.

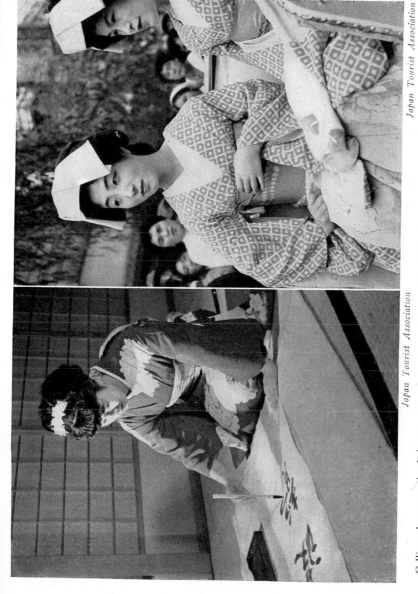

Calligraphy, practiced by means of brush writing, reaches high levels of artistry in Japan.

Traditional attire for Japanese women has by no means disappeared, even in Tokyo. Yet these pretty geisha girls attract appreciative stares.

Miyajima, popularly called Shrine Island, is a lovely ornament of Japan's Inland Sea. A vermilion-painted torii of camphor-wood rises from the sea 500 feet from the main shrine and through this "floating gate" dedicated pilgrims approach by boat.

This scene of Mt. Me-Akan, in Japan's northern island of Hokkaido, is typical of the enormous and widespread volcanic activity to which Japan owes its hundreds of thermal springs.

Japan Tourist Association

The Hairy Ainus that once inhabited all Japan are seen now only in a few villages of Hokkaido. This vanishing race, thought to be of Nordic or Russian origin, is reduced nowadays to catering to the tourist trade.

Hokkaido Island, paradise of Japanese ski enthusiasts, has a blanket of deep snow for nearly half the year.

Sumo wrestlers, each weighing 250 to 450 pounds, offer one of the strangest sports of any country.

Philippine Tourist and Travel Association

This view of central Manila, on both sides of the River Pasig, shows how the war-shattered Philippine capital is rising again, largely in Western style.

The 8000-foot Mayon Volcano, on the Philippine island of Luzon, is a perfect cone, without flaw, as seen from any direction. No other mountain in the world quite matches its symmetry.

Philippine Tourist and Travel Association

The Ifugao rice terraces of Banaue, in the northern Mountain Province of Luzon, are among the wonders of the world. Their construction was started by rugged farmers 4000 years ago and they have been maintained ever since on these steep Philippine slopes.

Hong Kong's "ladder streets," with their crowding shops and open-air stalls, are redolent of China.

Pan American Airways

Hong Kong's administrative and banking center (foreground) is on the island of Victoria. Across the roadstead lies the mainland portion of the colony, with busy Kowloon. The large, dark building on the central waterfront is the Peninsula Hotel.

Pan American Airways

(*Upper*) Chinese women, wearing umbrella-sized hats, work tirelessly transplanting rice in the paddies of Hong Kong's New Territories, which are the colony's hinterland, under long-term lease from China.

(*Lower*) The waters around Hong Kong are always alive with junks, propelled by means of their strange matting sails.

(*Upper*) This mansion, in the Portuguese Territory of Macao, which may be easily reached from Hong Kong, was the property of Sun Yat Sen, the revered founder of the Chinese Republic. Members of his family still live here.

(*Lower*) A vignette of Portuguese Macao, the Orient's oldest foreign settlement, founded in 1557. Macao can add its own touch of spice to the program of any traveler who visits near-by Hong Kong.

YOURSELF IN THE PICTURE OF TOKYO

CHAPTER 6

PLANNING YOUR DAYS–AND NIGHTS

Maps and Printed Guides

Tokyo is well equipped with clear maps, the best of them all being a JTB map of the city, with the environs shown on the reverse side. And in English-language pamphlets, all with maps, it is as well equipped as New York or London, some of these latter, having a view for trade, being offered free to foreign visitors. One comprehensive publication offered free is called *Metropolitan Tokyo and the City of Kyoto*, a monthly magazine found in various tourist shops such as that of the Ando Cloisonné Co., on Z Avenue just off the Ginza. This magazine is packed with practical information on what to see and do, where to eat and where to have fun and it has two maps of central Tokyo, plus a transportation map of the whole capital, plus a map of central Kyoto.

Another free publication (with two maps) encountered everywhere is a mere leaflet called *Tokyo, Only Guide Published and Edited by Americans*. This stresses the fleshpots of the city, restaurants, bars, nightclubs with accommodating hostesses and a "Night Tour Worth a Million." It's a thin thing, with almost no general information, but its maps are easy to follow and it will slide easily into your pocket.

A much fatter and vastly more comprehensive guide, selling in the hotels for 50 yen, is a weekly of tall and narrow format called simply *This Week in Tokyo*. This has two maps, a lot of solid information, some special weekly features and the facts about all current attractions. I have found it the most useful of all the publications, yet it is not too thick to slide into an inner coat pocket.

A more ambitious guide, selling in the bookstores for one dollar, is called *Your Guide to Tokyo*. This is good on sight-seeing but I am not much impressed by its cluttered cartography.

Some, if not all, of these maps and small guides may be secured from the PATA office (see Chapter 1) in San Francisco.

Before leaving the subject of Tokyo cartography I should state that Japan's system of street addresses seems to the Westerner as clumsy and incomprehensible as its written language. *Cho* means street, *chome* means lane, or narrow street, and *ku* means district, but few streets bear individual names, as with us. The minor ones, of which there are thousands in Tokyo, hitch themselves to some nearby street important enough to have a name. Thus we find that the famous Ando Cloisonné shop gives its address as Number 4, 5-chome, Ginza; the Nikko shop advertises its ivories, silks and woodcuts at Number 6, 6-chome Ginzanishi, Shuoku, and the Amita shop its Damascene ware at Number 13, 2-chome, Aoyamaminamicho, Minatoku. Yes, it's discouraging, and Japanese people, when caught in a candid mood, will admit that it sometimes discourages even them, but the maps for foreigners still use the MacArthur nomenclature of *lettered avenues and numbered streets*. Even this is vastly confusing, for Tokyo is like Boston on a mammoth scale, with streets that seem to have developed from cow paths, but at least this system was a valiant attempt to reduce chaos to some sort of order, and the Tokyo city fathers have generously left many of the MacArthur signs for our guidance, though they mean nothing at all to the Japanese.

I'd say in summary, *take it easy*. Learn what you can of the lay of the streets, especially the Ginza (with its long extension that is more strictly called Nihombashi Street, but which I shall call the Ginza to avoid confusion), X, Y, Z Avenues, Utility, Annex, Exchange and St. Luke's Avenues (there weren't enough letters in our alphabet to go the rounds) and 4th Street, 5th Street and

10th Street. That much will help you a lot. And the maps, ever eager to guide you through the maze, spot in the leading hotels, offices, embassies, theaters, nightclubs and shops. So let's cheer up and ask the kamikaze cabs to find what you and I fail to find.

City Transportation by Subway and the Yamate Loop

Most U.S. tourists in most large foreign cities depend for local transportation solely on taxis, but there's fun to be had, as well as money to be saved, by learning to use the subways and other means of public conveyance. In Tokyo, such personal explorations are admittedly more difficult because of the average visitor's total ignorance of the Japanese spoken language and his sense of frustration when looking at signs in the written language, but even here a lot can be done on one's own.

I would not recommend *any* attempt to use the public busses or streetcars, but the subways and some of the elevated electric lines are really easy to learn and—note this—the names of the stations are given in Roman letters as well as in the dreadful Chinese characters adapted by kana to Japanese. I'll try to make this as simple and comprehensible as possible.

Subways are now two in number (a third is under construction) and the fare on both, for any distance, is a uniform 20 yen, paid at any entrance. The two systems do not cross or connect at any point. The *old subway*, noisy and crowded, is very useful to visitors for it goes straight through the heart of the metropolis. One terminal point is *Shibuya*, an important station on the Yamate Loop (of which more presently) in a southwestern part of Tokyo, and the other is *Asakusa*, a rough-and-ready pleasure center and shopping center of prime interest in a northeastern sector. (For a glimpse of Asakusa's "candid strips," on Theater Row, see Chapter 8.) Connecting these terminal points the line passes the Diet Building, the important Shimbashi Station, near Hotels Imperial and Dai-ichi, then *directly along under the Ginza* to Kanda, to Ueno Park and so to Asakusa, with halts at frequent intervals.

The newer subway, much quieter and more modern, starts from *Tokyo Central Station* and proceeds in a general northwesterly direction, passing close to the big Korakuen Baseball Stadium and so to *Ikebukuro*, a station of the Yamate Loop. The third and newest subway, which will perhaps be the most useful of all for visitors, is fast approaching completion and may be in service when you read these words. Running in a general north-south course, it passes under Avenue A, just in front of the Imperial Hotel, and will halt also at Tokyo Central Station, thus tying in conveniently with the next-to-newest subway.

The *Yamate Loop* is just what it says, a *loop* line (elevated electric), running in an irregular circle, or oval, clear around the city, not too far out, in a big 30-station course that touches many important points. Yamate means, more or less, "residential" and indicates the general idea of the loop's service, though it does also pass straight through the heart of the city, paralleling the Ginza for a long distance and halting at Shimbashi, Tokyo Central and Kanda Stations. One of the Loop's halts, *Yurakucho*, is within a very short walk of both the Imperial and the Nikkatsu. The fare for most hauls on the Yamate Loop is a minuscule 10 yen, which is less than 3 cents U.S., and a big "score board" in each station indicates the 10-yen zone and the few, more distant, 20-yen stations. Tickets may be bought through coin-in-the-slot machines, but if you have any doubts you need only go to one of the ticket windows and give the name of your station, along with a 50-yen coin or a 100-yen note and you'll receive your ticket and your change.

With experience, you'll grow bolder and try some of the other elevated electric lines, all of which tie in with the Yamate Loop. A close study of the JTB map or some other will give you confidence. The two most important of the other lines are (a) the *Keihin Line*, connecting Tokyo Central Station and Shimbashi Station with *Yokohama*, and (b) the *Chuo Line* which runs west across the city to *Yoyogi*, on the Loop, and far beyond, and east to *Kinshicho* and *Chiba*.

Sightseeing by Pigeon Bus

Tokyo has a sightseers' tour service by so-called Pigeon Bus that is at least as good as those offered in London, Paris or any other world center and I use the words "at least" because I personally think them a bit better than any of their opposite numbers I've known in Europe. I think them better because of the expertness and "oomph" of the Pigeon Girls who guide them, dispensing floods of information in charming, slightly accented English. Maybe I've had exceptional luck in the quality of the girls who've handled the tours I've taken but I don't mind admitting that I'm deeply impressed. Dressed in a smart green uniform, with green cap tilted so sharply to one side that it must stay on her head by the girl's own magnetism, the Pigeon Bus hostess takes over the tour from the first turn of the wheel and her guests seem never to get out of hand.

To be reportorial, I recall with special zest the girl who conducted a night tour I took. Through her microphone she gave us a running commentary not only on what we were seeing but on Japanese life. She explained, with an oh-yeah twinkle in her eyes and her speech, that "women are now emancipated in Japan, so we're quite the equals of men. At least that's what the law says. The only trouble is that our fathers and husbands and brothers haven't heard about it yet." Her laugh was so charming and infectious that the whole bus burst into laughter with her. She made mistakes now and then and they always turned out to be as attractive as her commentary. Passing Asakusa Park she announced, "The traffic is so heavy here that we can only park the bus for three or four years—oh, I mean *minutes*" and she broke down in such lovely confusion that again we all roared with sympathetic amusement. Just possibly this was part of her routine, but if so it was a superb bit of acting.

The Pigeon Busses are operated by a concern called Shin Nippon Kanko Company, meaning New Japan Tourist Company, whose head office is almost opposite the northern entrance of the Tokyo Central Station, and the company enjoys the close co-operation of the JTB. The starting point of all the tours is the company's office, but always they stop at Hotel Imperial to pick up passengers and, when the tour is finished, to deliver them. An Up Town Tour is offered each morning, a Down Town Tour each afternoon and a special Shopping Tour twice a week. Twice a week also, on Wednesday and Saturday evenings, there is an ever-popular Night Tour, but I'll tell about this dazzler in Chapter 8, when Tokyo's electric lights and its myriads of neon signs are turned on.

Perhaps I am being "irresponsible" but I do not feel that a detailed, blow-by-blow report is needed on what the bus tours show their customers. The primary interest in Tokyo, quite unlike Kyoto and Nara and quite unlike large European capitals, lies in what the city *is*, not in what it was in times past. As a city of the past it has relatively little color. As a city of today, immense, ambitious, throbbing with life, seething with new ideas, replete with fascinating things to do, to eat, to watch, to experience, it has few equals in the world.

I haven't burdened you with many statistics so let me now toss a few into the hopper. Tokyo covers 828 square miles of rather yielding earth, more than half of which was under water until the Tokugawa Shogunate began reclaiming it in the 17th century. It has 309 parks, of which the most important to visitors are *Ueno*, with its three thousand cherry trees, and the Tokyo National Museum; *Hibiya* (opposite Hotel Imperial), with an amphitheater, a concert hall and a library; and blatant, blowzy, exciting *Asakusa*, to be described in Chapter 8 on "Entertainment." Two other garden parks, *Korakuen* and *Rikugien*, are worthy of visits for the sheer beauty of their landscaping and their special floral features. There are 600 movie houses in Tokyo, the film fare being roughly 60 per cent Japanese and 40 per cent Western, many of the Western pictures being Hollywood productions speaking the familiar language of Hollywood. The 1923 earthquake and fire destroyed about one hundred thousand citizens, one third of them in a ghastly funeral pyre which had been the Army Clothing Depot where they had taken supposed refuge. An *Earthquake Memorial Hall* now rises on the spot and in a three-story pagoda attached to it urns preserve the ashes of those who died here. The Ginza, perhaps *the* most sought sight of Tokyo, is four miles long, with the Nihombashi Extension, and it is lined in part with willow trees planted ninety years ago. Its name means Silver (gin) Mint and as an agreeable item of tomorrow's news I may mention that the streetcar tracks of this heart-street of the capital are to be removed and the sidewalks widened.

Of historic sights few demand tourist attention and only two, I should say, really get it, namely the *Imperial Palace* and the *Meiji Shrine*.

The grounds of the Imperial Palace are visited by the public only on the Emperor's Birthday, April 29, when vast crowds take advantage of the invitation, but the *fact* of the palace enclave, in the heart of the metropolis, is felt by all Japanese and by all visiting Westerners as one of enduring impact on city and nation. The Pigeon Bus tours all pass the Palace, and on the afternoon tour a halt is made in the Palace Plaza, where a group picture is taken. This is quickly developed and printed so that each guest may receive a copy, with Pigeon's compliments, at the conclusion of the tour.

The Imperial Palace is secluded within the 250-acre grounds originally developed in the 1600's as the Castle of the Tokugawa Shogunate. When the Meiji Restoration of 1868 called for the removal of the capital from Kyoto to Tokyo, then called Edo, the Emperor Meiji, grandfather of the present Emperor Hirohito, took over the castle and made it his palace. Various additional buildings were erected, but nearly all of them, as well as the palace itself, were burned to the ground in an American air raid on May 25, 1945. Since that time, the Imperial Family has lived in a temporary building that had been an air-raid shelter, but a new palace of appropriate quality is being constructed.

The grounds are surrounded by a chain of broad moats whose massive masonry, especially on the inner side, is wonderfully impressive, and for decorative effect pompous swans imported from Switzerland paddle about, lowering their dignity, along with their necks, to gobble up bits of bread tossed to them. The moats are crossed by various bridges, a double one called Niju-bashi being the main entrance. In prewar times, the palace, like everything concerned with the Imperial family, was sacrosanct and the Emperor was, of course, totally immune to public or even private criticism. Today, he can be publicly criticized in the press and even caricatured, yet so deftly and graciously has he altered his status from god to man and symbol of national unity that he is perhaps better loved than before. In this age of the new democracy, the Crown Prince walks the Ginza, milling with the crowds like any other shopper, whereas formerly any street which he proposed to traverse had to be cleared completely and cordoned off from the profane touch of the public. This meta-morphosis is all to the good, a patent benefit to the nation in its relations with fellow-democracies.

The *Meiji Shrine* is, in my view, the second of the two im-perative "sightseer's musts" of Tokyo's past, and this despite the fact that the sacred building was destroyed in a raid on April 1, 1945, and is only now being reconstructed. This is the only shrine ever built to an Emperor and its construction, completed as late as 1920, was due to a spontaneous demand of virtually the whole nation, which deeply venerated this great leader. His ashes, and those of his Empress and his mother, are enshrined here. The grounds consist of 175 acres, most of which are adorned by some 125,000 trees given by people and groups from all over Japan, so this forest-park is a thing of beauty, quite aside from its cen-tral feature. It includes a fine water-lily pond and a superb iris garden with nearly a hundred types of that lovely flower.

One reaches the shrine by a broad path graced by four very large torii, those graceful gateways by which *every* Shinto shrine is approached. The word torii means literally bird perch, but it is sometimes said that the gateway's shape represents the "mysterious channel of life" (i.e., the vagina). Leaving such symbolism to whom it may concern let us gaze at these gates to the Meiji Shrine for they are among the splendid and stirring sights of Japan. They are made of cypress wood over 1700 years old brought from Formosa and one of them, the largest wooden torii in Japan, is just a few inches under 40 feet in height, the supporting pillars being 4 feet in diameter.

Before the war brought such profound changes to Japanese religious thinking every person who passed this shrine honoring the Emperor-god was required to bow deeply, and so imperative was this rule that even the streetcars would come to a halt and the conductor would announce solemly, "It is the time to bow."

Shoppers in Paradise

Japanese cities, especially Tokyo, Kyoto and Nagasaki, rival Hong Kong in their wealth of exciting things to buy, and here you don't have to bother with the Certificates of Origin that are demanded by the U.S. Treasury Department (Foreign Assets Control) on many desirable items in Hong Kong—as proof that they didn't originate in Red China. In fact, Japan, as I've said in Chapter 1, gives the foreign tourist an added incentive to buy by remitting the 16 per cent Japanese Commodity Tax on many prized items, including cameras, binoculars, tortoise shell, cultured pearls, cloisonné ware, ivory and furs.

Perhaps the best testimony I can give to the temptation shops of Japan, and of Hong Kong, despite the hurdle of the Certificate of Origin, is that I personally, a mere male who has built up a strong resistance to shopper's fever, was bitten by the buy-bug so severely that I recently bought more in those two places than I have ever bought elsewhere on a single trip. I'd be inclined to bet that you will do the same. Just try a leisured window-shopping stroll through the Hotel Imperial arcade, the Nikkatsu arcade, Z Avenue and a dozen blocks of the Ginza and see what happens to your resistance, if any.

All of the guide-pamphlets I mentioned at the beginning of this chapter are packed with tempting advertisements and with lists of recommended shops, these lists being possibly susceptible of a little "slanting," dependent upon whether or not a particular shop's advertising has been secured, but *This Week in Tokyo* seems to have an especially helpful listing and the dollar booklet called *Your Guide to Tokyo* is almost totally free of advertising and may be presumed to be totally objective. It lists the shops, under each head, by alphabet. Furthermore, it gives brief, concise paragraphs on all types of goods and how they are manufactured, so I would think that for its shopper's guidance alone the book is worth more than its modest cost.

I should mention here also, and emphasize, that there is a *Japanese Souvenir Association* to which many of Tokyo's most dependable firms belong. The JTA publishes a list of them, with a short and well-done commentary, in a free leaflet called *Japan Souvenir Guide* which you will do well to acquire from that office or the JTB. You may, of course, have full confidence in this authoritative leaflet.

In the following report I shall by no means attempt to present all the recommendable firms but will name one or two in each field that are members of the JSA or that have an international reputation to maintain. In giving the addresses I'll omit the words Avenue and Street, it being understood that *letters* mean avenues and *figures* mean streets.

Bamboo articles include handbags, baskets and lampshades, all beautifully decorated. A good shop is *Takumi*, in the Nikkatsu arcade.

Bookstores abound in Tokyo. You'll find a lot of them on Z near the Ginza, but the chief publisher and seller of English-language books about Japan and the Orient is *Charles E. Tuttle*, on T, east of 10th, and the chief importer of general foreign books is *Maruzen*, on the Ginza between W and X. In the Kanda district there is a street with literally scores of bookstores, catering especially to students.

Cameras are a major achievement of Japanese industry. Such excellent makes as Nikon, Konika, Minolta and Flex—there are several others of equal quality—always excite shutterbugs and the prices, tax free, are as tempting as the articles. Two leading firms are Matsushima Optical Company, on the Ginza, near St. Luke's Avenue, and Miura Trading Company, in the Marunouchi Building.

Chinaware is beautifully and meticulously fashioned, a typically Japanese feature being delicate teacups with covers but no handles, which are becoming popular as tourist gifts for the home folks even though the recipients may exclaim, "Oh, what lovely jam jars!" Three leading makers are *Okura* of Tokyo, *Noritake* of Nagoya and *Arita Yaki* of Nagasaki. Noritake ware is favored by many shoppers as the best of all. Its chief Tokyo outlet is *Nitto Toki*, on 10th at B, in the Shiba district.

Cloisonné production is centered chiefly at Nagoya and the most famous shop is that of *Ando*, which has a branch on Tokyo's Z Avenue, close to the Ginza. The basic processes of manufacture will be outlined when this book reaches Nagoya, in Chapter 9.

Coral, skillfully and tastefully carved (brooches, cuff links, earrings, etc.), is found at its best in the Fujiya Shop in the Nikkatsu arcade.

Damascene ware, originating in Damascus—hence its name—has long flourished in Japan, though it is now made only in Kyoto. Its chief purveyor in Tokyo is the *Amita Jewelry Corporation*, whose shop is on F, opposite the entrance to Meiji Park. Here is the interesting 7-point process of manufacture, as outlined by Amita: (1) Numerous fine lines chiseled in steel foundation with delicate instruments; (2) design inlaid with 24-carat gold and sterling silver; (3) surface corroded with nitric acid; (4) surface rusted with ammonia, then rusting stopped by boiling in green tea; (5) several layers of lacquer baked on entire surface; (6) design polished out with charcoal; (7) final engraving and finishing. Originally, Japanese damascene was fashioned in Buddhist utensils, especially sacred mirrors, and in samurai swords and helmets, but in these effete times we find it worked as costume jewelry, room decorations and smokers' articles.

Dolls "made in Japan" have delighted the world's children for generations. The best doll shops cluster on R Avenue, near the Asakusa Bashi, which latter word means bridge. A conspicuous and well-stocked shop is that of the *Yoshitoku Company* in this area. Its Yamata, Sakura and Kohagi dolls are fascinating, as are its so-called dancing dolls and this firm also specializes in the manufacture and sale of gruesome and humorous Noh masks. (For a description of classic Noh drama see Chapter 8.)

Drugs (and lots of other things) are obtainable "in your own language" in the American Pharmacy, located in a street-floor corner store of the Nikkatsu Building.

Fans are an obvious and charming product of Japanese manufacture. The plain and inexpensive ones are made of painted rice paper and bamboo sticks, while the fancier ones are made of silk, lace or feathers, with fragrant sandalwood or ivory sticks. The designs are nearly always exquisite and "understated." Fans may be bought in any department store and in many shops in Asakusa Park.

Furs, especially mink accessories, are *very* inexpensive in Japan, perhaps a half to a third the price of similar ones sold in the States. Inquiry should be made, say at the U.S. Embassy or Consulate, as to the U.S. customs rules on importing them. *Soga Fur Company*, just off Annex and not far from the Ginza, is an important fur shop.

Ivory ware should be bought only from a well-known, dependable dealer such as *Kita Shoji Company*, on the Ginza, near W, for imitations in bone are often "plausible." Bone doesn't take the same lovely polish as true ivory.

Kimonos, obis and *happi coats* of fine silk, the last-named garment being a feminine modification of the long blouse worn by workmen, are immensely popular with American shoppers. *Fujiya*, in the Nikkatsu arcade, is one well-known dealer; and on 10th, at T, is another, called the *Kimono Mart*.

Lacquer ware is as typically Japanese as silk or cloisonné, and women shoppers buy it ecstatically. A recommendable store is *Yamada Heiando*, located behind one of the Ginza's big department stores named *Takashimaya*.

Pearls (cultured) are perhaps the most famous of all Japanese industrial products and certainly the firm of *Mikimoto*, with one Tokyo shop on the Ginza and another in the Imperial arcade, is the most famous of the producers. This industry, as many shoppers know, was discovered and founded by Kokichi Mikimoto, who was the grandfather of the firm's present president. So very interesting is pearl culture, as a romance of industry, that its processes will be discussed in a separate section when this book (in Chapter 9) reaches Pearl Island and the Mikimoto Pearl Farm, located respectively in Toba and in Ago Bay. Suffice it to say here that the Tokyo stores have for sale fabulous displays of pearls—Mikimoto alone produces about a ton of them a year—in the form of necklaces (one, two or three strands), chokers, brooches, earrings and ornaments of many kinds. A good single-strand necklace may be bought for a hundred dollars or so, but you may pay a thousand or more for one composed of very large pearls of special luster. Mikimoto has by no means any monopoly of the industry today and there are other very good firms, as, for instance, *Matoba and Company*, with a main shop in the Nikkatsu arcade.

Silks, especially the celebrated *Nishijin* brocades, are found at their best in the luxurious *Kanebo* establishment, on the Ginza, at the corner of St. Luke's Avenue.

Silverware, in small personal and household items, is very well made and inexpensive. Two good shops, both in the Imperial arcade, are *Okubo Brothers* and *K. Uyeda*.

Smoked silver, made by *Amita* (see above under Damascene), has its own unique fascination. Its 4-point handicraft process, as set forth by the company, is as follows: (1) Base metal is sterling silver (97 per cent); (2) metal surface chemically processed and black-colored; (3) design with fine silver sparkle hand-carved in the surface by expert engravers; (4) finished with rhodium plating on chains or screws and with special hard plastics on the remainder. I can say for myself that I think the contrast of this jewelry's dark plastic portions with its silver-sparkling portions is as unique as it is artistic. If you are visiting Kobe perhaps you'll want to wait and buy some smoked silver in the Amita shop of that city's *International House.*

Sword, or *Japan Sword,* is the name of a high-grade, much-advertising shop on B, at 12th, which specializes in hand-made samurai and parade swords, some with gold and jeweled handles. It also sells lesser things in *cutlery* and accessories, which last word can cover quite an area.

Tortoise-shell ware is closely identified with Nagasaki, where its manufacture centers, and the variety of offerings in that city is much greater than in Tokyo, but of course interesting items such as toilet sets, fancy combs, compacts and trays are on sale in various department stores of the capital.

Toys have long been an important product of Japan and many of them are ingeniously devised. *Kintaro,* on the Ginza between Z and Exchange, devotes its energies solely to the sale of toys.

Woodblock prints, in which Japan is generally considered to surpass all other nations, are found at their best and in fullest variety at the widely known shop of *S. Watanabe Color Print Company* on the Ginza near Utility Avenue.

I may conclude this report on specialty shops—some notes on Tokyo's fabulous department stores will follow—by stating that the Pigeon Bus Shopping Tour makes halts of approximately half an hour at four of the shops listed above, namely Watanabe Color Print (for woodblock prints), Mikimoto (for cultured pearls), Yoshitoku (for dolls and masks) and Noritake (for china).

The Dazzling Department Stores

I do not think the adjective above is too strong to apply to Japan's department stores, especially those of Tokyo, for their quality consists not so much in their size, though they are indeed huge, rivaling those of New York, Paris and London, as in their remarkable inventiveness and the broad range of their stock *and their cultural services.*

Tokyo has at least ten of these big marts and new ones are continually opening. In other cities of Japan, all over the country, you may be practically certain that the largest, tallest, most conspicuous buildings in sight, often quite dominating large sections, are local department stores or branches of those in Tokyo or in Osaka, which is another great breeding ground for them.

Of the capital's many department stores I shall present four as being typical of their race, but first let me repeat from Chapter 2 my mention of one pleasing feature of nearly all such stores. They have escalators (as well as elevators) to lift you to the upper floors and at the top of each "flight" of these moving stairways you'll find a cutely uniformed girl who will bow in welcome to each customer. It's a heartwarming custom, putting the shopper in a glowing, and buying, mood. I can only say, "American stores, please copy."

Now for my four of Tokyo.

MITSUKOSHI, located on the Ginza a little north of W Avenue, is the most important emporium in all Japan and what a place it is! In the main rotunda is a pipe organ where an organist, sitting at his console high up on a balcony, dispenses popular music and light classics. After roaming through the labyrinth of the vast street floor the customer mounts to upper floors—there are eight of them, plus two basements, plus an open roof with all sorts of attractions on it—by one of two full sets of escalators or by one of the elevators. The escalators are paneled waist-high with tasteful, illuminated walls. On the top floor one very large section is devoted to an exhibition of paintings, sculptures and other art works, an exhibition which is changed each week and which often contains priceless national treasures from Kyoto, Nara, Nikko and other historic centers. On the same floor is a big restaurant where meals are offered for 50 yen (14 cents) and an impressive theater, with balcony, where concerts, Japanese kabuki dramas and movies, both Japanese and English, are offered. This same floor still has room for the sale of many articles, especially those concerned with the fine arts and photography, and for an arcade devoted to various cultural displays. On a recent occasion when I visited this arcade the *Reader's Digest,* which has its own building in Tokyo and publishes a very popular Japanese edition, was displaying a magnificent collection of international color photographs ranging from Scandinavia to Thailand and from Switzerland to Mexico.

I have said that Mitsukoshi—and it is not alone in its pursuits—is a genuine cultural center, but its roof turns out to be chiefly a play center, with one section used as a flower market. The play roof, typical of those found on dozens of department stores throughout Japan, is an amazing thing to behold. Always there are myriads of schoolchildren, in their uniforms, milling about excitedly, for they find here sections that are labeled, in English, Playland, Dreamland, Frontierland, Adventureland and Disneyland, this whole group of "lands" being made still gayer by a feature very common in Japan, namely large colored balloons that sway in the breeze above. Many fun-gadgets that are operated by putting a coin of 10 yen into a slot induce gales of laughter from the children and an immensely good time is had by all, the fun being enhanced by a dog market where one may buy dogs of various breeds or merely look at them, as in a dog zoo. Animals are not unusual features of Japanese department stores. In a big corner window of one of them, on Z Avenue, I have seen two lion cubs and a panther cub rolling over each other like three kittens. Presumably they were for sale as pets.

TAKASHIMAYA, located on the Ginza, just south of W Avenue, only a few blocks from Mitsukoshi, is another department store of giant size, also with its big play roof, including a Ferris wheel, for children. A feature of this store is its catering to Americans and other English-speaking visitors. It publishes an excellent illustrated folder in English, with a street map and a list of its departments, with the floors on which they are found. On two of its floors, the 5th and the 8th, one may see "Special Events" of various types, the place and hour of each attraction being given out at a *General Information Office* on the street floor. The 8th floor, like that of Mitsukoshi, has an art gallery, a refreshment room and an auditorium and as a further feature it has a tropical aquarium, whose occupants you may select and buy. Takashimaya is rightfully proud of its above-mentioned information office, where all information is given not only about the store but about Tokyo in general and its attractions. It is proud too of its "I-Speak-English" clerks, each of whom wears an arm band by way of identification.

TOYOKO is a vast department store, perhaps the largest of them all, in the Shibuya district, in a southwestern part of the city but directly on the Yamate elevated line. The elevated does, in fact, roar straight through this emporium, on the third floor. Toyoko has the largest theater of any Tokyo store and it also has a dance hall which can be rented by any organization for special events or celebrations.

SOGU is Tokyo's newest department store, this being a branch of one in Osaka. It opened its doors in the late spring of 1957, but newer ones will be opened, are even now being constructed, for the capital's appetite for them seems insatiable. Sogu, which I mention because it is the nearest such store to Hotels Imperial and Nikkatsu, rises directly beside the Yurakucho Railway Station, on the same side of the tracks as those hotels. The escalator bowing-girls wear natty gray uniforms with pink rosettes and you'll find various departments marked with exotic English, French and mixed signs such as Necktie Fair and C'Est Bien Corner.

Japanese Sport, from Baseball to Sumo

The Japanese people are exceedingly keen on sports of all kinds, both native and Western, whether as participants or spectators, and in at least four of them they excel, namely judo and sumo, native to Japan, and baseball and table tennis, imported. Let's have a look at them, first the imported games and then the native ones.

BASEBALL, both amateur and professional, has attained first place in popular interest and I should say that the quality of play, so far as I have seen it, rivals, respectively, that of American college and professional league teams. The sport was first introduced to Japan in 1873 when a couple of American enthusiasts taught it to the students of Kaisei School, which is now Tokyo University. It caught on quickly and has become, in the course of time, *the* national sport.

In non-professional ball, the most important and feverishly followed games are those of the Six-University League of Tokyo, being the annual spring and autumn tournaments of the capital's six universities. The hottest rivals are always Waseda and Keio.

Professional ball was first organized as recently as 1936, but has become big business, with a so-called Pacific League of seven teams and a Central League of six teams. The baseball stadiums, like the game itself, are outright copies of their American models and four of them, two in Tokyo and two in Osaka, have a seating capacity of 55,000 to 85,000 each.

So much for statistics. Now let's watch a game, for example one in the Korakuen Stadium of Tokyo between the Dragons, representing a Nagoya press, and the Swallows, representing the Japanese National Railways. There are a few Japanese touches before the game starts. We find usherettes, cute little numbers in green uniforms, instead of ushers, and a girl announcer gives the line-up through a public address system in crystal-clear—Japanese. As the teams trot out onto the field to take their places two girls also trot onto the field bearing armfuls of flowers which they ceremoniously present to the opposing captains. When the ceremony has been concluded and the flowers stowed away, the game starts—and a mighty good game it is, with a lot of hitting, a lot of sharp fielding and few errors. The players wear uniforms identical with those worn by our players.

All the calls of the plate umpire are given in Japanese-accented English, "Strah-eek, boru (ball), ah-oot," and he wears a wrinkled navy blue suit, the pockets stuffed with extra baseballs. From a distance he looks precisely like a smaller edition of Umpire O'Rourke or Umpire Murphy. The base umpires likewise resemble their American counterparts and even their gestures, indicating that a runner is safe or out, are the same. The scoreboard is also about the same, though with some Japanese adaptations. A strong yellow light gleams within a hole in the board to indicate a strike, a green light to indicate a ball, a red light to indicate an out. The only difference I could notice in the Korakuen field from our fields was that the right and left field bleachers seemed substantially closer to the home plate—I was told that they are only 300 feet distant—making home runs to right or left easier. The Swallows alone made five homers in a game I watched here. But the farthest point of this park's center field is said to be 490 feet from the plate.

Small differences between the Japanese game and the American game only emphasize the amazing similarities. If you watch a game in any of Japan's great stadiums you'll be quite carried away with the mass excitement of it, for the crowds are bigger than with us and just as demonstrative. The capacity of the Korakuen Stadium is officially stated to be 58,000 and virtually every seat was taken for the game I saw there. Night games occur in that stadium every night from mid-June through September, as they do at frequent intervals in all of Japan's stadiums. I once tried hard to wangle a ticket for a night game in the stadium of Fukuoka, but it was no go. I couldn't beg, borrow or steal one, for every seat had been filled before the game started and hundreds, like myself, had been turned away.

TABLE TENNIS, or ping-pong, has won thousands of adherents in Japan and many of them have attained such skill as to make good showings in international tournaments. In any resort and any Japanese inn you may likely see eager players swatting the little white pill back and forth.

JUDO, formerly called Jujitsu, was a strictly Japanese invention but it is of such unique fascination and of such practical value that it has aroused widespread interest in many lands, France alone having now over a hundred judo schools and halls. In America there are judo schools in New York, Chicago, Los Angeles, San Francisco and several other cities. The fascination of the game consists, as everyone knows, in clever tricks to utilize an opponent's superior strength to one's own advantage and his undoing. There are said to be 48 different ways of throwing an adversary and there are also various ways of immobilizing him by grips that make him literally unable to move. But first of all every student of the game, or art, must learn how to fall in such a way that there can be no danger of brain concussion.

Judo, as an organized sport, originated nearly ninety years ago when an imaginative athlete named Kano Jigoro systematized and greatly developed it, founding, as its hearth and headquarters, the *Kodokan Judo Hall* of Tokyo, which is still its home, rebuilt since the war. This can be visited by the public and it is, indeed, included as one of the halts on the afternoon sightseeing tour of the Pigeon Bus. In the main practice hall one may watch forty or fifty pairs of opponents trying out their skills and there is always a loud and unceasing wham-wham-wham of bodies falling on the resilient matting. In the crowded, struggling mass one is sure to see some Americans, especially members of the Air Force.

The players, which term is more accurate than fighters, wear a special judo costume consisting of white coat and trousers and a belt of varying colors. There are ten well-defined grades of experience and expertness and the grade is evidenced, at least in a general way, by the color of the belt. The first five grades, beginners and learners, wear black belts, the 6th and 7th grades red-and-white checkered belts, the 8th, 9th and 10th grades all-red belts. Nearly all of those who attain the top grades are middle-aged or downright elderly men, for this sport, always remember, depends on skill rather than strength. A first-rate judo player seems to "float" in his motions, counting for success on perfect timing and footwork. Actually, the leading player of them all, a 10th-grade man named Kifune who is known everywhere in judo circles, is pushing 75! Another 10th-grade expert named Samura is over 80 and still very good indeed.

Girls also go in for judo and I have watched their workouts in a smaller room of the same Kodokan Hall. An interesting feature of their play is that each girl, upon entering the room, bows twice till her head touches the floor, first to a wall picture of judo's founder, Kano Jigoro, then to the hall itself.

SUMO is just about the *oddest* sport ever invented, oddest to watch and oddest, I should think, to engage in. It may be translated as Japanese wrestling, but it is completely different from Western wrestling. It is centuries older in origin than judo, having been an ancient traditional sport even at the period of the Tokugawa Shogunate. And the oddest of its odd features is the appearance and physique of the sumo wrestlers themselves, for they are huge, fat men, every one, in sharpest possible contrast to the small and slender physique of the average Japanese. A common question of foreigners is, "Who *are* these obese giants? Are they real Japanese, like others, or are they a race apart?" The answer is that they are Japanese all right, real Japanese, but, aspiring to this profession because they happen to be exceptionally tall and husky as boys, they deliberately fatten themselves, especially by eating incredible quantities of *chanko ryori*, a mixture of chicken, beef or pork with succulent vegetables, and at the same time they take special exercises for years to develop their muscles. The average sumo aspirant must weigh 250 pounds at the very least or he will seem, and be, like a "shrimp" in the ring. Many of them weigh 350 pounds and one man whom I saw in the ring tipped the scales officially at 48 kan, which is 465 pounds. His vast belly would have made that of a toy-store Santa Claus look puny by comparison and I thought he would collapse from sheer obesity, but he fought doggedly and won his match.

The wrestlers wear their hair, which is shiny black as always in Japan, in a strange feudal style, for it is allowed to grow long and is then fastened on top of the head in a queer topknot. Their fighting costume consists of a dark loin cloth, held on by a cloth belt, and *nothing* else. There are two 15-day tournaments annually in Tokyo, in January and May, and one in Osaka, in the autumn. Those in Tokyo are held in a big covered arena called the Kokugikan, in the Asakusa section, and on each day of each tournament there are dozens of matches, lasting from morning until late afternoon. The same wrestlers compete in all the tournaments and their total score determines their rank and their payments. The champion of champions each year receives a champion's flag and a cash prize and is lionized almost as a national hero. The Kokugikan Arena seats about 16,000 spectators and the better seats are arranged in cushioned squares holding four persons each. Customers take off their shoes and squat or recline on the matting. If they stay a long time they buy or bring their lunch and eat it while they watch.

The ring in which the contestants wrestle is 15 feet in diameter and is thickly sanded. It is on a raised platform over which is a canopy suspended from the lofty roof. This canopy represents the Shinto shrine of feudal days and from its four corners hang four enormous tassels, green, red, white and blue, representing the shrine's pillars. Thus sumo has a quasi-religious and a decidedly feudal background. There are always 60 "selected" wrestlers, who are public idols, and many lesser fry who are expected to kowtow to the selected ones, serving as devoted apprentices and performing all sorts of menial tasks, such as laundering all their clothes for them. In the case of the grand champion, the hero of heroes, devotion becomes a sort of fanatical dedication.

Now I will *try* to describe this indescribable sport as I have watched it. Two fat giants step onto the platform and into the ring and salute each other in traditional style. Then an announcer wearing ancient garb and an odd hat like a Noh player announces, without microphone, the names of the contestants in medieval language which few can hear and fewer can understand.

While speaking he holds a fan out in front of himself at arm's length. His announcement is followed by a real announcement, in modern Japanese, through a public address system by another announcer. Then the contestants go to their respective corners, rinse their mouths for purification and take a pinch of salt which they toss into the sanded ring, this being also a ceremony of purification. Then they straddle their fat legs and stamp the platform in an utterly absurd, but traditional, manner.

By this time you'd think the contest would start, and so indeed it seems about to do. They face each other, glare at each other, squat down and place their clenched fists on the floor preparatory to the attack. There they go! But no! According to ancient rules the two wrestlers must rise to the attack precisely together but they *never* seem to do so on the first, the second or the third squatting. So both leisurely get up, go to their corners, rinse their mouths again, toss another pinch of salt into the ring and go back to squat and glare again. This "fat men's ballet" used sometimes to continue for half or three quarters of an hour but nowadays the rules limit it to five minutes. When the time is up and they have done their rinsing-salting-squatting act five or six times they finally spring at each other as if by mutual consent, seizing each other by the belt of the loin cloth. Generally the contest is over within half a minute. It ends when any part of the body of one wrestler (except his feet) touches the floor or when he steps out of the ring or is forced out. Each then bows to the other, the winner squats once more in triumph, while the loser bows again to the winner. This contest is over and in a few minutes another will start.

This is sumo, a very ancient, wonderfully fascinating, queer-in-the-head sport. *Don't miss it* if you are in Tokyo or Osaka at the sumo season.

The Turkish Bath, Tokyo Style

A special institution of Japan that flourishes at its steaming best in Tokyo is the Turkish bath and massage, administered to all comers by young girls. A persistent advertisement appearing in every issue of *This Week in Tokyo* is of the *Rakutenti Onsen* (the last word means bath) reading: "For Gentlemen, steam bath, massage, shave, etc., by 100 young and lovely girls; For Ladies, beauty treatment and steam bath, facial massage, body massage, etc., by experienced cosmetician." There is nothing at all odd or "special" in such service, as the advertising might perhaps lead one to think, for it's an old Japanese custom for girls to scrub and massage the customers, both male and female, just as the bath women of Finland scrub all customers in the sauna baths. It's the same only different, for the Finnish women are big, muscular, blonde, middle-aged huskies and the Japanese bath girls really are young and lovely, wearing white halter bras and shorts.

The procedure, if you order the full treatment, is as follows. You undress, completely, and the bath girl installs you in a Turkish bath box from which only your head emerges. She turns on the heat and steams you like a boiled live tourist for some ten minutes. When you can't stand it any longer she lets you out and then proceeds to give you a thorough all-over soaping and rinsing, after which you sog for a few minutes in a tank of clean hot water. Then she bids you lie down on a padded pallet and when you've complied she massages you with expert and strictly impersonal fingers. You could be a horse or a puppy so far as she is concerned, but she does a fine and honest job, the whole bath and massage taking about an hour. When the job is done you give her a tip of perhaps 200 yen, or if two girls have worked on you, 150 to each girl, this being one of the very rare cases in Japan where a tip is expected and properly due. In the Rakutenti Onsen, if a good many of the "100 young and lovely girls" are free two of them will take you on, one massaging your chest and back, the other your legs, and they'll chatter and laugh together just as naturally as if they were making beds in a hotel. The price of the bath and massage is 800 yen, but sometimes, as in the most central of all the baths, called *Tokyo Onsen* (on Z Avenue, east of the Ginza), an inclusive price of 1000 yen, with tip, is to be paid at the desk.

To sum up the steamy subject, there are three large bath halls that chiefly concern Western visitors, namely: *Tokyo Onsen*, whose address is given above; *Rakutenti Onsen*, at T and 25th, beside the Kinshicho Station; and the *Santé Bath*, near 30th Street, in the Shinjuku area.

CHAPTER 7

THE FABULOUS FLESHPOTS OF TOKYO

Poly-National Gastronomy

THE greatest surprise I have had in Tokyo is the city's thoroughgoing cosmopolitanism in its poly-national restaurants, supplementing its expected temples of native gastronomy (sukiyaki and tempura) and, as a corollary, in its sumptuous coffee shops, tearooms, beer halls, barbecue dives and myriad bars. One could fall back on travel's hardest worked cliché and call it the Paris of the Orient, but that would tell only a part of the story for Tokyo has plenty of features quite unknown in Paris. Its coffee shops, to mention one, differ from Europe's sidewalk cafés as greatly as the Toshogu Pagoda differs from the towers of Notre Dame.

Tokyo had the advantage of entering the world scene only a century ago, long after Europe's eating and drinking customs had been fixed by the mordant of habit, and since the Japanese are born adopters and adapters they set about vigorously borrowing whatever they liked from foreign nations and, in many cases, improving on the originals.

I have an urgent personal message to convey and I doubt that I can make myself believed. Anyway, this is the message: I find Tokyo the most exciting city of fabulous fleshpots I have ever known and that phrase is not a mere exercise in alliteration. What I'm trying to say is that no great city in the world, and I believe I know most of them, can match Tokyo in its infinite *variety* of good eating and drinking places, sometimes in settings of rare beauty or exotic interest. Now it's up to me to document this claim and I'll do my best with it, though I need a couple of years more for epicurean research before pretending to master the subject.

First, let's have a look at the restaurants serving Western or international food.

This Week in Tokyo lists about ninety good restaurants of *all* types, plus a dozen or so more in the leading hotels, but I will attempt a drastic pruning of this restaurant jungle even though—please understand—I am forced to leave unmentioned many places of genuine excellence and elegance. Listers like myself always court sharp criticism from travelers and fellow-listers ("*Why* did he include that place and not this place?") but I'll thicken my skin and go ahead, taking the *types* by alphabet.

American. George's, just off A, between 10th and 12th, is outstanding in this type.

British. The King's Arms, in front of the American Embassy, is a reasonable facsimile of an English tavern, complete with a beefeater sign in front and a game of darts probably in progress inside. The food is, of course, British-in-the-good-sense.

French. There are at least half a dozen fair to excellent restaurants of Gallic inspiration, but two of them seem outstanding, namely *Franceya,* off B, between 42nd and 45th, and *Hananoki,* on 5th, between Annex and Utility, near Hotel Imperial. Franceya's setting is Japanese, but its filet mignon and other steaks are as French, meaning as tender and succulent, as anything you could find in Paris. The Hananoki will tease your taste buds from *soupe à l'oignon* through *langouste thermidor* or steak to a variety of Gallic desserts.

German. There are about as many German restaurants as French in Tokyo and most of them, of beer hall type, are run by owners who are *echt Deutsch* in looks and speech and in their outlook on cooking. Three that are easy to find are: *Lohmeyer,* on 5th, near Z; *Ketel's,* off Z, between 5th and the Ginza; and *Germania,* on Annex, close behind Hotel Imperial. This last is an unpretentious upstairs place featuring *Bier vom Fass,* which is draft beer. Any of these places will be happy to supply you

with *Wiener Schnitzel, Sauerbraten* and of course frankfurters
and sauerkraut to go with your beer.

Hungarian. Irene's Hungaria, in the basement of the Nikajima
Building just off St. Luke's on the first lane north of 5th, is
the only important Hungarian eating place in Tokyo. Its proprietress, Irene Haar, is a well-known "restaurateuse."

Italian. Chez Marta, near the junction of A and 10th, is sometimes listed as a "Mediterranean" restaurant, but I'd say it is
primarily Italian, good on all *pasta* dishes and very good on
such special items as *lasagna,* cooked in the rich style of
Bologna. *Nickolas,* on 15th, between B and D, is a newer place,
run by an undoubted Italian named Zappetti, who is a specialist
in pizza, offering it in no less than 15 styles.

Mexican. Papagayo, located directly under the railway tracks
back of the Shimbashi Station, offers a full kit of hot Mexican
tacos, tamales, enchiladas, etc., along with synthetic Mexican
atmosphere, but the food is nothing to write home about. The
girls who strip-dance every evening and some afternoons at 5
are very bold, and pretty. In fact, this place seems to live
largely on its much-advertised reputation for presenting "the
most daring show in Tokyo." Maybe you won't care whether
the food is good or not.

Russian. Troika, off Utility, on the Ginza side of the railway
tracks, only a slingshot from Hotels Imperial and Dai-ichi, is a
veteran Russian restaurant, with a veteran Russian chef. *Borsch,
blini, beef-Stroganoff* are among its typical dishes.

Steaks are hardly a nationality, but they are so strongly featured
in certain restaurants that few patrons visit these places to order
anything different. One such restaurant, a bit distant from the
center (10th, between K and Pershing Heights; get your hotel
porter to direct the taxi man) but superior in food and service
and highly popular with Tokyo's American residents, is *Frank's.*
This is not a luncheon place, being open only from 4 P.M. to
2 A.M., but a candlelight dinner here, with a filet mignon, a
T-bone steak or Frank's Cut, the whole lavish affair priced at
three to four dollars, can be a memorable one. Your selected
steak will be *branded* with a hot iron by the waiter and then
it is your personal master-slice of beef. While eating it you will

be soothed with soft music suited to the candlelight. *Suehiro*, on Annex between the Ginza and 10th, is a very good, easy-to-find restaurant specializing on charcoal-broiled steaks, but serving Japanese fare also.

Sea food is the specialty of three places all bearing the name *Prunier*. One is the *Prunier Room* in the Imperial Hotel; another is the *Hibiya Prunier*, on a corner of Z, at the Yurakucho Station; and the third is the *Prunier Room* in the *Tokyo Kaikan* (Building) on A, near Z, a pretentious (and good) five-story restaurant with large dining rooms, banquet halls 'neverything. This huge place is touted, and I dare say correctly, as "the largest restaurant in the Orient." The Prunier dishes of the sea are all French-inspired.

Wild game is the featured offering of *Akahane*, located on a lane off D, between 10th and 15th. Everything that flies is meat for this excellent place, whose style and *décor* are Japanese.

Japanese Foods and Restaurants—with Geisha Girls

Japanese fare, and also Chinese and Mongolian and Thai, surely warrant more research by the explorer-of-food, when in Tokyo, than do even the best steaks and lobster thermidor in plush Western restaurants, so let's see what's what first in the fare of Japan itself.

Sukiyaki, familiar to diners-out in many an American city (e.g., in the Japanese teahouses of Honolulu and in New York's authentic new *Saito Restaurant* at 70 West 55th Street), is, of course, at its superlative best in Tokyo and other Japanese cities, where it is indigenous. It is self-evident that a genuine Japanese meal of this type, served in the Japanese style and setting, is far different from its pale counterparts in most U.S. cities, so a brief description of the real thing seems in order here.

A sukiyaki dinner should always be taken in company with other people, as there's a lot of preparation and ceremony and a single person would feel a bit silly and lonely. First, invariably, you take off your shoes and squat or recline on the tatami matting floor of the sukiyaki room around a low table. An axiomatically graceful cook-waitress, clad in kimono and obi, warms a heavy iron saucepan over a charcoal brazier, which she fans to brighten the flames, and when everything is set she prepares in the pan, which sizzles with suet, a sauce consisting usually of soy and a sweet spirit called *mirin*, distilled from rice. Into this sizzling sauce she then puts the various delicacies, with basic chunks of beef, chicken or pork, that are to be cooked. And what an assortment these make, liver, bamboo shoots, pieces of *tofu*, which is bean curd, quartered onions, egg yolks and assorted vegetables, especially *shirataki*, which is translatable as "white cascade," the whole potpourri seasoned by pinches of sugar, salt and ajinomoto, which America has substantially borrowed and now makes under the name A'ccent. Often, a raw egg is broken onto your individual plate and the cooked items placed upon it in rapid succession while you ply your chopsticks with ever-increasing skill. And of course there is sake, *much* sake, to accompany the food. This drink is brewed, as I've said, from rice and served hot in tiny porcelain cups, which the waitress constantly refills whenever you take a sip. Sake may take a bit of learning, but if you are like most visitors you get to like it more and more and after eight or ten cups you always begin to experience a pleasant glow, enhancing the aroma and taste of the succulent viands. All in all, a sukiyaki dinner, as served in Japan, is a delightful blend of good food, gracious service and companionship. Few types of meals in the world can match it.

Geisha girls, in the geisha teahouses and restaurants, not to be confused with the general public restaurants listed here, are a common feature of many Japanese meals, whether of sukiyaki or tempura persuasion—the latter type of meal to be described below—and perhaps this is the best place to present them and explain their true nature and service.

Jean-Pierre Hauchecorne in his treatise on Japanese women and children in "The World in Color" series sounds off with this statement: "Despite everything that has been written, they [geishas] are nonetheless an outdated survival of the 18th century." Well, if this is true, the anachronism is an astonishingly virile and lively one. The geisha may be outdated but she just won't roll over and die. She is everywhere in Japan. Thousands of her flourish in Tokyo and hundreds of her in other large cities, especially in Kyoto, where she is an institution in which the city takes enduring pride. And as for foreign interest, I can state in personal vein that practically every friend who has spoken to me or written to me about my experiences in Japan has asked first of all, "How did you make out with the geisha girls?"

As Americans all know since it was forcefully explained in *The Teahouse of the August Moon*, geishas are not prostitutes but "art persons," which is the literal meaning of the word. However, the nature of their life and bondage is such that in very many cases the girl sooner or later becomes the protégée (i.e., mistress) of some well-to-do Japanese businessman or public official, who sets her up in business with a bar or restaurant and maintains a sugardaddy-san interest in her. By present law, girls cannot be legally apprenticed to a geisha house as young children but must be at least fifteen years old. Then the apprenticeship commences in earnest. The girl is tied to a "house" by a contract running five or ten years and her madam, if the term is not too rough, buys her expensive (often $300) kimonos, her ivory samisen, a long-necked stringed instrument which she must learn to play, and other accouterments and pays for her long years of instruction by a full-fledged geisha. She pays for the girl's "accessories" too and these are by no means negligible, since her toilet is an exceedingly elaborate business, the kimono being only the main feature of her get-up. Her hair, for instance, must be piled high on her head and held by a complex array of combs and ornaments, as prescribed centuries ago and hardened into custom during the gay years of the Tokugawa Shogunate. There's nothing altruistic about these aids, for the madam's outlay becomes a debt which must be paid back out of the girl's earnings (actually withheld from them) when she becomes an accomplished entertainer.

This entertainment consists of singing, to the accompaniment of her samisen; formalized, almost ritualistic, dancing, with intricate symbolism suggested by her graceful arms and hands and the expert wielding of a fan; light conversation; tinkling, cascade-like laughter, which she must *learn*, like her other arts; and above all a continuous patter of flattery, which need not be too subtle, of the male customer who is buying her cheerful company. Occasionally the geisha develops such talent that she can actually earn enough to pay all her debts without ever accepting a "paying lover" or protector and this is said to be especially true in Kyoto, the historic shrine of geisha art, but since she must expect to become passé by the time she reaches her mid-thirties she must "work fast" to become and remain solvent for life. In summing up the sexual side of geisha life, one can hardly improve on the wording of a guide-bulletin prepared some years ago for the American armed forces of occupation: "They take lovers but choose them themselves. They are not for the casual visitor with a few dollars to spare."

That brings us to the question of what *is* the role of the geisha, so far as tourists—you and I—are concerned? She speaks only Japanese, so her light conversation will hardly serve to entertain us, but nevertheless she is such an intrinsic part of today's Japanese life, however "outdated," that every visitor should certainly go at least once to a geisha teahouse or restaurant. Such affairs are always *parties*, never solitary dining, so perhaps you have Japanese friends who will arrange one. If not, you can always fall back on a tour visit by Pigeon Bus or otherwise. The nightly tour of the Pigeon Bus always includes an hour or so in a geisha teahouse and I think you'll be surprised by the verve and good fun of it. One teahouse visit that I was involved in became a hilariously folksy frolic of the first order. Two geisha girls sang and danced and then lured the whole group, by successive invitations, into participation in games and folk dancing.

Of course that was not a Japanese-type geisha evening, but other opportunities came my way to join with Japanese groups in the real thing. Typical of these was an evening with three Japanese men in the tiny but well-appointed *Ki Bun Restaurant* in Kyoto. The fare and cooking happened to be of the tempura type, but the entertainment was pure geisha.

At my right at the low dining table, sat Masugiku, whose name means Increasing-Joy-Forever, and at my left sat Kotake, meaning Little-Bamboo, the diminutive syllable ko being placed, in this case, at the beginning. The Japanese men, my hosts, disposed themselves at various points around the table, while the end was graced by a pleasant mamma-san holding a samisen. There was point in this, for Masugiku was but 15 years old, being what is known in Kyoto as a *maiku* girl, and in Tokyo as a *hangyoku* girl. Both of these terms mean "apprentice" and the girl can be no more than an apprentice geisha until she is at least 18 and preferably 20. Kotake was all of 22 and was indeed a full-fledged "art person."

Increasing-Joy-Forever was an excessively timid but lovely young thing, with full, elaborate geisha garments and make-up, including a mountain of sleek black hair piled up in the feudal-age style. She could not talk with me, nor I with her, but she had mastered four words in English "Thank-you-very-much," which she brought off from time to time with a gracious little silvery cascade laugh that she had learned well. Little-Bamboo, on the other hand, was as lively as an uncaged cricket. She laughed constantly, talked volubly in Japanese and, for my benefit, uttered a few phrases in what she said was French, her accent being among the world's worst. The accent didn't matter, for she was "a barrel of fun" and even engaged in some minor tricks and foolery. Then, in turn, Masugiku and Kotake sang and danced for us, while mamma-san strummed her samisen. It was a grand evening and that, I was able to report to my friends back home, was how I made out with geisha girls.

Tempura cooking means frying in a pot of deep fat (vegetable oil) various delicacies that have been dipped in batter, this process being performed, in tempura restaurants, before the eyes of the guests by a cook who sits on the floor on the opposite side of the usual low table. The chief and favorite ingredient is usually shrimps, but bits of eel, octopus, flounder, clams and sometimes chicken may be tossed in, along with mushrooms, peppers, onions, chunks of sweet potato and other vegetables. As the many items become lusciously ready for the guests' enjoyment the cook takes them out with chopsticks and puts them on the plates.

Now it's the guests' turn, *our* turn, to complete the preparation. This we do by mixing the fried dainties with a sauce composed of soy, grated white radish and a sort of bonito broth. That done, we stop teasing our olfactory glands and begin to *eat*.

Other popular Japanese dishes, which, however, may take a bit of learning by Westerners, are *kabayaki*, *sashimi* and *sushi*. The first is eels, split and broiled over a charcoal fire and dipped in a sweetened soy sauce. The other two are raw fish in slices—pink bream is a favorite kind—sashimi being the said slices dipped into a sauce much like the one described above for tempura meals and sushi being a mixture of the fish slices with rice that is seasoned by vinegar and soy sauce. Perhaps I should say, in this connection, that the usual diet of 95 per cent of the Japanese people is composed of *fish* (with much rice), meaning raw fish, broiled fish, fish steeped in vinegar, fish mixed with vegetables. Both sukiyaki and tempura are *restaurant* foods, genuinely Japanese but rather more for foreigners, in these days, than for the Japanese themselves. A special food that is grown in great volume in the shallow coastal waters of Japan is *edible seaweed*, eaten as an accessory food in many dishes, including the complicated concoctions prepared by Chinese chefs.

In Tokyo's many Japanese restaurants there is, of course, considerable overlapping in the types of food offered, meaning that some serve sukiyaki in certain rooms and tempura in others, but generally they are better known to gourmets for one type than another.

Kegon, near the Yoyogi Station of the Yamate Loop, serves first-rate sukiyaki and tempura in a genuine Japanese setting, in a specially appointed room of the Kegon Hotel.

Doh-Hana, on N, between the Ginza and 4th, in the Ueno district, is a tourist-conscious place that also serves both types of food. Its catering to Westerners may prove an advantage in comfort even though it doesn't enhance the food.

The *Sukiyaki Room* in the Imperial Hotel is one of the very best of its kind in Japan.

Suchiro, on Z between the Ginza and 10th, has been mentioned as a steak restaurant, but it is also first rate in sukiyaki, served in its Okazaki Room.

The *Takeuchi Restaurant,* in neighboring Yokohama, is one of the leading sukiyaki restaurants in that port city.

Among Tokyo's tempura specialists three of the best are the *Ten-ichi,* on 5th, at Z; the *Inagiku,* on 17th, between W and X; and the *Hanacho,* on V, near the Meiji-za Theater.

Chinese restaurants, if they may have mention here alongside those of Japanese type, abound in Tokyo and some well-traveled gourmets who have been everywhere will tell you that they are better here than even in Hong Kong, or anywhere else in the world. Among the topflight places, and there are many, three may be selected, perhaps arbitrarily. These are the *Sunya,* on A, between 10th and 12th; *King Ling,* on F, near Mampei Avenue; and *China House,* on A, between 10th and 12th. A fourth place, called *Forbidden City,* at the corner of Yoyogi and 30th, is proud of both its Shanghai and Szechwan cuisines. This place, parroting the name of a famous San Francisco nightclub, makes an earnest play for tourist trade.

I might mention in passing that both Yokohama and Nagasaki have a true, though not very large, Chinese Quarter, with many Chinese restaurants. One of the very best in all Japan is the sumptuous *Shikai Ro* in Nagasaki.

Chinzanso for Mongolian Feasting and Fireflies

Perhaps the most famous of all Tokyo's myriads of restaurants, and deservedly so, is the *Chinzanso*, a superb garden restaurant in a 17-acre park so lovely and remote-seeming that patrons can imagine themselves many miles from the big, roaring metropolis. Actually, it is in a northwestern quarter, on M, near 15th, well within the Yamate Loop. Chinzanso means "Camellia Mountain," but it is hardly that. More precisely, it is a hill-and-dale park with a brook running through it and with 8000 trees and handsome shrubs planted in it, all of them set out after fire bombs, launched on May 26, 1945, destroyed most of the previous vegetation, along with most of the buildings. Fortunately, they did not destroy a lovely 3-story pagoda built in the 9th century in Hiroshima Prefecture and moved to the Chinzanso in 1924 by Baron Fujita, nor did they destroy an ancient Oratory that was likewise moved to this spot in 1924, this coming from Kyoto.

Chinzanso, as a park, was conceived and developed during the Meiji Period by Prince Aritomo Yamagata and the great Emperor Meiji himself often came here for conferences with his ministers. Its development as a garden restaurant occurred much more recently, but it is now at its peak of attractiveness. There is a small Japanese-style dining room for 40, a Western-style restaurant for 200, with outdoor dancing, an open garden-grill for 400 and space for garden parties of up to 2000 persons. Its specialties are Genghis Khan-style barbecue, which is served for four or more persons seated around a brazier in the garden-grill, and Hakone broiled chicken.

For the Genghis Khan barbecue, which is Mongolian fare at its superlative best, each guest is draped with a sort of butcher's apron so that he may protect his clothing when he uses his chopsticks to take from his plate the sauce-dripping delicacies. If I were asked to name the very best meal I have had in Japan, giving glamour some part in the point score, I would certainly name a

Mongolian dinner I enjoyed here with Japanese friends on a balmy evening late in May.

That date has its bright significance, for every year from May 25th to June 25th the Chinzanso has a *Firefly Festival* that is one of the exotic spectacles of Tokyo. From all over Japan fireflies gathered by country folk are dispatched to Tokyo at so much per hundred, or thousand, sparklers and the Chinzanso alone claims, or implies in its advertising, that it buys a *million* of them each year, to be loosed in the garden by the thousand every night during that month for the entertainment of its patrons. Most of the fireflies are of normal size and brightness such as we know them in America but about 10 per cent of them are giant-sized ones, with brilliant lamps, called *genzi*, captured on the island of Shikoku. Many Tokyo shops sell fireflies in cages during the firefly season and the Chinzanso does likewise, vending small cages of them at 100 yen. Each cage contains 3 or 4 normal ones and one big genzi, along with a bit of green stuff for them to feed on. For 200 yen anyone may have tea and cakes along with the firefly cage. After my Genghis Khan feast I went back to my hotel with one of these cages, hung it up in my room and enjoyed the company of the flashing insects during the night.

Temples of Coffee and Tea

The coffee houses and tearooms of Tokyo reach levels of splendor and musical entertainment that never fail to astonish visitors, and the American, upon seeing and enjoying them, invariably asks himself and others, "Why don't *we* have such things?"

Coffee houses are found in thousands all over Japan and though their range of size and elegance is considerable they all have musical entertainment of some sort and most of them have a pleasant and soothing effect on the visitor. In every small city dozens of these places exist, sometimes mere dens with room for only eight or ten guests, but almost always there is good music, even if only from a record player. More pretentious houses have elaborate hi-fi instruments and the *most* pretentious ones, consisting of several stories, have good popular orchestras, supplemented by soloists playing and singing light classics and the better popular songs, or, in some cases, providing dance music. There are more than 4000 coffee houses in Tokyo alone and many of them are very good. In general, the majority of them aim to provide a romantic atmosphere and one of my more articulate American friends living in Tokyo once referred to them collectively as "the catalytic agent in the chemistry of love." And they are *so* inexpensive. For the price of a cup of coffee or an orangeade, say 100 to 200 yen maximum, you may linger for hours enjoying the music and the crowds. No waitress will bother you or suggest that you buy another drink, in the manner of nightclub hostesses.

In central Tokyo there is one outstanding temple of coffee and one of tea, while several other houses demand special mention for some special feature.

The coffee house to which I refer is the *Shirobasha*, on Annex between the Ginza and 5th, hence very near the Imperial Hotel. This is a four-story place of dim lights and considerable luxury, with an open well in the middle for the orchestra and singers, whose music, genuinely good and smooth, may be enjoyed from any seat on any of the floors. The place is open from 11 A.M. to 11 P.M. and to keep the music going continuously several orchestras spell each other.

The outstanding tearoom to which I refer is the *Yie-Lai-Shian*, a 3-story Chinese-style place of soft carpets, luxurious décor and relaxing atmosphere on Z between A and 5th, this too being near the Imperial and still nearer the Dai-ichi. The name of the place means "Jasmine Flower." This, like the Shirobashi, is open from 11 to 11 and the music, emanating from a platform that can rise or descend by electric power, is perhaps even more soothing to tired patrons.

Three other coffee houses shall have mention in this drastically condensed listing, namely the big *New Mimatsu*, where three dance bands alternate; *L'Ambre*, which, despite its French name, resembles a 17th-century English coffee house; and the *Albion*.

This last, which confuses us by *calling* itself a tea saloon, is the very strangest place of public refreshment in the world, so far, at any rate, as I have seen the world. An American resident who first took me there warned me "The Albion is a place for deep, concentrated thought. The management tries to keep it dead silent and you even have to write out your order lest your whispering to the waitress should disturb other patrons." I took this all in, hook, bait, sinker, line and reel, and prepared to tiptoe in—but we were met at the door by a *blast* of noise fit to crack a body's eardrums. Jazz music of the most strident, tinpanic type created part of the din and some thirty singing waitresses created the rest. The girls were all clad in spangled blouses and spangled knee pants with the sides open to their hips and in addition to their yelling they kept up an odd, jittery weaving of their hips *all* the time. Also, as every guest entered, they *shrieked* a cheerful welcome to him and as he left they *shrieked* an equally piercing "Arigato! Arigato!" This amazing place is in a basement room of the Nichigeki Theater, a conspicuous rounded building on Z, just east of the railway tracks. Do, by all that's incredible, make a visit to the wildly cacophonous Albion but before you go insure your eardrums.

The Ten-Course Barbecue Dives

One of the surprises and delights of exploratory eating in Tokyo is the multitude of tiny barbecue dives where a few guests, seldom over ten, may enjoy a chicken barbecue meal as big as the establishment is small. The word for such an eating den is *yakitori* and a typically good chicken barbecue, in a central location, is *Isehiro Yakitori*, at 6, 1-chome, Kyobashi, Chuoku (Tokyo). This, like hundreds of similar dives, is essentially a family affair run by papa-san, mamma-san and one or two grown-up daughters. Their domain is no larger, all told, than an average American kitchen, but it is wonderfully compact. The guests perch on stools at a rude wooden counter behind which the proprietor and his family cook and serve the meals, most of the items being skewered on sticks and handed to the customers.

Consider a meal, course by course, that I tackled at the address mentioned above, a meal that proved to be at least four courses too big for me, though I thought myself half starved when I entered the place. I made such a poor showing that the proprietor looked unhappy, thinking he hadn't pleased me, though actually everything was delicious.

1. Bits of chicken meat with horse-radish
2. Chicken livers barbecued with a sweetish sauce
3. Chicken livers barbecued with salt
4. Quail's egg
5. Ground chicken meat
6. Chicken with a small Japanese onion
7. Barbecued duck
8. Barbecued chicken skin
9. Chicken bone with its meat
10. Chicken wing and joint

The servings were big and generous, every one, and I began to fade after the first four courses, but with lubrication from a bottle of cold beer I struggled happily on for two or three more skewers of the wonderful fare. Do try one of these dives, I urge, and prove yourself a better tackler than I.

Bars by the Thousand

Sometime when I have a half year to spare I am going to undertake a census of Tokyo's bars, of course engaging a large staff of assistants to aid me in the research. A Japanese official count, or estimate, of them made a while ago, set the figure at 15,000, but this must now be far too low. In many of the narrow lanes (chomes) on either side of the Ginza virtually every building has one or two bars, most of them even tinier than the barbecue dives, and each one has dainty waitresses or hostesses, usually dressed in Western clothes but sometimes in kimono and obi. The bars are quite as numerous in the vicinity of Shimbashi Station and most of the other stations of the main railway line and the Yamate Loop. There are said to be 2000 of them in Asakusa Park alone. The going drinks are beer, sake and shochu, a cheap and powerful beverage distilled from rice, others being awamori, a brutal liquor distilled from millet, and various Japanese whiskies, one of them being the widely advertised Suntory. The beers of Japan, I should emphasize again, are very good indeed and no visitor need order expensive imported beers unless he simply *must* have some familiar, favored brand. Some of the best Japanese brews, as previously listed in Chapter 3, are Sapporo, Asahi, Kirin, Gold and Nippon.

How do these thousands of bars all flourish? *Why*, if they do flourish, aren't the Japanese a drunken nation? These questions every foreigner asks himself and others as he strolls the many bar areas of the capital and other cities. I suppose one answer is that five or six average bars in the Japanese pleasure lanes can accommodate no more customers than one average bar in a Western city. Another answer is that it takes quite a lot of either sake or beer to bring on inebriety. Whisky is too expensive for most of the patrons, but cheap shochu has a massive kick and this *does* cause drunkenness, as you may see by walking through the Shimbashi pleasure lanes of an evening. Most of the bars close at midnight and a characteristic sight of Tokyo's zero hour is the sight of thousands of lovely young bar girls and hostesses, many of them in striking, provocative garb, hurrying from the center to catch subway trains or streetcars to their suburban homes.

The *names* of the bars, to conclude this bibulous essay, are very often given on signs in English or French and I'll set down a score or two of them that I've culled at random from Tokyo and other cities: *Subrosa; G-String; Gloria; Coppelia; Magnolia; Lumière; Bar Jhonny* (*sic*); *Club Opera; Bar Moses; Black Bar;*

Bar Pony; Bar St. Moritz; Bar Dom; Golden Bell; Silver Kitchen; Capri; Bar Swanee; Bar Happy; Bar Again; Bar Betty; Moon Palace; Black Rose; Clover Bar; Stag Bar; Duffy's Tavern; Club Million Dollars; Café Suez; Club Night-and-Day.

The last two named are in Yokohama and each has its advertising gimmick. Club Suez has individual table telephones for flirting and pickup purposes, in the manner of Berlin's famous Resi. Night-and-Day is more of a nightclub and its advertisement reads: "Our Hostesses Are Most Desirous And Beautiful Young Ladies." So—if you wish some desirous and beautiful young ladies this may be your golden goal.

CHAPTER 8

ENTERTAINMENT IN ALL KEYS

The Festival Dances and Girlie Revues

SPRING busts out all over in Japan and this is very understandable when one thinks of the grim winter from which its people have just emerged, a winter of raw, cold days, cold homes, cold Japanese inns. Not least active in this vernal exuberance are the theaters of Tokyo, Kyoto and Osaka, for they produce huge, spectacular girlie revues that would captivate audiences in Paris, London or New York quite as surely as they do in Tokyo. These revues set the tone for a season of lavish and varied entertainment that is scarcely surpassed anywhere in the world. Indeed, I think it is fair to say that except in opera, concert music and stage plays of Western type Tokyo surpasses all other cities of the world in what it offers in after-dark entertainment. To make up for its lacks it offers its amazing kabuki and noh stages.

To be specific about Tokyo's gay theaters, there are at least three that regularly offer "spring spectaculars," namely—and please don't let these names throw you—(1) the *Nichigeki Theater*, on Z; (2) the *Shimbashi Embujo Theater*, in the Shimbashi district; and (3) the *Asakusa Kokusai Theater*, just beyond Asakusa Park. All three of these, and there are one or two other settings for extravagant shows, such as the *Shinjuku Koma Stadium*, think nothing of having girl dance groups as large, and almost as well trained, as the Rockettes of New York. The Asakusa Kokusai Theater has an even larger group, much larger in fact, for no less than 300 pretty girls crowd the vast stage in some of the more elaborate scenes. This, like the others, is an all-girl show, no mere man having a chance on such a stage.

A warning about the hours of performance is important here, for they differ radically from those of our big revues. The shows are usually given three times a day, the first one starting in the forenoon, the second early in the afternoon and the third about 6 or 6:30 P.M.

An idea of the nature of the Asakusa show may be gathered from the titles of some of the 18 numbers in a show I saw. Here are a few: Cherry Trees; The Flower Romance; Spring Night; Arizona Poppy; New York; Trip to Arabia; Galaxy of Legs; Ballet of the Violet; Spirit of the Carnation; Grand Parade. In the scene called New York a girl met and fell for a charming but sinister gangster but was rescued just in time by her true love.

The spring shows in the Nichigeki Theater are more or less similar to those at Asakusa, but the *Shimbashi Cherry Dance*, offered at the Shimbashi Embujo, is *quite* different, being definitely a Japanese, not a Western, spectacular. Like the others it has only girls in the cast, but here they are clad in lovely kimonos, and an orchestra composed only of samisens plays in a large alcove at the left of the stage. Some of the numbers in a show I enjoyed here were: Hana no Irodori, translated as Colorful Flowers; Nuregoromo (Wet Clothes); Furisode Monogurui (Crazy Sleeves); and Ensetsu Saiyu-ki, a story of love. Conforming to the title of the whole show there were several lovely cherry dances by large groups of kimono-clad girls and during these beautiful scenes stray petals of cherry blossoms drifted down upon the dancers, not *showers* of petals but one and then another—and then perhaps two. This, I thought, was still another evidence of Japanese artistic taste, the taste for "understatement."

In deference to sound reporting I should mention that not only in spring but at other seasons of the year, especially autumn, when Lantern Dances reign, there are elaborate girlie shows; and I should state too that the most celebrated troupe of dancing girls in all Japan, comprising the world-known *Takarazuka* company, performs for one or two weeks every second month in a big theater now called the *Tokyo Taka Theater* but formerly called the Ernie Pyle Theater, on Annex, directly opposite the side doors of the Imperial. But the dramatic story of the founding and growth of Takarazuka belongs in a later chapter (9), when this report reaches the theater-town of Takarazuka itself, not far from Osaka. In all the theater world I doubt that there is a more stirring story of enterprise.

Kabuki on Its Native Heath

Kabuki is about the strangest form of drama that any civilization has developed, or it would be so if this same Japanese civilization had not developed the drama style called noh. This latter has not gone abroad but kabuki has, at least in its dance form, and on these foreign tours its novelty made a smash hit, especially in New York, a few years ago. In Honolulu, it is seen, in a small way, with some frequency.

Kabuki is wonderful to watch, a shock to the senses, a challenge to credibility, but it is almost impossible to describe it in words. I will not attempt even a short treatise on it but will tell a few basic facts and indicate where you may best see it for yourself.

Kabuki is supposed to have developed from some religious dances performed in public in Kyoto by a priestess named Okuni, from the Great Shrine of Izumo, and later in Edo (Tokyo) in the early 1600's. It caught on with the public as a departure from the stiff formalism of the existing noh stage and gradually developed as a strange complex of acting, singing and dancing, all of these vehicles being used to develop the story. A few decades after Okuni's pioneer work women were sternly forbidden to appear on the stage anywhere in Japan, for it seemed that many of the plays took on a hot-sexy turn and the presence of women in them was felt to be demoralizing. From that day until the Meiji Restoration of 1868 the ban remained in force and in kabuki, believe it or not, it is *still* in force, though by custom rather than by law. The inevitable result is that men specially trained to it for years invariably play the women's parts, and their voices, in quavering, squeaky falsetto, are weird beyond one's imagining. Even the men who play men's parts have voices that you just can't believe until you hear them. It is said that in training they go out into remote places in wintry weather to scream and shout until they wreck their natural voices, proceeding then to build up the stark, distorted, often violent timbre that seems able to project itself to the farthest corner of the gallery of great theaters. Often it has seemed to me a cross between a wild man's wail and a person in the throes of seasickness.

In the 18th century, kabuki sharply declined in popular favor, due to the success of the puppet theaters, but on the theory that "if you can't beat 'em jine 'em," it borrowed many of the livelier plots of the puppet shows, while clever playwrights devised new ones, as they are doing even now, so kabuki was able gradually to regain the ascendency until it finally pushed puppetry far into the background. Even so, every play for the kabuki stage is written in the old feudal style and the settings are pre-Meiji feudal settings. About 500 plays exist, the best and most famous classics being those of a dramatic genius named Mokuami Kawatake. The most enduring sure-fire plot is still and always the deathless story of the Forty-Seven Ronin, which never fails to rouse audiences to fever pitch.

Many plays start with a traditional oddity borrowed from the puppet theater. As the curtain rises, a narrator and a musician twanging a samisen are seen at the side of the stage, which is *very* broad. The narrator proceeds to reveal the plot, reciting from a book in an unearthly, wailing voice, and the actors illustrate by gestures and facial contortions what he is reading. But they are not *merely* mimes, for they make their own comments and rejoinders to the narrator's story. Sound effects are produced by a hidden orchestra of samisens, flutes, assorted drums and pairs of wood slabs struck sharply together to produce resonant, clacking sounds.

The actors resort to fantastic make-ups to add terror, consternation or fury to their expressions and in big scenes these displays of violent emotion reach Everests of dramatic feeling. When one of these scenes is "coming on," usually at the point where an actor, bent on vengeance or some deed of heroism, is about to rush from the stage by an extension of it called the *hanamichi* that passes clear through the audience to the rear of the theater, a stage hand appears at the side of the stage and clacks two slabs of wood sharply together. The actor freezes to the spot where he stands, plants his feet apart to indicate stern determination, makes the most ghastly grimaces a human face can make and distends his eyeballs as if he would pop them from their sockets. He waits for urgent cries from the galleries, "Go to it! Give it all you've got! Pile into it!", and then, uttering a weird cry or a retching wail, he stomps up the hanamichi to disappear behind a curtain at the theater's rear. Many in the audience become weepy or semi-hysterical and even the Westerner who may have come to scoff remains to be strangely moved by the eerie intensity of the scene. The beholder is exhausted after it and slumps down in his seat to rest and recover.

The hanamichi, which I have mentioned rather incidentally, is an essential part of any kabuki theater. Actors often enter the main stage by it, with dramatic flourish, as well as leave by it. Another essential feature is the revolving stage, which permits one setting to follow the other, always in full view of the audience, as the stage slowly turns. This was invented, in a primitive form, about the year 1760 and such Western theaters as now use this device must, it seems, have borrowed it from Japan. When changes in the furniture or costuming become necessary during the course of a play these are taken care of by property men called *kurogo*, who are invariably shrouded and hooded in black. They sneak on and off the stage as quietly and surreptitiously as possible in order to avoid distracting the audience.

By far the best known of some seven or eight Tokyo theaters offering only kabuki is the *Kabuki-za*—za means theater—handily located on Z, a few blocks east of the Ginza. Outwardly it is of Japanese architecture but inwardly it is more Western in style, with comfortable seats, and it has ample lounge and lobby space, souvenir shops and tearooms. Put the Kabuki-za on your calendar of certainly musts. If you take a Pigeon Bus night tour you will probably have an hour in this theater as one of the evening's features, but this taste of kabuki may be only enough to whet your appetite. A full show, which may consist of five separate plays, historical or tragic and of formalized dancing, usually starts at noon and lasts until 4 or 5 o'clock. A second series consumes a long evening. Patrons often bring their lunch, or buy it at the theater snack shop and munch as they watch.

Snail-Paced Noh for the Curious

If kabuki is weird, noh is positively creepy, and if kabuki is slow-paced, noh is snail-paced. Noh is of 14th-century origin and was built up as *court* drama, intended for aristocrats, as opposed to kabuki, which was and is for the masses. Today, it lives only by government subsidy and by the dedicated support of several dramatic schools in Tokyo, Kyoto and Osaka. The speech of the actors is even more hollow, belching and unnatural than that of the kabuki actors, seeming to come from the depths of a disturbed stomach, and the language is so ancient that even Japanese patrons understand little of it unless they are proficient noh students.

But that doesn't matter, for noh isn't meant to tell a story or to entertain in the ordinary sense. "Its main aim," writes T. Kawanishi, a noted authority, "is to make the audience feel rhythmically and musically the sense of beauty through song, dance and music." To this end, a man playing the part of a priestess obsessed by a divine spirit can easily take three-quarters of an hour to convey beauty by teetering about the stage and gently shaking a fan or a stick with a string of paper prayers attached to it.

The very *stage* of noh is one of its peculiarities, for its nature and dimensions are rigidly prescribed. It is 18 feet square, raised 3 feet from the ground and is topped by a roof supported by four pillars. Back of this square is a rectangular back stage for the orchestra (flutes, drums, resonant sticks) and to the left, as we face the stage, a corridor, which must be 9 feet wide and 53 feet long, leading from and to the greenroom. There is no curtain whatever and there are no changes of scenery, but behind the back stage for the orchestra there *is* a backdrop and on it is painted a pine tree, one tree only, to symbolize the early times when noh was staged in the open air.

Masks, often of wonderful cleverness and power, are an essential of noh and their range of representation is from old man to child, from potent god to monster and from fairy to wild animal, but only the chief actor wears a mask, whatever character, old or young, male, female or beast, he may be playing. A second actor, and perhaps some companions, support the protagonist, but he is really the whole show. Occasionally, in these free days, it is *she,* for it is not now absolutely against custom, as it still is in kabuki, for a woman to play a part. In a play called *Sakura Gawa,* meaning Cherry River, I actually saw an actress, but this was rare luck. Another play, offered as part of the same show, was called *Maki-Ginu,* meaning The Rolls of Silk. In both plays the costumes were of utmost magnificence, as they invariably are in noh, and this goes for *every* player, even the most poverty-stricken beggar. The reason for this is intrinsic. In the words of a guide to noh, "The play does not aim at realism but tries to create a special world of beauty. The dress is always adapted to promote this conception."

I would say in conclusion that if you "bore" easily while watching a play which you cannot hope to understand, then noh is not for you, for the movements are sloth-slow, even a romping child moving at a barely perceptible creep. But if the Japanese world of six centuries ago stirs your curiosity and fascinates your imagination then give it a try. You need not sit through the whole show with the dedicated few. There are, at present, about half a dozen exclusive noh theaters in all Japan, three of them being in Tokyo. One of the newest and best is the *Kanze Noh Theater*, in the Shinjuku section.

Undress Shows and Candid Strips

Tokyo has one undress theater, small but very gay and uninhibited, that attracts tourists in droves, like an Oriental Folies Bergère, namely the *Nichigeki Music Hall*, which is located on the 5th floor (elevator) of that circular building on Z that houses the big Nichigeki Theater, the raucous Albion Coffee Shop and a movie house. The Music Hall is open throughout the year, presenting three shows on weekdays, four on Sundays, and there is rarely a vacant seat. The best seats may be reserved, but the rest may be scrambled for, as in our movie houses, and you may come when you like and stay as long as you like, one show following another. At every show tourists take flashlight shots of the more beautiful and bizarre scenes and the bulbs flash like mammoth fireflies.

The shows of the Music Hall are fast and funny and very much undressed, being of the type called by the trade "b and b," for breasts and buttocks, but with very few and minor exceptions the girls do not strip, nor do they bump and grind, as in American burlesque. For each scene they appear, right off, in whatever they wear, or don't wear, and that's that. Mostly they don't wear. Bras are virtually unknown and in some scenes a fancy g-string is the whole costume. In another way the shows differ sharply from American burlesque, for the comics are genuinely comic, not merely tramps and bums saying dirty and unfunny jokes. No doubt there are many lines of *double-entendre*, spoken in Japanese, but the whole atmosphere of the comic scenes is one of uproarious humor and I, for one, have more than once been "in stitches," over a scene in which I did not understand a single word of the dialogue except the occasional English phrases tossed in as a sop to the tourists in the house. In general, one might describe the typical show of the Nichigeki Music Hall as a small-scale French revue, with touches of forthright U.S. vaude-ville, almost every scene emphasizing nudity, as does the adver-tising. The costumes, when there are any, are clever and some-times lavish, but toward the end of a successful run they often get spotty and frayed, so don't look closely, except at the bodies, which are always graceful and creamy-smooth.

The names of the shows, always advertised in English (or French) as well as Japanese, give a clear indication of their gen-eral nature, such names *L'Amour de Printemps, Angels Don't Wear Petticoats* and *Tickle My Ears Gently.*

The candid strips of Asakusa Park are something quite "else again." If the Music Hall offers "nude follies," the favorite phrase of its advertisements, Asakusa offers outright sex shows, as naked and bawdy as anything New Orleans or Chicago could hope to show.

Asakusa Park, since nudity has led me to this area, is a sight that no visitor should miss. Its gridiron of lanes, made gay with banners and neon lights, resounds with the life of common-or-garden Japan. It is said to have 2000 bars and coffee houses, a like number of restaurants, scores of *pachinko* dens, these being pinball parlors whose clicking sounds fill the air like surf on a pebbly beach, and heaven knows how many thousands of tiny shops, most of them with wide-open fronts. And it has its Theater Row, where some thirty movie houses stand "elbow to elbow." Here too are the candid strip shows, six or eight in number. They are given in tiny theaters, usually in a basement, with seats for perhaps a hundred persons and standing room for another hun-dred, and always a runway for the strippers, extending straight through to the rear of the house. A bevy of perhaps a dozen girls puts on one fleshy number after another in rapid succession and here, both on stage and runway, they bump and grind, weave and wimble and do all in their expert power to inflame their all-male audiences. In one scene that I saw here a girl clad in the most tenuous of g-strings lay on her stomach on the floor and with undulations and writhings of the most primal sort simulated the most primal of human acts. A man in the audience called out something to her in Japanese and a big laugh swept the house. I asked the patron standing next to me—all seats are nearly always filled—what the man had said. Fortunately he knew a little English and understood me. With some effort he managed to tell me: "He say 'What are you doing?'" This, I suppose, was funny because what the girl was doing was a hundred times more than obvious.

In the quieter reaches at the edge of Asakusa Park men and boys offer invitations to "special shows," both live ones and movies, which *must* be tolerated by the police, for literally hundreds of such invitations are offered, and not only in Asakusa but along the central portion of the Ginza and on Annex Avenue, near Hotel Imperial, and on 5th Street and on all the little lanes in that whole area, and in Shimbashi. Every conceivable show that turgid imaginations can dream up is offered openly, with no pretense of furtiveness or secrecy. In this department, Montmartre is kid stuff by comparison with Tokyo. But maybe that's enough on this topic.

Big and Little Cabarets—with Hostesses

To report adequately on Tokyo's nightclubs is just as difficult, and I mean this literally, as to do so on those of Paris, for they are almost as numerous and even more varied in their style and in what they offer for the entertainment of the customers. I don't believe you want a directory of scores of them, to compound confusion on the subject, so I shall offer a few "observations" and then try to give a fair report on some of the better-known places and on samples of other types.

One thing that all the nightspots of Tokyo have in common—

with the single exception, so far as I know, of the *New Golden Gate*—is hostesses, hostesses and more hostesses. They are beautiful creatures, petite and winsome, like almost all Japanese girls, but axiomatically "on the make," and in some cases positively predatory. I don't mean, and I would stress this, that they are any *more* predatory than nightclub hostesses in any great city of the world, but there are far more of them and they all exert themselves to make a living, with the result that they often seem to descend on the male patron like a swarm of pretty seventeen-year (-old) locusts. They all have a big thirst and make it very easy for the male to order repeated drinks at 300 yen and up per drink. In addition to this, their company alone is priced, in the plushier places, at 1000 yen an hour if the patron selects a hostess, less if he takes any girl whose turn it may chance to be; and in addition to *this* there is usually a cover charge of 300 yen per person; and in addition to *this* the girls, unlike servants in hotels and restaurants, expect tips and will ask for them if they are not offered. The bolder ones may even suggest 1000 yen apiece but that is real and inexcusable rapacity, since 200 or 300 is ample.

The charges, in general, are modest enough and much less than one would pay in New York or Paris, but the part of it that can be ruinous to the budget is the drinks bought for oneself *and* the hostess. Of course she gets a cut on everything and of course she tends to get restless if her glass and the patron's glass are not filled and refilled frequently. Also, she will likely have a girl friend or a "sister," equally thirsty, who would just love to meet the charming gentleman and, in fact, why here she is right now, cheerily settling into a chair, and it is *so* hard for a polite patron to say "Please get up and go away." The result can be that what looked, at first glance, like an inexpensive 5- or 10-dollar hour can readily become a 25-dollar hour and what looked like a 25-dollar evening can become a 50-dollar evening.

It would be naive to set down this warning, which is basic to all the world's nightspots, were it not that the threat is so *subtle* in Japan; and when the lovely things descend upon a customer with their sweet and gracious smiles and he cannot talk with them freely—the girls' English is usually very limited—he finds it doubly hard to rid himself of their expensive company. Furthermore, the girls are deliberately, seductively sexy. That too is no rarity in the world's nightspots, but in Tokyo it is often carried to an extremely provocative point, at least by the girls wearing Western clothes, as they do in most places, the necklines plunging to the dizziest depths and the skirts often split to the thighs, in the Chinese style.

The hostess threat can be met and countered if you go to these smart places as a mixed group, or even as a couple, but it is very difficult for males, whether singly or in twos or groups, to fend the girls off. Only by taking seats at the bar can this be done with reasonable *sang-froid*. But having said all this I would say, to lend comfort, that the male who is cool and firm and keeps his wits about him *can* enjoy a gay hour, with a hostess and with entertainment by a first-rate floor show for ten dollars. It will help to achieve this if he quietly insists that beer, Japanese beer, is the drink he desires for himself *and* his hostess. Beer is commonly served, even in the most luxurious places, as it is *not* in fancy nightclubs of Western cities, and it can "save the night."

Now to name some names.

The *Queen Bee*, on the Ginza, is one of the smartest of all the city's night clubs and it offers a good show twice each evening. A very good dance orchestra plays in an alcove at the right of the stage, and at the back of the stage there is an interesting illuminated stained-glass window representing, of all things, a scene of Merrie Olde England. The Queen Bee hostesses are divided into two groups, those who speak English, sort of, and those who don't, the former group, setting their sights for tourists, being far more sexily clad, or unclad, than the others.

The *Crown*, on 5th, near Annex, is about as plushy as the Queen Bee. At each table where there is a group of men patrons one hostess has the status of "head girl" and if other girls swarm in, as they surely will, she alone is responsible for the proper division

of the hostess fees, the drink credits and the tips. Everything is
supposed to be settled by the patron with her alone. The Crown
offers a good show twice every evening on a circular stage that
sinks out of sight and rises again as the different acts come on.
An aperture in the ceiling also opens to let down performers by
chains or cords and other performers descend to the stage by a
long, winding stairway. The bright boy who dreamed up these
gimmicks seems to have made them a success, but the show would
be good without them.

The *Show Boat* is a very big, very self-conscious, very noisy
and raucous place that can be a lot of fun if you're in a Coney
Island mood. It is an exhibitionist 5-story affair of steel and
chrome on a lane (called 8-chome, as if *that* would help) near the
Ginza and in the attempt to suit its style to its name it is got
up to represent, if your imagination can manage it, a Mississippi
river boat. Around the perimeter of a big well in the center aluminum dinghies circle on tracks on the second and fourth floors,
stopping to sell cold beer to customers who stand at the railings
of the well. There are said to be no less than 600 hostesses, waitresses and girl-gobs in service here, at least 400 of whom are always working. The hostesses who have worked at the Show
Boat less than twenty days must wear a sort of badge on a halter
to indicate that they are greenhorns. The waitresses wear skirts
and jumpers as of mariner-girls and the humbler gobesses are
clad in sailor pants and blouse, for their job is to swab down the
decks, wipe up spilled beer and so forth. A special task force of
girls dressed as streetcar conductors collect the money from each
table. They and the waitresses may dance with the customers,
competing with the hostesses, but the humble swabbers may not
dance. Each hostess, by the way, is named for some country or
city, by way of identification. Two that eagerly attended to my
needs and helped me drink up my beer were Miss New Zealand
and Miss Seattle. I asked for Miss Boston, that being my city, but
Boston-san was busy entertaining another customer.

The charges at the Show Boat are unique, for they are based on a ticket system, each ticket having a value of 420 yen. You pay a basic 1320 yen for a table and then 420 yen for each item purchased, whether it is a bottle of beer or sake or Suntory whisky or a "sand wich" or a "fry eggs." Imported whiskies, such as "John Walker" (sic), call for 2 tickets and French "shampagne" calls for 6, which is 2160 yen, which is $7.00, but Japanese champagne may be had for 3 tickets.

Dancing is done on a tiny floor to the music of a band that rides up and down on an electrically operated platform but since 400 couples, or even 40, can't dance on a space 10 feet square, the dancing becomes merely teetering and hugging, which is all right with the customers and certainly with the accommodating hostesses and mariner waitresses. What the Show Boat lacks in exclusiveness it makes up in *noise*, running a close second in that department to the Albion Tea Saloon. So much for the Show Boat, House of Blare!

Benibasha, on 10th, between D and F, is pleasantly different in that the hostesses don't descend on the customer en masse. They remain behind a barrier and are more than ready to accept any invitation, but it must actually be a customer's invitation, not theirs. This place has a 500-yen charge, and for the company of a hostess, if one is desired, the usual 1000 yen per hour is charged, but the Benibasha is known for its fairness and for *not* being predatory. It offers a good floor show.

Casino Tokyo, on 10th, near 5th, also seems to have a reputation for fairness, but I haven't had personal experience of the place.

The *Mimatsu*, on a lane near Z, between the Ginza and 10th, is a hostess-nightclub after dark, offering the "Mimatsu Follies" twice each evening, but before dark, in the afternoon from 1 to 5:30, it is a public ballroom, being different in this respect from all the other big cabarets.

The *Montevideo*, a small upstairs place on a lane off Z, east of the Ginza, is an earnest advertiser of its "three nude shows every evening," but despite this, it seems to me more folksy and less sexy than many of the nightspots and it is unusual in making no charge for the company of its hostesses.

The *Nikkatsu Family Club*, open to members and their guests and to all registrants at the Nikkatsu Hotel, is a large and luxurious nightclub, with a good dance orchestra, located on the 5th floor of the Nikkatsu Theater, on 4th, between Y and Z.

And so on and on and on, to the *Ginbasha*, the *Monte Carlo*, the *Golden Ginza*, the *Club Cherry*, the *Minato*, the *Hibaya Club*, *Club A-1*, *Club Silver Star*, et cetera ad infinitum, and again one asks oneself *"How* do they all manage to live?"

A word of Nestorian warning may be in order here about the places marked "On Limits." There are literally dozens of these smaller nightclubs on the lanes on both sides of the Ginza and in other crowded centers and they usually advertise "No cover, no hostess charge, no minimum, no tipping." Well—that sounds fine to the exploring male, but many (not all) of these places tend to be on the clip-joint side. Often they advertise drinks at 200 or 250 yen, but that proves to be the price for beer only and unfortunately the pretty little hostess is allergic to beer and must have whisky, a thimbleful of a Japanese brand diluted with water priced at 500 yen. Even so, the *customer* may drink beer and if he keeps his head he may spend an hour at one of these places, most of which offer shows, for well under $10.00. The last two places named above are On Limits places, located respectively on 5th, and on a lane north of Z, and both candidly advertise their main attraction. Club A-1, calling itself "An Oasis for Thirsty People and Lonely Souls," stresses its "Sexy A-1 Girls and Soothing Drinks," while the Club Silver Star, calling itself "Your Earthly Paradise," calls attention to "a wide selection of hostesses and a setting of extremely dim lights where customers literally have to feel their way around." Both places make good, in a big way, on their basic promise of sex.

Are the Red Lights Turning Blue?

For centuries all Japanese cities have had extensive "gay quarters," as they are called, operating in a wide open way with full legality and with regular medical inspection of the prostitutes, but in 1956 the impossible happened. After the war, the subservient, downtrodden, humiliated women of Japan won the right to vote and within a decade they brought such pressure to bear on the Japanese Diet that that body voted to abolish legalized prostitution all over the country, following the lead of various European countries, including France and Spain. This was an earth-shaking decision, hardly to be grasped and understood by the average Japanese, for the prostitute population of Japan has long been numbered in tens of thousands and little or no stigma has been attached to the profession. Every small town has had two or three gay quarters, the larger towns four or five, and Tokyo over a dozen, led by the famous quarter called Yoshiwara. It was a common and accepted tradition for poor parents to sell their "extra daughters" into this life, but if a girl was ambitious she could often earn enough to pay off the purchase price and even build up a little dowry. Then she could return to her home town, marry and live a respectable and respected life. Many of her neighbor-wives had achieved home life by the same route.

Well—the unexpected thunderbolt struck Japan and the Diet was goaded, seemingly much against its will, into passing the law that was to abolish prostitution, but the date for the closing of the multitude of brothels was set well ahead, the deadline being April 1, 1958. Now the big question is: How will this work out? Will the law really be implemented by police action? Will there be a *token* closing, to appease the feminine clamor, or will a genuine attempt be made to effect a real and permanent closing? I have asked a number of Japanese these questions and the answers seem to reflect a general, widespread opinion that the red lights will turn to blue lights, meaning that the houses of prostitution will *call* themselves hotels, bars, restaurants, coffee houses, even shops, but will continue in the old business, using some slight camouflage and perhaps altering their outward appearance. I, as one of the tourist onlookers, won't attempt to prophesy, or even guess, what the authorities will do. Perhaps the degree of enforcement of the law will vary from city to city and from ward to ward. Time will reveal the interesting denouement.

YOURSELF IN THE PICTURE OF JAPAN

CHAPTER 9

FROM NIKKO TO KOBE, A PLAN FOR SHORT-TIMERS

The Heart of Honshu in Ten Days

IT is customary for travelers who have a lot of time at their disposal to deplore, generally with fine touches of sarcasm, the rushers-around who have only a fortnight or so to spare and who try to see a lot in a short time. It is axiomatic that leisured travel is more fun than hasty travel, but I have a deep-rooted sympathy for the rushers. They have come a long way to see, for instance, Japan, and if business or other demands are so urgent that they can have but a short vacation they may still pack a *lot* into that short period by intelligent advance planning. If a fortnight is all the time available for Japan I personally would vote for putting four days of that time into Tokyo (with a single afternoon or evening of it devoted to nearby Yokohama) and the other ten days into touring the heart of Honshu. But if the amazing metropolitan modernities and excitements of the capital do not much thrill you and the temples, shrines and grand scenery of Japan do, then Tokyo may be cut to two or three days, allowing a bit more time for the provinces.

This present plan shall presume that you are dividing a Japan fortnight as above, allowing ten days for the sights of central Honshu outside of Tokyo. Chapters 10 and 11 will visit more remote portions of Japan that cannot very practically be packed into the short-timer's tour. Here, then, is a Honshu Tour that experts of the JTA and JTB once worked out, at my request, to offer the traveler the maximum return in travel pleasure with the minimum wear and tear.

First Day. Take morning train from Tokyo's Ueno Station to *Nikko*, spending the rest of that day and most of the next in Nikko, with a side trip to *Lake Chuzenji*. Stay overnight at Nikko's *Kanaya Hotel* or at *Lakeside Hotel* on the edge of Lake Chuzenji.

Second Day. Return by late afternoon train from Nikko to Tokyo and spend the night in Tokyo. (Important Note: Nikko can be pleasurably visited from Tokyo in a special JTB tour of one day or two days. If you wish to steal this day or two from your Tokyo time you can ease the rest of your provincial tour.)

Third Day. Leave Tokyo by private automobile for Kamakura (for the great Daibutsu image of Buddha and the Hachiman Shrine). Continue by private auto to *Enoshima Kanko Hotel* for luncheon, and thence to *Miyanoshita*, in *Fuji-Hakone National Park*, putting up for that night at *Fujiya Hotel*.

Fourth Day. By auto past Lake Hakone and over the *Ten Provinces Pass* (for close-up views of Fuji, clouds permitting) to *Atami*, a famous hotspring resort. Bathe in the pool of *Atami Fujiya Hotel* and then lunch in the hotel. Early afternoon take limited express train called "The Pigeon" (Hato) to *Nagoya*, spending that night in the first-class *Nagoya Kanko Hotel*.

Fifth Day. Devote the morning to Nagoya, with special attention to its famous cloisonné industry. Afternoon ride by auto to *Gifu*, on the Nagara River. Dinner there in the *Nagaragawa Hotel*. Evening excursion on the river, in a boat furnished by the hotel, to watch the exciting spectacle of "cormorants fishing for fun." (N.B.: The cormorant fishing season is from May 11 to October 15.) Back to Nagoya Kanko Hotel for the night.

Sixth Day. Morning train from Nagoya to *Toba*. Side trip by auto to visit the Ise Grand Shrine; then back to Toba for a visit to Mikimoto's Pearl Island. Auto from Toba to *Kashikojima* (Island), on Ago Bay, where Mikimoto's Pearl Farm is located. Overnight in *Shima Kanko Hotel*.

Seventh Day. By auto back to Toba and thence by rail to *Kyoto*, staying at lovely Miyako Hotel, built on a wooded hillside.

(There are various routes, by JNR and private lines. Have the
JTB arrange a convenient routing.)

Eighth Day. A long, but memorable day of sightseeing in two
historic cities, *Kyoto* and *Nara*, that were quite untouched by
the war. (N.B.: Here, more than anywhere else in the program,
an extra day, if you have it, could help a lot.)

Ninth Day. Train or auto to *Osaka*, lodging at the luxurious
Hotel New Osaka. Visit mighty Osaka Castle. Afternoon and
evening (transportation by electric train, in 45 minutes) in
nearby *Takarazuka*, Japan's unique theater town, returning to
Osaka for the night.

Tenth Day. Train or private car to *Kobe*, the "Rio of Japan,"
with afternoon visit by car or funicular to Mount Rokko. Return, if limited time bids, to Osaka, taking evening plane of
JAL to Tokyo. If your time is more lenient spend a night in
Kobe's modern *Oriental Hotel*, returning to the capital next
day by plane (from Osaka) or by the limited express train
called "The Swallow" (Tsubame).

Yes, I agree that the above is fast work, approaching, at times,
a scramble, and I hope for you that you can do the same tour
half as fast in twice as many days.

A Close-up of the National Railways

Japan has long been a *railway country* and only of recent years
have serious nation-wide efforts been made to plan and build a
complete network of good, paved highways worthy of so great
and populous a nation. A ten-year development plan is now being
pushed and a major strand in this network is to be a new four-
lane speedway between Tokyo and Kyoto, a distance of some 300
miles. Meanwhile, it is entirely feasible to drive almost everywhere in Japan, but the highways, with some notable exceptions,
are rather narrow and bumpy.

I have stressed (in Chapter 2) the amazingly dependable punctuality of Japanese trains, but perhaps you'd like a close-up of
what they look like and how they ride. Most trains consist of

what are called second and third-class coaches, only the aristo-cratic name trains having first-class service, consisting usually of a single air-conditioned observation car at the rear. Actually, second and third might well be called first and second, as has been the universal custom in Europe since 1956, and the observation car might well be called Pullman. The change in Europe has been of psychological benefit, and hence trade benefit, and could have the same effect, I think, in Japan. The coaches are all open, in contrast to the compartment-and-corridor coaches of Europe, and in most cases the seats are double ones, in pairs, so that two people riding forward face two people riding backward, but the limited express name trains, comprising a small but growing family, have only forward-facing seats, slightly narrower than ours because the gauge is narrower, and these recline, for the comfort of passengers. The trains also have Western-type toilets as well as those of Japanese type and this is by no means an "of course" item. Ordinary trains have Japanese toilets and the seat in these is not a seat at all but more like a king-size porcelain toidy for boys. Anyway, each toilet room, whatever its type, is decorated with a vase of flowers! The name trains have dining cars where good Western-type meals are served at moderate prices. There are sleeping cars on most of the long-distance night trains, some of the berths being in compartments and some merely curtained double-deckers.

The name trains are the ones you will want to use whenever possible, so a little further description of their names and services may be in order here. There are forty or more of them, all expresses, but only a few, often bearing the name of a bird, are the *limited* expresses, the nobility of the race, and all are on the main line (Table 1 in the English-language timetable) that extends south from Tokyo all the way to Fukuoka, the largest city on Kyushu Island, and on to Nagasaki. In each coach of these special trains there is an English-speaking hostess to dispense personal service, information and charm. To be specific, the first four put into service were the Swallow (Tsubame) and the Pigeon (Hato), both running between Tokyo and Osaka; the Sea Gull (Ka-mome), running between Kyoto and Fukuoka (whose station is called Hakata); and the Sea Breeze (Asakaze), a night train running between Tokyo and Hakata-Fukuoka. Late in 1957, two new fast services went into effect, one between Tokyo and Nagoya, another between Nagoya and Osaka; and as this is being written a 12-car Blitz train is being readied, at a cost of over half a million dollars, to cover the distance between Tokyo and Osaka, about 385 miles, in 5 hours, as against the present 7½ hours. It will leave Tokyo at 7 A.M., returning late in the afternoon from Osaka. This will be, or maybe *is*, by the time you read this, Japan's first venture in "lightning" rail service. All these limited trains are in great demand and the traveler must make reservations, presumably through the JTB. These are accepted one week in advance and should be made as early as possible to avoid the rush.

Railway fares are figured on the so-called tapering system, as in many European countries, meaning that the longer your journey the less you pay per mile. For instance, in ordinary second class the fare for 100 kilometers (60 miles) works out at about $1.40 whereas for a journey of 1000 kilometers, ten times as long, it is only $8.00 instead of $14.00. For the use of the limited express trains there is a substantial extra charge, figured on a zonal basis, the charge for the first zone (600 kilometers, or 375 miles) being 1440 yen ($4.00). Tickets have a validity of two days for journeys of 200 kilometers, with an extra day for each additional 200 kilometers, and within this limit of time the traveler may make as many stopovers as he likes. Children under six years of age travel free and those from six up to eleven are charged half fare.

The size and importance of the network of the Japanese National Railways (JNR), which came into being in 1872 with a modest line between Tokyo and Yokohama, may be judged from the fact that in this less-than-California-sized country there are 12,500 miles of National rails, supplemented by 700 miles of JNR-operated bus routes and by about 500 miles of privately operated rail lines. A 2½-mile railway tunnel links Honshu, the main island, with Kyushu and an ambitious 25-mile tunnel to connect Honshu with Hokkaido is at least being vigorously "talked." Over 1200 miles of the trunk routes are electrified and *all* of them are being electrified gradually. Many Diesel rail-cars are also in use, so the glorious railside scenery of Japan is being less and less obstructed by engine smoke. It *is* obstructed, however, by thousands of billboards in the neighborhood of the towns, this being presumably one of the less happy importations from American civilization.

The density of railway traffic is almost beyond belief, until seen. By statistics, nearly *four billion* passengers are carried an-nually by the JNR alone, the average being over ten million a day. About a quarter of a million passengers arrive at and leave from Tokyo Central Station daily. The main JNR lines are con-nected at various stations (Tokyo Central, Shimbashi, Shinjuku, Ueno), with the Yamate Loop, and from this belt line fourteen or fifteen private suburban electric lines fan out to all points of the compass—with which report and statistics it becomes high time for this chapter to start actually rolling.

Glorius Nikko, Curtain Raiser or Climax?

The plan at the beginning of this chapter contemplates starting the provincial travels with a visit to Nikko, but that shining goal of tourism can just as well be the climax of the tour and if you are in Japan in the spring it is worthy of special effort to arrange your itinerary, if possible, so as to be in Nikko on May 17 (oc-casionally May 18 instead), when the Grand Festival of the Toshogu Shrine takes place, for that is one of the most elaborate costume festivals in the country's calendar. A similar festival, of almost equal splendor, occurs in the autumn, on October 17.

There is no good road from Tokyo to Nikko and most visitors go there by train. There is a National Railway line, whose fast trains make the trip from Tokyo's Ueno Station in about two hours, and a private line, leaving from Asakusa. This private line owns *all* the transportation in Nikko itself, the street railway, the taxis, even the cable car to a lofty belvedere called Akechidaira.

Nikko National Park and its great religious structures are of such fabulous beauty and so universally revered by the Japanese and their visitors alike that it is practically impermissible for anyone writing or lecturing about the place to omit mention of Japan's most famous and historic cliché. It seems that in the early 1600's some 15,000 carpenters, carvers, painters and artisans were conscripted by the Shogun Iemitsu Tokugawa to build the Toshogu Shrine to his grandfather Ieyasu Tokugawa, founder of that shogunate, and when they looked upon their completed work they exclaimed with reverence: "Never say '*kekko*' (magnificent) until you have seen Nikko." This adjuration, in a class with "See Naples and die," must have been written and uttered some millions of times since it was (presumably) spoken in 1636, but like all clichés it has a foundation of solid sense. Nikko is indeed a magnificent welding of the best that man can achieve, set amid the best that nature can achieve. Nikko Park is 200,000 acres of forested mountain land, rich with pine, maple and birch forests, with glamour-avenues of Japanese cedars, with towering hills, a stupendous waterfall (Kegon Falls) and a resort lake 20 miles in circumference nearly a mile above sea level (Lake Chuzenji), on whose shores hundreds of cherry trees come into bloom in mid-May, a month after they have drooped in Tokyo.

The *Kanaya Hotel*, at the edge of Nikko town, is the place to stay if you can get a reservation, for it is a lovely hotel of Japanese architecture but Western comfort and it rises on a knoll directly above one of Nikko's most striking ornaments, the *Shinkyo*, or Sacred Bridge. This bridge, crossing the Daiya River, is largely decorative, for it is never used except on the greatest ceremonial occasions. It is a lovely vermilion-lacquered wooden cantilever bridge resting on two massive stone supports shaped to resemble torii.

The sacred buildings of Nikko are a conglomerate of three incredibly elaborate Shinto shrines and as many Buddhist temples, indicating, for one thing, how closely these two expressions of religion are interwoven in Japanese tradition and daily life. This book, I may as well state now, will go easy, meaning *very* easy, on shrines and temples, for I am sure that nothing is more confusing to the reader than to struggle with detailed printed descriptions of such structures. They are marvelous to see, to revel in visually, even to study closely, with the help of a guide, but their intricacies do not lend themselves to a general book of travel. In Nikko, I shall limit myself to certain basic facts about the central Toshogu Shrine and about one other wonder, the Mausoleum of Iemitsu Tokugawa, generally neglected by tourists because one must climb 130 very arduous steps to reach it.

The *Toshogu Shrine* was built at shogunate expense, with no limit set on the cost, and it is far and away the most lavish of all Japan's shrines. So important is it, in official view, that it is meticulously kept up, at great expense, a complete repainting job being undertaken every twenty years, and when you see the shrine you'll think it must take the whole twenty years just to go over it. To toss in a statistic or two, I may say that two and a half million sheets of gold leaf, each about four inches square, were used in its decoration, this total of gilding alone amounting to six acres. The timbers of the shrine are estimated to total 330 miles, which is more than the distance from Tokyo to Kyoto.

At the outer entrance to the shrine there is a granite torii, a symbol of Shinto, and immediately beside it the treasured Five-Storied Pagoda, a symbol of Buddhism, with the Tokugawa crest on black doors on each of the four sides of each story above the first. This pagoda is the one whose miniature replica has sometimes stood in the lobby of Tokyo's Imperial Hotel, as mentioned in Chapter 4. Proceeding, and climbing a flight of stone steps, one passes the Front Gateway, of Buddhist inspiration, guarded by two horribly grimacing wooden guardians, and so to the Sacred Stable (of a former "Sacred Horse"), copiously decorated with carved monkeys. On the second plaque is the world-celebrated "simian trinity," being the three monkeys that "Hear no evil, Speak no evil, See no evil," one covering his ears, another his mouth and the third his eyes. So, walking ever on and up, to the Sacred Cistern, built to contain holy water, with its granite pillars; through a bronze torii to the Sacred Library, with its 7000 volumes of Buddhist scriptures in a huge revolving bookcase; continuing between two Leaping Lions of stone to the Middle Court, which has a belfry to the right and a drum tower to the left, both over 40 feet high, and boasts three big candelabra of bronze. On the left, beyond the drum tower, is a purely Buddhist structure, the Honjido, with a curiosity called the Crying Dragon painted in India ink on its ceiling. The huge dragon "cries," with an odd echo, when you clap your hands beneath him. But perhaps it is doubtful that you will visit the Honjido to make the beast cry because directly in front of you as you walk between the Leaping Lions is the most overpowering spectacle of the whole Toshogu Shrine, namely the *Yomeimon Gate* to the Inner Court.

This Gate of Sunlight, for such is the translation of Yomeimon, is a two-story structure so gorgeous-gaudy that it would take a separate book to describe the details of its gold-and-white splendor, with 320 carvings of children and sages on its parapet alone. It is flanked by galleries extending 720 feet in all, whose floors, pillars and ceiling are painted with cinnabar to produce a flame-red effect that almost sears your eyeballs.

The Inner Court is full of special wonders, one of them being the Sacred Palanquin House containing the three Sacred Portable Shrines that feature the spring and autumn festivals of Nikko, each shrine so heavy that it takes fifty men to carry it in the festival procession. Whom do these shrines honor? They are Yoritomo Minamoto, Japan's first shogun; Hideyoshi Toyotomi, the great dictator-shogun who built the Castle of Osaka as his stronghold; and, of course, Ieyasu Tokugawa, founder of the

Tokugawa Shogunate, the deified leader in whose honor the whole Toshogu Shrine was built. All of these personages are discussed in the "Great Periods and Persons" section of Chapter 5.

Other buildings of the Inner Court include the Sacred Dance Stage; the Upper Shrine Office; the Chinese Gate; the Oratory; and the Main Hall containing the Inner Sanctum, where, in a gold-lacquered shrine surrounded by the finest art works of Nikko, repose "the three deities" (the deities are *mirrors*) of the personages mentioned above. This shrine is ordinarily closed to the public.

The actual tomb of *Ieyasu Tokugawa* is reached by a path culminating in 200 steps, at the top of which is a torii, a second oratory, a solid bronze gate, and finally the mausoleum itself, a bronze affair shaped like a small pagoda. Here—*requiescat in pace* —are enshrined the ashes of the central figure of Japan's most sumptuous complex of religious structures. (The tomb of Yoritomo Minamoto is near the Hachiman Shrine in his own Kamakura and that of Hideyoshi Toyotomi is in Kyoto.)

*   *   *

The *Daiyubyo*, or *Mausoleum of Iemitsu Tokugawa*, who built the Toshogu Shrine to his grandfather Ieyasu, is on a separate steep knoll and its shrine buildings are even richer in dazzling gold leaf than are those of the larger shrine. On the steep and toilsome steps, 130 of them, leading to this shrine I once met, and was presented to, "Mister Tokugawa," who was none other than Prince Iemasa Tokugawa, eighteenth in direct descent from Ieyasu. This courtly gentleman, who received his higher education in British Columbia, dropped his royal title after the war and is now known simply as Mister Tokugawa. On the occasion when I met him he had been performing his annual ceremonial duties before the tombs of his ancestors.

*   *   *

Lake Chuzenji, high in the mountains above Nikko, may be a relief, even a very welcome relief, from the overpowering grandeurs and complexities of the shrines, for it is a cool play-lake set within a rim of gloriously wooded heights. Nikko itself tends to belie its name, which means "Sunshine," for the unkind records show that its region is hazy and damp seven days out of ten and often steamy-damp in summer, but Chuzenji village and lake have a bracing and exhilarating atmosphere.

The best way for the visitor who is staying at Nikko to reach Chuzenji is to take a streetcar from just below Hotel Kanaya to the end of the line; then an aerial cable car to the exciting belvedere of Akechidaira, mentioned above; and then a bus on a toll road about a mile and a half long to the lake; returning by bus on the regular road from Chuzenji all the way down to Nikko. The belvedere provides a grand view of the lake, of the striking Kegon Waterfall, which is the lake's effluent, and of many miles of park and mountain scenery.

The *Kegon Waterfall* itself may be easily viewed in its thunderous, close-up splendor by taking an elevator from Odaira, a halt on the regular road, *down* to a ledge above the deep gorge, where a snack bar and shop are maintained for the hordes of visitors. The fall is 330 feet high and it plunges into a rock basin with such force that the rising mist mingles with the wind-blown spray of the fall itself to create an unforgettable spectacle as of liquid lace.

Chuzenji village is a little community straggling along the lake's edge and it is filled with a succession of Japanese inns, most of which seem always to be filled with Japanese schoolchildren on sightseeing excursions, but *Lakeside Hotel*, mentioned above, is a pleasant inn of Western type, with wooded grounds sloping down to the water. This could be an ideal spot for the leisured visitor to rest, with intervals of yachting and fishing, the open season for trout fishing being from May 20 to September 20. Many foreign diplomats enjoy summer homes on the lake shore.

Motored Steps to Fuji

(Yokohama; Kamakura; Enoshima)

One may reach the flanks of Fuji by a national rail line from Tokyo Central Station; or by a private rail line from Shinjuku Station; or, much more enjoyably, by unhurried motoring along the shores of the Pacific, with halts at Yokohama (if this has not been already visited from Tokyo), Kamakura, Enoshima and Odawara. This latter route is the one that will be followed in the ensuing pages.

Yokohama didn't exist a century ago except as a fishing hamlet of perhaps 300 inhabitants, but today it is Japan's fifth city, with well over a million inhabitants. It is a port city, handling about a quarter of Japan's foreign trade, and an industrial city of steel mills and heavy industry. Of course its cultural life and entertainment life suffer from the city's proximity to vast Tokyo but even so it deserves an afternoon or evening from the most crowded schedule, for there are interesting things to see and do, and if you stay overnight you'll find the *New Grand Hotel* one of Japan's best, even though it was first built in 1927. It has every modern comfort of Western living and its top-floor grillroom commands a superb view over a street lined with ginkgo trees to a newly landscaped seaside park and the ship-filled harbor.

The sights of Yokohama can be handily ticketed. They consist of a local *Chinatown;* the *East Bluff Area Hill,* where a considerable colony of foreign businessmen, including some Americans, have built their pleasant homes; the raucous Gay Quarter of *Hommoku,* where the sailors of the seven seas pursue their favorite lusts; the lovely 30-acre seaside *Sankeien Garden* (it closes sharp at 5 P.M. daily), developed by a wealthy family named Hara; and, above all, two throbbing streets of souvenir shops called Motomachi and Isezaki-cho. If you enjoy seeing life with its throttle wide open don't miss strolling one or both of these streets. They reach their peak of animation late in the afternoon. There are other things to see in this million-plus city, such as the *Nogeyama Hill,* with its zoo and children's park, and the *Foreign Cemetery*, dating from the opening of Japan by Commodore Perry, but it is inevitable that amid Japan's wealth of tourist "musts" Yokohama gets less attention than it warrants.

* * *

Kamakura, on the shore of Sagami Bay, 30 miles from Tokyo and 14 from Yokohama, is a rare combination of a historic town of the first importance and a beach resort popular with summer throngs.

As a town of history it has been mentioned in Chapter 5, for here Yoritomo Minamoto, one of the three great ones enshrined in Nikko, set up Japan's first shogunate government and here the Minamoto family and its offshoots maintained the national capital from 1185 to 1336. This was a period of notable development in the fine arts and the most admired achievement of the Kamakura Period still exists, right where it was set up in 1252. This is, of course, the fabulous *Daibutsu,* or *Great Buddha of Infinite Light,* a giant bronze statue of the Buddha sitting contemplatively with legs crossed and with hands in his lap, palms upward and thumbs touching, in symbolic indication of steady calm and faith. This statue is a wonder of Japan, even a wonder of the world of art, and not only for its great size but for the artistic perfection of its conception. It weighs, in case you go for statistics, 103 tons and is 42 feet, 6 inches high, the face being 7 feet, 8 inches high. The statue was originally enclosed in a wooden building, but this was destroyed by a typhoon and tidal wave in 1369 and a replacement building was wrecked by a similar storm and wave in 1495. The Buddha of Infinite Light merely sat there in untroubled serenity, as he still does, quite untouched by these violent paroxysms of nature. Since 1495 the figure has remained in the open air.

Among other existing relics of Kamakura's great era is the *Hachiman Shrine*, reached by an avenue lined with pine and cherry trees and brilliant azalea shrubs. This was built in another location in 1063 but was removed and set up in its present location in 1191 by Yoritomo Minamoto. It is on a knoll, attained by a flight of 70 steps. At the left of these steps you'll see an enormous ginkgo tree, behind which, in the year 1219, a chief priest of the Hachiman Shrine took ambush to assassinate the third Kamakura shogun. It seems that politico-religious murders are not a recent invention. The remains of Yoritomo Minamoto lie in a modest tomb on a hillside on the northeastern edge of Kamakura, for it is only his "deity" (symbolic mirror) that is enshrined in Nikko.

Kamakura has many other historic shrines and temples. They include the *Hase Kannon Temple,* containing a 30-foot, eleven-faced gilt image of Kannon, the Goddess of Mercy, supposed to have been carved in 721 from a single huge log of a camphor tree; the *Ennoji Temple,* containing a frightful image of Emma, the Buddhist Satan; and the *Engakuji Temple,* containing a tiny quartz tabernacle enshrining an alleged tooth of Gautama Buddha himself—this recalls the sacred relics in so many of Europe's cathedrals—but I promised to go easy on shrines and temples, so this is my cue to halt my report on Kamakura.

*   *   *

Enoshima means "Picture Island"—*shima,* or *jima,* is the standard word for island—and it is just that. It is a lovely miniature, a mile and a half in circumference, lying close to the shore four miles west of Kamakura and is reached by a 1300-foot concrete footbridge. From the crest of a hill rising from the center of the island you can see, some thirty miles to the south, Oshima (O Island), with a constantly smoking volcano whose crater is so tempting to would-be suicides that policemen are stationed near its rim to keep them away. Equally distant to the west you *may* see—Fujiyama! Fuji is very often veiled in clouds, so you'll need a bit of luck to have this distant view of its summit.

On a bluff on the mainland opposite Enoshima Island is the attractive, Western-type *Enoshima Kanko Hotel,* which is a good place for a meal, a tea, a siesta or a game of golf, for it has its own scenic 18-hole golf course with dramatic views from every tee and green.

The coastal highway continues some 25 miles along the shore, as does also the main line of the National Railways, to *Odawara,* which has a ruined castle of the Kamakura Period beautified in spring by masses of azaleas overhanging the moat, and from here the road and an electric mountain railway climb inland and up, only a few miles, to the wooded seclusion of the *Fuji-Hakone National Park.* For those who love grand scenery nothing can surpass this area, dominated as it is by Fuji itself, and fortunately it is enhanced and made easy for visitors to enjoy by one of the loveliest and most altogether enticing resort hotels in all Japan, the *Fujiya Hotel* in Miyanoshita.

Hotsprings in the Lee of Fuji

(Fuji-Hakone Park; Atami and the Spas of Izu)

Fujiyama, or Mount Fuji—*yama* is the common word for moun-tain—means more to the Japanese people than does any other mountain on earth to any other people. Not only is it Japan's highest mountain, soaring 12,380 feet, and its most beautiful and photogenic one, with a symmetrical volcanic cone, snow-mantled most of the year, but it is even a kami, or Shinto spirit, and is still reverenced and, in effect, worshipped by millions of those who dwell within sight of it. Pilgrims clad in white robes adorned with the seals of various shrines climb its sacred slopes in thou-sands every summer. Before the war, this veneration was genuine and intense with the *average* Japanese, except perhaps the more emancipated of the city dwellers, but Fuji's failure to deter American airmen from bombing sacred places jarred the faithful and dissipated some of the spiritual glow. Anyway, Fuji is one of the most superior mountains nature ever made and it is doubtless *the* most incessantly photographed one, by pious and impious alike.

Fuji-Hakone National Park, as its hyphen suggests, is actually two parks, considered by the authorities as one unit. Mount Fuji and its extensive flanks, dotted with five lakes amid virgin forests, is one part and near-by Hakone, boasting a dozen hotspring resorts, is the other, the combined area being 177,000 acres.

Fujiya Hotel, at Miyanoshita in the heart of the Hakone part, is my ideal as Japan's most perfect resort hotel. The beauty of its Japanese architecture, with its main building and various cottages climbing a wooded slope, in a setting of gardens and cascades seen, along with the mountains, from picture windows and terrace lounges, is matched by the comforts of its better Western-style rooms and by the excellence of its Western-style meals, served with untippable Japanese courtesy. But perhaps the hotel has, after all, one flaw. It has a never-ceasing abundance of natural hot mineral water (176° F.) flowing into its Dream Pool, its Roman Aquarium Bath, its Mermaid Bath, its Goldfish Bath, its Bath of Eternal Youth and Perpetual Spring, its main indoor and outdoor pools, but in all of the public pools the wearing of bathing suits is compulsory. This is in obvious deference to Western squeamishness, since much of its clientele is international, but the other spas of Hakone and the big one of Atami and the multitude of them on the Izu Peninsula all adhere to the Japanese custom of mixed nude bathing. Oh, well, when in Fujiya let's do as the Fujiyans do and enjoy its varied bathing facilities in a mood of Western modesty. If you take a bath with your spouse or family in one of the smaller private baths Japanese-style nudity is still the accepted custom *of the Japanese,* and that will doubtless challenge *your own* built-in inhibitions. (*Warning:* What seems like hot water to the average Westerner seems merely warm, or even tepid, to the average Japanese, and what seems to us scalding seems to them merely hot, so *watch out* and dip an experimental toe or finger into any pool before plunging in.)

The Fujiya Hotel is almost a "self-contained" resort, for it has its Arcade Gift Shops, its New Ginza Shop of Arts and Crafts, its window displays in a corridor called Rue de la Paix, its movies every evening, its Sengoku Annex for golfers, adjacent to an 18-hole course, and by way of fascinating reading it has its own encyclopedic but popularly written book of general information called *We Japanese*, authored, as I've said, by the hotel's president and manager, K. Yamaguchi. This book, I assure you, is not stuffy or propaganda-laden, but rather an intimate study of the traditions, daily life and special customs, including odd foibles of the Japanese people.

* * *

If you can stay two or three nights at Fujiya Hotel you might well devote half a day to an automobile tour, with guide, of the most interesting parts of Hakone Park, for which I will offer an itinerary that I followed, based on plans suggested by the JTB. A small map of the region is printed on a hotel folder, but a much better one may be had from the local JTB office.

1. *Gohra*, or Gora, the terminus of the electric railway line from Odawara, which passes through Miyanoshita, is one of Hakone's twelve spas and here there is a very big hotspring bathing pool (160° F.), where, if I'm correctly informed, a hundred or more persons at a time "mix-bathe" *in puris naturalibus*. Unfortunately, a too-full schedule prevented me from researching this pool. The *Gohra Hotel* has long been occupied by American "Security Forces," as the official *Japan Hotel Guide* puts it, but I believe it is, or soon will be, restored to public use. High on the mountain slopes above Gohra you will see dozens of furiously gushing steam vents and they cause park engineers a perpetual headache, for they loosen the soil and cause frequent landslides. To prevent these from endangering human lives and valuable property vast and expensive masonry work has been done to channel the slides.

2. *Sengokuhara Spa* is a golfers' paradise. There are two small courses and one full course of 18 holes, as mentioned above. The

greens fee for this course is 600 yen ($1.65) for guests of the
Fujiya and its Sengoku Annex, more for non-guests.

3. *Lake Ashi,* popularly called Lake Hakone, is about 13 miles
in circumference. The road route followed by this itinerary
touches the lake at Umijiri and here a fleet of busy little excursion steamers operates on a 20-minute frequency. There is
also scheduled motorboat service from here to Hakonemachi
(40 minutes), where the first-class *Hotel Hakone,* affiliated with
the Fujiya, rises on the lake edge. It is quite practical to make
this stretch of the tour by boat, instructing your driver to meet
you with the car at Hotel Hakone, but you would thus miss a
pleasant drive along the lake's edge.

4. *Hakone Shrine,* on the lake near the village of Motohakone,
is in one of the country's finest groves of Japanese cedars. These
magnificent monarchs of the forest rival Douglas firs and even
redwoods in their soaring majesty. A splendid lane of them leads
up from a lake steamer wharf directly to the shrine. Historically,
this shrine is famous as the refuge of Yoritomo Minamoto in
1180 during his war to establish his shogunate government at
Kamakura.

5. *Hakonemachi,* the leading summer resort on the lake, is
reached from Motohakone by a twisting road of wonderful
beauty through an almost unbroken double row of giant cedars,
for this was a portion of the Old Tokaido Highway between
Tokyo and Kyoto and Hakonemachi was a major post station of
that famous road. The reason for its fame, aside from the fact
that it was bordered by splendid pines and cedars the whole
way and still is in many parts, brings to our attention one of
Japan's most fascinating items of political history. When the
Tokugawa Shogunate was set up in Edo (Tokyo) in 1615 the
shogun thought up an ingenious plan to keep an eye on his un-
ruly feudal lords and to prevent them from ganging up against
him in rebellion. He required that the *families* of all the important warrior-lords live permanently in Edo, but that the lords
themselves live with their families only *every other year,* return-

ing to their own homes for the off years. So it came about that on each trek to and from the capital the central and southern lords, with their retinues, formed a long politico-pilgrim procession as they passed along the Old Tokaido Highway, northward one year, southward the next. This must have been one of the most colorful spectacles of that colorful feudal age.

6. *Hakone Hotel,* bordering the lake, is an ideal spot to stop for a meal or a snack, or even for a quick drink if time presses. Its big, cheerful lounge gives straight on the lake, and across the lake, if the day is clear, looms incomparable Fuji in the distance. It soars up into the blue of the sky while its reflection plunges down into the blue of the lake.

7. *Mount Koma* (Pony Mountain, 4400 feet in altitude) is passed on a returning road that winds through the mountains to Miyanoshita. In the near future, this peak will be of major holiday interest, both summer and winter, for an aerial cableway is now being constructed from the village of Ashinoyu, on the highway, to the summit, and on the summit a hotel is being built, with a skating rink as one of its features.

*   *   *

The road from Miyanoshita to Atami via Hakonemachi climbs up and over the *Jikkoku Pass,* from whose highest point a cable car ascends to a rounded hilltop. From that crest Fuji is seen, more closely than from Hakone Hotel, and also no less than *ten provinces,* if the day is clear, suiting the sight to the name, for Jikkoku means Ten Provinces. Descending from the pass, the road makes a great many hairpin turns to reach the seashore, finally, at one of Japan's most popular resorts for bathers, both in the numerous hotspring pools and in the sea.

Atami and the spas of Izu need but brief mention here, alluring though they are. Atami is to Japanese city dwellers, especially those of Tokyo, what Niagara Falls is to Americans of our eastern cities, a honeymoon goal, par excellence, and it is a goal too for all Japanese who feel the urge to shake off work and worry and just relax. The resort is typical of Japan's hotspring spas, of which there are nearly 800 large and small, throughout the country. The baths at these spas, speaking generally, reach levels of variety, number and quality never equaled anywhere since the days of Imperial Rome. Some, even indoors, are as large as Olympic swimming pools and many are half as large. Some are tiled in white, some decorated with fancy mosaic art works and stained-glass windows illumined with soft lights behind them. Some have cascade-curtains showering down the walls. Some are in sheltered nooks in the open air, with hot water gushing eternally into them. In content they are as varied as in form. Some are iron baths, some sulphur, some manganese, and a few are mildly radioactive, to be used under a physician's directions.

The Japanese guest who arrives at one of these spas throws off his cares with his clothes. He may loll in a warm pool several times a day, sharing this pleasure with his bride, his wife of many years, his children, his friends, his fellow-guests of both sexes at any one of scores of spa-inns having their own pools.

The best hotel in Atami, with the best pool, is the *Atami Fujiya*. It has a dining room on an upper floor and above that a belvedere café whose broad windows look down on the beach and the crowded town. It has a small palm-patio, a large "Danceland" for the guests and a tatami-matted dining hall for Japanese-style dinners. The *Atami Hotel* is another good place, with hotspring pool, and immediately adjacent to the Atami Fujiya is the *Kan-ichi Hotel*, built in the oddest style I've ever seen. The whole top of the hotel, perfectly round, *revolves* continuously, like a revolving stage. It turns so very slowly that you can hardly see it move, yet it completes a full revolution about once every 15 minutes. If you book here your bedroom windows will face every point of the compass about four times an hour, or 96 times in every 24-hour period.

There is little to see in Atami itself except, perhaps, one interesting curiosity, namely a spring called *Oyu*, meaning "The Great Hot Water." Its temperature is a constant 226.4 degrees Fahrenheit and it is the hottest spring in all Japan. Until 1923 it was a geyser, spouting at exactly regular intervals like one that now spouts in Beppu (see Chapter 11), but the earthquake of that year somehow managed to put it out of business as a geyser. Since then it has been only a bubbling spring.

The *Izu Peninsula*, which juts into the Pacific south of Atami for a distance of nearly 40 miles, could almost be called one great spa for it has almost 30 well-established hotspring resorts and in one of them, a coastal town named *Ito*, there are more than 800 inns, public baths and private homes that have unceasing natural hot water flowing into them. The whole shore line from Atami to Ito and beyond is often referred to by enthusiastic posters and folders as the Riviera of Japan. Between Tokyo and Ito there is a daily steamer service (12-hour run), with a halt at the aforementioned volcanic island of Oshima, and on that island good accommodations of Western type are available at the *Oshima Kanko Hotel*, but in Ito the traveler must lodge in one of the many Japanese inns, two good ones being the *Kaniyajuraku*—please pardon its syllables—and the *Masuya*. At *Kawana*, on the other hand, located only six miles southeast of Ito, you will find one of Japan's very finest resort inns, the de luxe *Kawana Hotel*—a name that should be italicized in your memory. It is a modern concrete structure with over 60 Western-style rooms, most of them with private bath, plus four of Japanese type, but the comforts and luxuries of the hotel, welcome as they are, may be overshadowed, in the golfer's view, by the fact that it is located between *the two finest golf courses in the Orient*, each course having 18 holes. The Kawana is considered of such sure tourist appeal that an overnight halt is usually provided here for passengers taking luxurious round-the-world cruises on such famous ships as the *Caronia*.

Nagoya, the Cradle of Cloisonné

Nagoya, with well over a million inhabitants, is now the third city in Japan in population (after Tokyo and Osaka), but the first in the production of fine pottery, porcelain and, most glamorous of all, cloisonné ware. It is an industrial city of no great tourist interest except for its special factories, which may be of strong interest to those who have no "mental allergy" to factory visits.

Until May 14, 1945, when American bombs reduced it to blackened ruin, *Nagoya Castle* was another very potent attraction, a magnificent affair whose construction was started in the time of Hideyoshi Toyotomi and brought to completion in 1612 by Ieyasu Tokugawa as a stronghold for his son. Its dungeon, 144 feet high, was topped by a pair of famous nine-foot dolphins made of pure gold. One of these was loaned to the city of Vienna for an exposition in 1873, but the steamer *Nile*, which brought it back to Japan, was wrecked off Izu Peninsula and the dolphin sank to the ocean floor, where he must have been a puzzle to live dolphins if they glimpsed his gleaming skin. The water was not too deep at that point and this treasure of art was finally salvaged and restored to the top of the dungeon beside its mate. The castle has "gone with the war," and the gold dolphins have gone with the castle. Today, it is a park surrounded by a moat walled with the massive masonry that one comes to expect in all of Japan's strongholds, but plans are now actively advancing for the complete rebuilding of the castle, at an estimated cost of six million yen, by the beginning of 1960.

So the factories are about all that is left to draw tourists to Nagoya. Fortunately they are enough, for the interest, at least in cloisonné, is intense and widespread. I once heard a gushy lady exclaim, upon seeing an attractive vase of this ware in an American home, "Do you know, if I had *my* way I'd have *nothing* but cloisonné in my house." I presumed aloud that this would include the tableware, the toaster and the washing machine, whereupon she hedged, ever so little. Anyway, it *is* utterly fascinating and the making of it may be watched in the factory of *Ando*, leader of them all, or of *Yamamoto* or of *Akagi*.

The word cloisonné is a French participle meaning "partitioned," and that's exactly what the product is. To describe how it is partitioned I will quote the leaflet that Ando puts out, thereby saving myself from technical errors:

1. The silver or copper base is shaped.
2. Ribbon shaped wires of silver or gold brass only a fraction of an inch in width are glued edgewise very carefully over the outline of the design drawn on the base.
3. The multitudes of cells so formed are filled with the various colored enamels.
4. Vitrification is next. The coloring and baking must be repeated at least three times, because of the shrinkage, to obtain the needed thickness of the enamel color.
5. After an even thickness and the desired shades of color have been acquired the surface is ground, smoothed and finally polished with several grades of whetstones. The recipe for making enamel colors is the secret of the artist, inherited from his father and his ancestors.

The last sentence calls to mind the secrets of the medieval glaziers who created the inimitable colors of the stained-glass cathedral windows of France. Actually, these two somewhat parallel arts developed at about the same period, in the 13th century. In France and other European lands the secrets were lost and have never been fully recovered. In Nagoya they have been passed from father to son for 700 years and the work of today's best colorists is as fine as any that has ever been done. In the apt words of the compiler of *Japan, Town and Country* Nagoya's workers in cloisonné "produce vases, bowls and boxes in studded opaque effects, in melting fused lines or glowing with hidden fires beneath the transparent surface." The hidden fires do indeed glow, especially in the rich reds, and time is never able to extinguish them.

Gifu, Where Cormorants Fish for Fun

Gifu lies about 20 miles due north of Nagoya on the River Nagara, which is such a large and swift and scenic stream that it has to submit to the tourist tag "the Japanese Rhine." It is a pleasant tourist goal in itself, with special holiday attractions and special industries, but it becomes an irresistible goal during the season when trained cormorants fish for the benefit of men, this period being the same every year, from May 11 to October 15. I'll get to the cormorants presently, but first a word about Gifu's all-year attractions.

On the left bank is *Gifu Park*, with a riverside promenade nearly a quarter of a mile long, and from this park a cable car ascends to the hilltop known as *Kinkazan* (Golden Flower), with a café and an ancient castle. At the base of the hill, near the lower station of the cable car, is a statue of Count Itagaki, the Meiji-era statesman pictured on Japan's 100-yen note, and this has real interest for it rises on the exact spot where the count was wounded by an assassin and uttered his famous cry "Itagaki may die but liberty will live!" Not far from this monument, near the park's entrance, is a religious curiosity, a 45-foot "Basket Buddha" built of basket-work and finished in shiny lacquer.

The numerous industries of Gifu include three products that catch the eye, namely fans, paper umbrellas (long standard in Japan but gradually yielding to dull cloth ones of Western type) and colored paper lanterns, usually in a luminous shade of "Gifu blue."

The Gifu lanterns are at their best in their home town, brightening boats that are out on the river to let their guests watch the fishing cormorants. The procedure is to assemble a group, or join in a group, and set out in one of the boats about 8 o'clock in the evening with plenty of beer and sake aboard and, if possible, with two or three geisha girls to add their tinkling samisen music and tinkling cascade-laughter. These boat parties are gay affairs and they get gayer as the sake flows. Roman candles are set off by the participants and "fire fountains" on tiny rafts are launched to float downstream. Excitement grows as the time draws near for the evening's big and unique spectacle.

For sheer oddity nothing I have ever seen in any country

surpasses this spectacle of trained cormorants fishing for ayu, a miniature but trout-like fish greatly esteemed by the Japanese. This sport, or industry, has been going on for at least 1200 years right here on the River Nagara. Formerly, it was done chiefly for the benefit of emperors and daimyos, but today it is a profitable fishing industry *and* a tourist spectacle, occurring every night from May 11 to October 15, with the exception of full-moon nights when the handlers knock off work to indulge in their own celebrations. There are only six families, or clans, entitled by tradition and law to carry on this industry and they cherish this right as a proud, inherited distinction passed from father to son for centuries.

About 9 or 9:30, when full darkness has settled over the river, six cormorant boats, each manned by members of one of the six privileged families, are seen floating down the river toward and past the clustering tourist boats. Each of the fishing boats has a crew of three or four. The master, wearing a traditional grass skirt and a ceremonial helmet called a *kazaore-Eboshi*, stands at the bow of the boat. With skilled hands he controls twelve cormorants, each on a tether about twelve feet long, as the birds bobble about in the water looking for ayu, while his mate, standing amidships, controls another six birds if the fishing is good enough to warrant it. A third man keeps a decoy fire blazing in an iron cradle that protrudes several feet from the forward gunwale and a fourth man steers the boat. Whole schools of ayu, attracted by the bright blaze, swim near the surface while the fishermen urge their tethered birds to catch them. They need little urging for they are bursting with eagerness. Spotting a tempting ayu, the cormorant makes a queer little jump, lifts his rump, tips forward and plunges for his prize, nearly always coming up with the fish.

Unfortunately for the bird he cannot swallow his catch, for his neck is tied with a cord so that only the tiniest baby fish can slip down his throat, but he is a good sport and this frustrating experience seems only to heighten his pride in performance.

He gorges his gullet, but not his hungry stomach, with fifteen to thirty ayu until it is so distended, to several times its normal thickness, that he is neck-heavy and swims clumsily in foolish circles. Then the master (or mate) hauls him aboard, squeezes the catch from his neck into the boat and sends him forth again for a new catch. An experienced bird can catch sixty to a hundred ayu, weighing a total of ten to fifteen pounds, in an hour or two, so an evening's catch can well amount to 150 or 200 pounds per boat. This, one can see, is Business with a big B. The fishing that is done for the benefit of the visiting watchers is only a prelude to the serious work that is done later at points farther up river.

One might think that the birds would quickly tire of this frustration fishing, but the fact is that they love it, as their whole performance shows. To attain this professional status calls for intensive training. The birds are caught in winter in northern Honshu, bought by the Nagara fishermen and strenuously trained for three years. Then they have a working life of about twenty years, after which they "retire." While working they give every evidence of a sportsman's pride. In each boat, when the birds are preparing for their assault on the ayu, a veteran cormorant is stationed in the place of honor at the bow of the boat, for he is the respected "head bird," captain of the flock. Each bird under his chieftainship has his own number and his proper place in line and there he must stay. If Bird 5, for instance, should presume to take a more favored position, ahead of Bird 4, a terrible hullabaloo would promptly ensue and he would be quickly driven back. The head bird seems to say, almost in words, "See here, Five, there's to be no cheating on *my* boat."

To Pearl Island and the Mikimoto Pearl Farm

Upon arriving at the seacoast town of *Toba* and before succumbing to the lure of pearls the visitor should allocate a couple of hours to a side trip by private car or train-and-car to *Ujiya-*

mada for a visit to the *Grand Shrine of Ise*. Why select this from the multitude? Because it is the central shrine of the whole Shinto religion; because it is the oldest shrine in Japan; because it is the repository, and has been so since the year 5 B.C., of the Sacred Bronze Mirror (see Chapter 5) handed down to earth by the Sun Goddess Ameratsu, one of the Three Sacred Treasures—Mirror, comma-shaped Jewel and Sword—that constitute the Imperial Regalia; and because it is the Imperial Shrine, to which the Emperor and every newly elected Prime Minister comes to worship.

Ise is a substantial city composed of the two former towns of Uji and Yamada (the railway station, opposite which is a JTB office, is still called Yamada) and here is the Grand Shrine, consisting actually of two units, the Outer Shrine (*Geku*) and the Inner Shrine (*Naiku*). The latter is the historic heart of the whole sacred area and to it leads a splendid road lined by 5000 cherry trees donated long ago by Kokichi Mikimoto. From the entrance to the grounds of the Inner Shrine one must walk a good quarter of a mile on a pebbled path, but it leads through one of the country's finest groves of giant cedars. You should not expect magnificent buildings, as in Nikko, for the Naiku Shrine is simplicity's own self, and for the best of reasons. By an old and ancient tradition, whose purport is lost in the shadows, it is razed every 20 years and a new, identical shrine constructed in a plot beside it. The last such razing and reconstruction occurred in 1953 and it was the 59th time!

For a good meal of Japanese type, with an interlude of sightseer's relaxation, the visitor who has trudged about the parks of the Naiku and Geku would do well to make a halt, perhaps for lunch, at the lovely, pine-shaded seaside resort of *Futamigaura*, where there are several high-grade Japanese inns. One of the best of them is the *Futamikan*.

Along the shore directly in front of this inn is a beautiful seaside promenade continuing around a jutting point, opposite which are two celebrated rocks in the sea called the *Wedded Rocks*.

The groom is naturally larger than the bride and he wears on his head not a hat but a torii. The two are united by a heavy rope, maybe a Japanese version of the ball-and-chain, which is replaced every year, on January 5th, when thousands come here to witness an annual quasi-religious ceremony.

*   *   *

Kokichi Mikimoto was born in 1858 in Toba. His father was a manufacturer of noodles and young Kokichi, the eldest son, inherited the business but he was destined to escape this drudgery and induce others, millions of them, to work for him in building up one of the most imaginative and fabulous industries the world has seen. The millions who worked for him, and still work for his grandson, were and are, of course, pearl oysters.

Pearl Island, off Toba, is a memorial to Kokichi Mikimoto rather than a place where the industry of producing cultured pearls is carried on, but it gives the visitor an authentic close-up of the methods and processes of production. Mikimoto has been compared to Thomas Edison and in a sense the comparison is apt, for he did what others before him had tried to do and had finally pronounced impossible. A German scientist named Hesling, for one, had devoted years to experimenting with oysters in the attempt to induce them to build pearls around an irritant inserted within the shell but was never able to produce a single pearl. Either the irritant was inserted too deep and caused the oyster's death or it was not inserted deep enough, or not in the right place, and the oyster soon ejected it. If the oyster lived and the irritant remained he just ignored it and wouldn't co-operate. The thing was clearly impossible and Dr. Hesling gave up in discouragement.

But Mikimoto didn't give up. He must have said, like the U.S. Armed Services, "The impossible takes a little longer." He started his experiments in 1888 at Shimenoura, in Ago Bay, and two years later he started another experimental farm at this very Pearl Island, off Toba. In January, 1893, a "red plague" in the sea water all but wiped out his whole establishment, destroying most of his oysters. Even his best friends began to tap their heads and say "Poor Kokichi! He's daft on this thing and it will never work." But his wife, Ume, who was his only partner, stayed with him and supported him wholeheartedly.

He tried again. A few oysters had survived the red plague. On July 11, 1893, he and his wife were examining one of their oysters on the beach of Pearl Island when suddenly they saw—a pearl! It was a poor, semi-spherical thing but it *was* a pearl. With tears of joy and jubilation Kokichi exclaimed "We have it!" This was the beginning. Today, the Mikimoto Company, of which Kokichi's grandson is president, produces, as I've said, about one ton of perfect, spherical pearls annually, and since the Mikimoto patent, or monopoly, ran out, some years ago, hundreds of other firms have been producing them in Japan, where it is a $10,000,000 industry, and a few are making headway in other countries, especially France, whose leading old-line jewelers were, and still are, hostile to the idea.

Of course a terrible hue and cry went up from all the established jewelers of Europe, who had invested great sums in natural pearls. They poured ridicule and contempt on Mikimoto's "fake pearls" and filed lawsuits against him. But respected scientists such as D. Lister Jameson of Oxford University and Professor Boutane of Bordeaux rallied to his defense, proclaiming that cultured pearls were no different from natural ones, and David Starr Jordan, former president of Stanford University and widely known as an expert zoologist, stated that "both have the same luster and sheen, a quality which cannot be imitated by any form of paste or artificial pearls." The conventional jewelers were forced to subside, though they are still prone to say to their customers, "Of course you would not give to a loved one any jewel that is not genuine." Cultured pearls *are* genuine, but they have the unforgivable fault of being far less expensive.

On Pearl Island the processes of production are graphically set forth in a small Pearl Museum. Oysters live eight or ten years, but they aren't able to produce good nacre till the third or fourth year and it takes at least four or five years of labor to perfect a good-sized spherical pearl, so the mollusks have to work fast. A tiny round pellet of—guess what—Mississippi River mussel, or "pig toe," is inserted by the "surgeon" in the oyster's mantle so that it does not touch the valve but is completely surrounded by mantle flesh. To ensure this a small piece of flesh is taken from a "sacrifice oyster" and grafted onto the mantle of the host oyster, which—or should it be who?—is then placed in the water with many others in one of the wire-mesh cages suspended from rafts. This is the merest start, for the oyster must be nursed for years as it is exposed to many hazards. Too-cold water is a threat, so in winter all the thousands of cages have to be moved to warmer coastal waters. Too much rain, swelling the rivers, can sweeten the sea water to such extent that the oysters die. Plankton masses sometimes come in such volume as to absorb the oxygen and suffocate them. Barnacles and other growths on the shell harm them, so the oysters must all be hauled up and cleaned three or four times a year. And of course there are natural enemies in the sea, such as the octopus, but all these hazards are met and overcome by the expert oyster nurses.

The market price in Japan of a good single-strand necklace of cultured pearls is, as I have said, from about 35,000 yen to 350,000, which is roughly from $100 to $1000, but in the leading stores, of course including those of Mikimoto, the tourist may present his Specified Stores Tax Exemption Card (see Chapter 1) and thus have the 16 per cent Japanese Commodity Tax *deducted* from the quoted price. The value of a pearl, whether natural or cultured, is based on its color and its luster. A delicate pink is specially favored by buyers, but this is only one of many hues. Due to the oyster's constitution, to the condition of the sea water, to light refraction and other factors, oysters produce pinkish-gold, light gold, silver, green, blue, red and even, very rarely, black pearls. In producing this last color they achieve what the tulips of Holland have never been able to achieve.

Three other features of Pearl Island always attract tourist attention. One is a bronze statue of Kokichi Mikimoto wearing a kimono and carrying a staff, his head topped by a queer-looking derby. The second is a stone pile, with a round stone on top, marking the exact spot where Kokichi and his wife opened an oyster and saw their first cultured pearl. The third is the succession of demonstrations by the *ama*, or diving girls, whose task is to find and bring up young oysters. At frequent intervals two or more of them, always clad in white, which scares away sharks, enter the water, taking their oyster buckets with them, and then dive under, swimming about underwater for as long as two full minutes at a time. Always it is girls, or even women up to the age of fifty or more, who perform this task, the officially given reason being that the female body can stand cold water better than the male.

* * *

The *Mikimoto Pearl Farm,* in Ago Bay and several other adjacent bays, cannot be visited by the public without special, hard-to-get permission. By persistence I did secure such permission and was fascinated by what I saw. In one of the work sheds hundreds of "surgeon girls," working in absolute, concentrated silence, were prying open one oyster after another by hand, then inserting a wedge to keep the shell open until they could place the nucleus of mussel shell and a wrapping of grafted mantle flesh in the host oyster. In another shed the operators were matching pearls for necklaces, a job requiring the keenest vision. In another they were drilling holes in the pearls, for stringing. I learned here a further pearl fact that surprised me. The host oysters are given several irritants, not just one, and their average production, according to statistics, is two and a half pearls per oyster!

* * *

The Japanese have developed at least one important process in culturing oysters *for food*. They plant the seedlings in different shells, wire the shells to ropes, attaching fifty to a hundred to each rope, and lower them in the water. Within ten months, instead of some three years, the baby oyster has grown up and adapted himself to his host shell, thus greatly speeding up production. So effective is this system that it has been adopted in certain American oyster parks, notably those in Puget Sound.

Kyoto and Nara, Great Capitals of the Past

Kyoto and *Nara,* only 25 miles apart, go together like apple pie and cheese. Both were early capitals of Japan, Nara from 710 to 793, Kyoto from 794 to 1185. Both are replete with great temples and shrines. Throughout the war, both were completely spared by the bombers, in accordance with orders from the U.S. High Command. Both are darlings of tourism, with as strong a pull as Nikko.

Kyoto, being the unchallenged center of Japanese Buddhism, has 899 temples, and there are also some hundreds of Shinto shrines. In Nara there are "more of the same," which facts bring me sharply up against my promise not to overdo these subjects. Before we meet that problem let's look at the practicalities and pleasures, first of big Kyoto, which pushes Nagoya as claimant to be Japan's third city, and then of Nara. A first-rate folder entitled "How to See Kyoto and Nara," published by the JTB, tells all in succinct style, with map. By far the most glamorous hotel of Kyoto is the *Miyako*, built on a steep wooded hillside in a quiet part of the city. It is constructed *against* the hillside in such a way that each floor of its seven becomes in part a ground floor. A spacious bar-lounge is on the third-ground floor, the lobby and handsome dining room are on the fourth-ground floor, and a fine open-air swimming pool is located in a glen just off the seventh-ground floor, the bedrooms being at "assorted levels." From all the public rooms and bedrooms facing the city there is a striking view.

Other high-grade hotels are the *Kyoto Hotel,* a big and very well-run place in the heart of the city, and the *Kyoto Station Hotel*, located where its name says. There are many good restaurants of all types in the city, general, Western, sukiyaki, tempura, kabayaki (broiled eels) and Chinese. The folder I have referred to above lists about forty of them, three popular ones of Western type being the *Fujiya*, the *Alaska* and, for sea food, the *Prunier*. An excellent sukiyaki restaurant is the *Mishima-Tei*, centrally located near the Fujiya.

Kyoto has a calendar of festivals hardly equaled by that of any other Japanese city, so it will be bad luck indeed if nothing special is going on at the time of your visit. Also, this city, as I have said earlier, is the home and habitat of the art-persons, meaning geisha girls. They are at their superlative best here and if possible you should arrange, perhaps with the aid of the city's JTB office, a group dinner at one of the geisha restaurants in the famous Gion district. I have described one such Kyoto dinner in Chapter 7.

Shops specializing in woodblock prints, lacquer ware, silks and brocades, chinaware and dolls are as tempting as those of Tokyo and the big department stores are almost as interesting. And for stage entertainment, which may have to consume some of your hours of daylight, nothing in Japan can surpass Kyoto's all-geisha festival spectaculars in the big theaters. One of the best of them is the *Miyako Odori* (known to tourists as the Cherry Dance), which occurs every day during the month of April. The entire cast, including fascinating groups of line dancers, all in full and elaborate dress, is composed of geisha girls and the music is furnished by an orchestra of samisens at one side of the stage and another of drums, bells and flutes at the other. Some of the numbers in a Miyako Odori show that I saw here were entitled: A Plum Flower in the Quiver; Terrific War Cry; Mushroom; Sofaren, A Famous Song for Koto; The Snows of Awazu; and Robes of Flowers. A concomitant of the Cherry Dance for ticket holders is the privilege of participating in a brief tea ceremony, *not* the long-drawn-out kind of formal custom.

A most interesting late evening hour may be spent strolling the bright quarter, being one chief street and its offshoots, named *Shinkyogoku*. This is typical of such bright-light streets in many Japanese cities and not unlike the main stem of Tokyo's Asakusa Park. Its multitudes of shops stay open till all hours and interlarded with them are dozens of movie theaters, bars, little coffee shops and pachinko gambling dens, the characteristic staccato rattle of their machines filling the air for blocks. In front of one of the movie houses I noticed a flamboyantly sexy poster advertising the bosom and swivel-hips of Tempest Storm, American burlesque queen. Such films lure huge and eager throngs in Japan.

*   *   *

How shall I cope with the problem of presenting Kyoto's historic sights, its palaces, temples and shrines? I think the only way to do so short of ignoring the subject altogether, which would be ridiculous in view of their importance, is to list the very most outstanding of them in each category, with the briefest possible mention of what each one signifies or has to offer the visitor. Let's take them in the order named above, remembering, however, that sightseers, following local JTB advice, should combine these sights *geographically*, to save wear and tear, rather than by category or relative significance.

PALACES

1. The *Old Imperial Palace* (*Gosho*), whose earliest building, in a different quarter of the city, was erected for the Emperor Kammu in 794, is now a sort of compound, with many different buildings, all extremely simple in style. This rambling affair is open to the public only twice a year for brief periods, but foreign visitors may obtain special entry permits (see the JTB office) through the Kyoto Office of the Imperial Household Agency. The *Serene and Cool Chamber* (*Seiryoden*), so called because a cool stream has been diverted to run under its steps, is among the diverting sights of this compound and another is the

Ceremonial Hall (*Shishinden*), built by the father of the great Emperor Meiji.

2. The *Katsura Imperial Villa*, also requiring a special permit, easy to obtain through the JTB, lies on the southwestern edge of the city. It was built in the late 1500's by order of Hideyoshi Toyotomi and, like the Imperial Palace, consists of many buildings, but its special interest for visitors is its wonderful garden, perhaps the most flawlessly artistic garden in all Japan. Its combination of pines and palms and shrubs—gorgeous azaleas predominating in spring—around a placid body of water, with pavilions and a teahouse, gives every visitor a sense of peace. Wherever you stand and in whatever direction you look you seem always to be in just the right spot, looking at just the right scene.

3. The *Nijo Detached Palace*, called also *Nijo Castle*, was built by Ieyasu Tokugawa as a personal residence for use during his visits from Tokyo to Kyoto and its lavish decorations put the visitor in quite a different mood from that felt in the plain-Jane Imperial Palace. The first two of the Nijo Palace's several connecting buildings are enriched by large and superb paintings on sliding screens done by Tanyu Kano, the most famous artist of the early Tokugawa Shogunate. On entering this palace all visitors must leave their shoes at the threshold and pad about on the matted floors in slippers. The corridors have what are whimsically called "nightingale floors," built purposely to "sing" or squeak loudly. The purpose of this was to prevent would-be assassins from sneaking unheard into the quarters of the shogun. An interesting turn of history's wheel is seen in the fact that in this palace of the Tokugawa shogun Emperor Meiji established his temporary seat of government and here issued the Imperial edict that abolished the whole shogunate system. The moated grounds of the castle are impressive, brightened as they are by rocks, trees, a water garden with a cascade, and a section devoted to varicolored tulips. Just within the main gate is a massive roofed torii.

TEMPLES

1. *Nishi Honganji Temple* is the so-called senior headquarters of what is perhaps Buddhism's purest and noblest sect, rejecting all clairvoyant and superstitious follies, namely the *Jodo-Shinshu Sect.* (See Chapter 2.) This splendid temple is considered a nearly perfect example of Buddhist architecture.

2. *Higashi Honganji Temple,* the junior headquarters of the same sect, is approached through a colossal two-roofed gate. The massive character of the temple itself, with its huge, dim interior and its tall, smooth pillars, carries out the initial suggestion of strength through calmness. This temple has been four times destroyed by fire and was last rebuilt, in the same historic form, in 1890.

3. *Kankakuji Temple,* or Golden Pavilion, was built by a court noble about six centuries ago as a villa, but was turned into a Buddhist temple in the 15th century. It lasted for some 500 years as a marvelous relic of the past, but in 1950 it was deliberately burned down, for the sake of a thrill, by an arsonist, who must rate as one of the world's meanest criminals. In 1955, it was rebuilt and brilliantly re-gilded exactly as before and today it gleams in golden splendor on the edge of a tree-fringed, azalea-fringed pond.

4. *Ginkakuji Temple,* or Silver Pavilion—you remember that the Gin of Ginza means silver—was built in 1479 by a shogun named Yoshimasa and converted into a temple upon his death. Its fanciful name is a complete misnomer, for it was never actually covered with silver as had been originally planned. One feature of special interest about this pavilion-temple, aside from its very lovely garden, is a tiny tearoom of about 80 square feet, which is the model for all the ceremonial tearooms in Japan.

In Kyoto, by the way, is one of Japan's most important schools of the tea ceremony, by name Urasenke. I have visited the school and have listened and watched, but the extreme, slow-motion formalism of the ceremony, with every conceivable implement and move precisely and unalterably prescribed by tradition, is one thing in Japanese life that I simply cannot go for. The slow-ness of the noh stage I really find fascinating, if taken in moderate doses, but the glacier-paced ceremony of preparing and drinking a cup of tea in two hours or so, is not for me. Perhaps if I were to cultivate Buddhist repose I could learn to like it.

5. *Chionin Temple*, grand headquarters of the Jodo Sect is of importance in various ways but its chief interest for tourists lies in its immense temple bell, the largest in Japan, weighing 74 tons. The ultimate act of faith by members of the Jodo Sect is to re-cite, day and night, as many times as possible, a prayer formula called *Namu-Amida-Butsu.* In another Kyoto stronghold of this sect, the Chionji Temple, the abbot ruling it in 1331, when a plague was raging, held a service in which this prayer was re-cited *one million times in succession,* which is quite the opposite theory of prayer from that of Him who said: "they think that they shall be heard for their much speaking." It suggests, rather, a full-throated filibuster of the U.S. Senate, which might be hand-somely extended if the prayer formula were said one million times. I offer this suggestion in a spirit of helpfulness.

6. *Sanjusangendo Temple*, erected in its present form in 1250, is called the longest wooden building in Japan, being 396 feet in length. In Western eyes it is one of the weirdest in Japan, for it houses a statue of the "Thousand-Handed Kannon," goddess of mercy, carved by a famous sculptor named Tankei when he was 82 years old, and it houses also *one thousand and one* smaller gilded figures of Kannon, each of exactly the same height, 5 feet, 7 inches. The figure 1001 is supposed to represent, in the words of a temple leaflet, "one step higher over infinitude," indicating, I suppose, the infinite mercy of the goddess. A pleasing thing about this forest of statues is that they actually have high artistic merit and are much admired by experts in Japanese sculpture.

7. *Kiyumizu Temple*, dating in its earliest form from 805, rises from a cliff ledge, extended by a wooden platform, half way up Mount Otowa. You have to climb 144 steps to reach it, but you'll have your reward, for the view of the verdant valley

immediately below the belvedere-platform and of the city and its surroundings will provide one of the thrills of your Japan tour.

Perhaps you feel a touch of vertigo from so rich a diet of temples, but I would call your attention to the fact that I have reported on only seven out of the 899, which is seven-ninths of 1 per cent of the city's total.

SHRINES

1. The *Heian Shrine* is a recent one built in 1895 to commemorate the founding of Kyoto as the national capital by Emperor Kammu 1100 years earlier. It is a big and showy affair, modeled in general on the original Imperial Palace of the 8th century and strongly attesting Chinese influence. The bright two-storied vermilion gate, with blue tiles, is especially colorful. One of Kyoto's greatest festivals takes place at this shrine on October 22nd and another one, almost as important, on April 15th.

2. The *Gion Shrine*, more officially called the *Yasaka Shrine*, is important as centering another tremendous event in Kyoto's calendar, the *Gion Festival*. This occurs in July, lasting from the 16th to the 24th, but the big days, when gorgeous floats pass in parade, are the 17th and the 20th.

*   *   *

Nara, with but 80,000 inhabitants, is now a sort of moon to big Kyoto, from which it is only 26 miles distant, but its modest size is no measure of its tourist importance, for it was the "cradle of Japan's arts, crafts, literature and industries," in the words of a local folder put out by the JTA, and, as we've seen, it was the very first fixed capital of the nation. Previous to its selection that honor had shifted from place to place in nomadic fashion with each incoming emperor. Today, it doesn't try to compete with Kyoto in creature comforts, though it does, at least, have one excellent place where tourists may stay, namely the *Nara Hotel*, which is of Japanese architecture but Western accommodations and comforts.

The first thing that every visitor wants to see is *Nara Park*, a 1250-acre area of meadows and splendid trees, mostly oaks and towering cedars, commonly called the Deer Park, for the most obvious of reasons. Many very tame deer roam its broad acres and tourists buy packages of wafers to feed to them. A pretty, willow-fringed pond and some small, scattered temples serve to decorate the park but there is one thing of real importance, a *National Museum* containing valuable works of art of the early Nara Period, especially paintings, sculptures in wood and engraved gems.

Of course Nara has its galaxy of Buddhist temples and Shinto shrines but this report will limit itself to two temples and one shrine, presenting them, in this case, in a sort of counterclockwise walking tour, since Nara is small and the most important sights can be comfortably seen by good walkers in half a day.

1. *Kofukuji Temple* is on the north side of a body of water called the Sarusawa Pond, lying west of the Park, about ten minutes distance. Its chief attraction is a handsome 5-story, 165-foot-high pagoda, this "recent edition," from the year 1426, being an exact copy of an original of the year 730. As seen from the south side of the pond it is beautifully reflected in the water.

2. The *Kasuga Shrine*, rising at the far eastern edge of the Park in the midst of dense woods ennobled by many cedars, was founded in 768 as the tutelary shrine of the Fujiwara Family. Actually it consists of four small shrines, all painted bright scarlet. Another feature of this shrine is *three thousand* sacred stone lanterns, all of which are lit at the time of the *Satsubun Festival*, on the night of February 3rd or 4th (it varies) and again in high summer, on August 15th.

3. *Todaiji Temple*, or the Great Eastern Temple, consists of a vast main building and two lesser halls. The main temple, or Hall of the Great Buddha, called "the largest wooden building in the world,"—this begins to sound like Texas talking—houses

what is undeniably the largest bronze statue in the world, a Great Buddha (*Daibutsu*) that dwarfs the one in Kamakura. These claims obviously call for some statistics and here they are, taken straight from the *Official Guide:* "The statue weighs 452 tons, measures 53.5 feet in height and has a face 16 feet long by 9.5 feet wide, eyes 3.9 feet wide, a nose 1.6 feet high, a mouth 3.7 feet wide, ears 8.5 feet long, hands 6.8 feet long, and thumbs 4.8 feet long. The materials employed are estimated as follows: 437 tons of bronze; 165 lbs. of mercury; 288 lbs. of pure gold; 7 tons of vegetable wax and an amazing amount of charcoal and other materials."

After eight discouraging failures this statue was successfully cast in the period from 745 to 749 and the question that rises in everybody's mind is: "HOW did the Japanese artisans succeed in making it?" The year 749 was 51 years before the crowning of Charlemagne in Rome, 742 years before Columbus' first voyage of discovery, yet the Buddha is twice as massive as the Statue of Liberty, which weighs but 225 tons. HOW, again, did the men of that primitive age achieve it? If you can't answer that riddle you may let off your pent-up amazement by paying 10 yen for the privilege of whamming a heavy wooden plunger against the big Buddha's big bell that hangs in the belfry, this being second in size only to the one in Kyoto's Chionin Temple, mentioned above. The bell may not give an answer to your query but it will at least give a resounding and satisfying BOOM.

Nishijin, the Nursery of Silk

Silk is woven into the life and thought of Japan far more widely than pearl culture and of course this industry has had a far longer period of expansion, for it was a going thing, in Kyoto at least, as early as 794, when that city became the capital. The same city, and specifically the northwest corner of it, called Nishijin, is one of the chief nurseries of silk, as it has been for some twelve centuries. The industry languished here for a while because of local wrangles and internecine strife, but in the 17th century the Tokugawa Shogunate issued an edict that henceforth all silks for the use of the Imperial Court and the nobility should be manufactured by the weavers of Nishijin. This gave the quarter, and all of Kyoto, a tremendous industrial fillip and the looms of Nishijin have been racing their shuttles at top speed ever since. Today this quarter is just about 100 per cent silk-conscious, for the whirring of the looms in almost every home fills the air like the drumming of a swarm of cicadas. Silk weaving is still, in considerable part, a home industry and the product is literally *manu*-factured. The textiles are also dyed in Kyoto and in the three rivers that flow through the city much of it is washed and then laid out in long, bright strips on the banks. Nishijin silks, especially the superb brocades, are prized above all others and the weavers of this quarter enjoy special favor and protection from the government to ensure the continuance of the industry as a fine art.

The making of silk fiber would seem like some sort of mystic miracle or fairy tale if the facts were not so universally known. The common silkworm of Japan is of an "off white" color and about three inches in length. He doesn't live long but *how* he lives during his brief span! He is the "compleat glutton," unconcerned about his figure, for he spends literally *all* of his life voraciously eating and at the same time casually spinning gossamer thread around his body. If he has plenty of his favorite diet, his only diet, the leaves of the mulberry tree, he can easily spin 1200 to 1500 yards of it in a single day, and we may be very sure that he does get plenty of these luscious leaves. The Japanese farm families take care of that, hundreds of thousands of them being busily engaged from May to October gathering the leaves.

The worms, in thousands, are laid on forms of straw provided for their convenience and there they spin their cocoons. At the reeling mills the cocoons are softened in hot water so that the filaments can be unwound and reeled into shiny bales, ready for the looms.

The variety of finished silks is one of the wonders of this fiber, ranging from the sheerest gauze fabrics, as delicate as mist, through crepes, taffetas and satins to damasks and heavy brocades. Dyed fabrics called *yuzen*, from the name of a 17th-century priest who inventd the process, are a treasured specialty of Kyoto. Intricate and highly artistic designs are printed on the fabric through a special "working partnership" of designer and dyer.

Japan produces by far the greater portion of the world's silk and it is still and always an important item in the national economy. Nylons, orlons, dacrons and other synthetic fabrics have created formidable competition, but they haven't been able to put the silkworms out of business.

Osaka and Its Mighty Palace

Osaka, with two million of Japan's most hustling inhabitants, is to Tokyo what Manchester is to London, or São Paulo to Rio de Janeiro, in other words the humming capital of the country's industry and trade. For this reason, and even though it has two of Japan's finest hotels, the *New Osaka* and the still newer *Osaka Grand Hotel*, whose 1958 opening aroused wide interest, it commands limited attention from tourists but very close attention from businessmen and bankers. However, the city is not all business. It is Japan's center of stage drama, as it has been for nearly three centuries, and for tourist bait it has the most striking castle in the country (unless one must except the White Heron Castle, of Himeji, to be presented later) built by Hideyoshi Toyotomi in 1584.

Let's look at the castle first, since it looms up so imposingly, its five stories, "accented" by serried roofs and cornices, soaring from a high foundation of masonry. Hideyoshi required his generals to furnish the materials for its construction and they developed such enthusiasm that the sending of immense stone blocks for the surrounding walls became a competitive game. Many of these blocks are as large as the fabulous stones quarried for Lebanon's Baalbek and a few are even larger. The mammoth of them all measures over 48 feet in length and 19 feet in width. The superstructure of the inner castle, or citadel, was burned almost to total destruction by the retreating Tokugawa troops in 1868 when they were forced out at the time of the Meiji Restoration, but its reconstruction, this time in reinforced concrete, was ultimately undertaken and finally brought to completion in 1931. It is now open to the public and you will be pleased to know that elevators have been installed for the ease of sightseers. Of course its upper "peaks" command a very broad view of the city and its environs.

Osaka's role as the drama center of Japan may come as a surprise, but it attained this eminence long ago when Japan's greatest dramatist, Chikamatsu Monzeimon, who was born in 1653, devoted his talents to writing exclusively for the Osaka stage. The city has retained its leading position all through the centuries and still does so. In addition to the theaters that offer classical and modern kabuki drama there are two that offer noh classics and one, the famous *Bunrakuza* (Theater) that offers puppet shows in their purest form. In fact, this is the only real puppet theater in Japan, though traveling troupes occasionally give shows in Tokyo.

Do not think of the *Bunraku*, which is Japanese for puppet show, as a sort of glorified Punch and Judy affair, for it differs from such kiddie entertainment as much as kabuki differs from circus clowns. The puppets are at least three-quarters life-size and they are remarkably lifelike and handsomely dressed. They are not manipulated by persons hidden above or below the stage but by men in classical robes who frankly stand beside their big dolls and "work" them, by hands or cords, in full view of the audience. Bunraku is *adult* fare and was once extremely popular, even overshadowing kabuki, but it has lost much of its appeal and nowadays the young theatergoers, in Tokyo at least, give scant thought to it.

The Hankyu Line and the Girls of Takarazuka

The story of the *Hankyu Railway Line* is one of rare imagination and business enterprise, its high point for all visitors to Japan being GIRLS.

Early in this century a young man named Ichizo Kobayashi, who had a strong interest in the theater, became president of a tram line that connected Osaka with a small, little-known spa called Takarazuka (pronounced by the Japanese Takarázka, with the *u* more or less suppressed). Kobayashi, a keen businessman and a bold promoter, saw the need for more railway transportation in the densely populated area centered by Osaka and bounded by Kyoto and Kobe, so he undertook the building of a railway network that was at first known as the Hankyu Railway and later by the long-winded name, now used, *Kei-Han-Shin Kyuko Electric Railway*. The system sprouted half a dozen short branches, one of them, quite naturally, being a line from Osaka to Takarazuka. The whole network, comprising only 82 miles of track, is now one of the best-operated and most important transportation systems in Japan, carrying the incredible average of a million passengers a day.

Of course the splicing of Kyoto and Kobe to Osaka accounts for the bulk of this immense traffic, but another contributing factor is the existence of Takarazuka and that brings us to the story's climax, for there was no such demand, nor perhaps the hundredth part of it, up on the little tram line with which Kobayashi started his business career. To develop a two-way reason for the mass use of the Takarazuka branch he built up a major attraction at either end of it. To lure city folks to the country he created the *Takarazuka Amusement Center*, whose core was and is the all-girl *Takarazuka Opera Troupe* and to lure country folk to the metropolitan centers he built two big Hankyu department stores, handy, respectively, to the system's Osaka and Kobe terminals.

The fame of his all-girl troupe gradually became, and is today, world-wide. Discipline is very stern, but the girls are all proud of being selected for it, and they respond with whole-souled devotion. To be chosen they must first pass a formidable entrance examination and then they must attend the Girls' Operatic School, an institution unique in Japan, and devote at least two years of hard study, not only to acting, singing and dancing, in both Western and Japanese styles, but even to standard academic courses. The results of this discipline and devotion are seen in the finest presentations in the Orient of the types of show offered.

These types come under three general heads, kabuki drama; folk dances from every corner of Japan; and Takarazuka versions of Western musical revues and operettas. These Western-type spectaculars are especially popular and are thunderously applauded. The line dancers, called the Zukettes, put on quite as finished a performance as do their American or European counterparts. Small groups of Takarazuka Girls have been seen in Honolulu, Hollywood, Paris and Rome and requests now pour in from all over the world, but the place to see them at their superlative best is right at their home theater in the pleasure-spa of Takarazuka, where there's something doing every day of the year. If that is not possible, the next best place to see them is in Tokyo, at the Tokyo Taka Theater (see Chapter 8), adjacent to the Imperial Hotel, where they have short runs about six times a year. In both theaters, and indeed in most of Japan's theaters where lavish revues are offered, the stage is of enormous width, rarely if ever matched in Western theaters.

The Main Building in the Takarazuka Amusement Center houses a Grand Theater, with 4000 seats, the Shingei Theater, the Second Theater, the Picture Theater, various restaurants and tearooms and a public bath. Among countless other features of the Center are a zoo, a botanical garden and a children's garden where parents may park their kiddies safely under the eyes of specially trained policemen while they watch the show of their choice. In any one of the three theaters in the Main Building *one hundred yen*, less than thirty cents, buys a reserved seat!

Kobe, a Japanese Rio

With close to 900,000 inhabitants, *Kobe* rates as the sixth city of Japan, yet it is hemmed in so closely to the shore of the Inland Sea by an almost unbroken range of steeply rising 3000-foot mountains that it can expand only lengthwise. This it does with a will, for it is actually 23 miles long in a fan-like crescent from east to west. If you pass to and through it in a JNR train you feel that you will practically never emerge to the open countryside again, but you'll hardly care, for Kobe is so beautifully situated that you feel yourself in a Japanese Rio, skirting a Japanese version of Guanabara Bay.

The chief mountains hemming in the city are, from east to west, Rokko, Maya, Futatabi and Takatori. The first two are ascended respectively by a cable railway and an aerial cable car, and there is a connection between the two by a new road now approaching completion. Mount Rokko, especially, is a goal of sure appeal and one may reach it not only by the cable railway but by a well-maintained toll road that ascends in many a tortuous curve. The views of city and sea from the roadway and from the mountain's crest are stunning and at one of the most beautiful points rises the *Rokko Oriental Hotel*, an affiliate of Kobe's *Oriental Hotel*, the leading one in the city.

Kobe is the second largest open port in Japan, yielding precedence only to Yokohama, and for this and other reasons it is a very cosmopolitan city. It has a Chinese temple, a Moslem mosque and, most surprisingly, 46 Christian churches, 40 being Protestant and 6 Catholic, although Christianity has captured less than 1 per cent of the people throughout Japan.

Central Kobe does not have many Buddhist temples or Shinto shrines, but it has certain modernities that make it a city of today rather than of the past. One is the gleaming City Hall, opened in 1957, its grounds enhanced by Japan's only floral clock, recalling to travelers similar clocks in Edinburgh, Ostend and other cities of Europe. Another modern feature is the *Kobe International House,* opened in 1956. This tall and massive building houses an attractive Shopping Nook (featuring Amita Damascene ware and Mikimoto pearls); a series of Exhibition Rooms; a 2300-seat auditorium for concerts, kabuki plays and other assorted events; and, on the 6th and 7th and 8th floors, the ultra-modern *Kobe Kokusai Hotel*—you remember that Kokusai means International—with the dining room and bar on the 8th floor, commanding a close-up view of the harbor.

In the heart of the Ikuta Ward, which can be called "Kobe Proper," is one of Japan's more famous and crowded shopping thoroughfares, *Motomachi Street,* where you'll find just about every kind of merchandise you can imagine, from big sides of beef hanging in a spic-and-span butcher shop—Kobe beef is famous throughout Japan—to the kimonos, delicate porcelains, lacquer ware and art bibelots offered in such well-known marts as the *Peony Shop.*

Almost anything can happen, and does, on Motomachi Street. I once encountered a folk dance carnival in full swing in an open area at the side of this street, so I passed a flimsy barrier and entered the enclosure to see what was going on. Great was my reward, for I witnessed some exceedingly lively folk dances, performed on an open stage at one side of the enclosure. The various dances were executed by different groups, competing for honors, and I was fascinated by them. One was an *Awaji Island Dance,* another a comic *Awa Dance,* like a wobbly mambo, wherein drunken villagers of both sexes, tippling freely, rendered thanks to a feudal chieftain for favors, while a third was a *Lion Dance,* performed by a single very cute 10-year-old girl named Kyoko Kinno, whose given name, I learned, means Child-of-the-Metropolis. But perhaps the most surprising number was the *Dekanso Dance,* translatable as the Philosophers' Dance. Of course you have guessed—or have you?—that Dekanso stands for *De*scartes-*Kan*t-*Scho*penhauer!

CHAPTER 10

SEAWAY OR RAILWAY TO KYUSHU

By Steamer Through the Inland Sea

JAPAN is one of the world's great maritime nations, as everyone knows. What everyone doesn't know, though Western shipping circles are only too painfully aware of it, is that Japan is currently surpassing all other nations except Great Britain in the construction of new ship tonnage. That it has reached this eminence in the short period since the vast destruction of its shipping in the war is dramatic proof of Japan's industrial capacity and drive.

So far as tourism is concerned the come-back of Japan's merchant fleet is all to the good for it has opened up many pleasant possibilities for sea trips, especially on the beautiful and sheltered Inland Sea, which extends for a distance of more than 300 miles, from Osaka to the northern coast of Kyushu and the Shimonoseki Straits. Most of this expanse is an island-dotted chain of smaller seas connected by channels, lying between Honshu and Shikoku. Since 1934 it has been officially designated *The Inland Sea National Park* and in 1950 the confines of this marine park were greatly extended. One of the important shipping concerns concentrating to a considerable extent on Inland Sea services is the *Kansai Kisen Kaisha*, or Kansai Shipping Company, which operates a fleet of over forty ships, to which it is constantly adding newer and faster ones, with speeds up to 18 knots. The trunk route of KKK through the Inland Sea is from Osaka, and nearby Kobe, to Beppu, a port and hotspring spa on the eastern shore of Kyushu. This trip, consuming only 17 hours from Kobe, I have taken on one of the company's ships bearing the delightful

182

name of *Kogane Maru*, which may be translated as *S.S. Yellow Gold*. I loved it and can heartily recommend it, not only for its convenience in bringing you to a fascinating destination but for the sheer beauty of the 220-mile passage, threaded through a maze of isles and islets whose total number is almost a thousand. Stops are made in the evening and early morning at two lively ports on Shikoku Island, namely Takamatsu and Takahama.

Shikoku Island, smallest of Japan's four main islands, being about the size of New Jersey, seems content to sit by the side of the sea and let the rest of the world go by. In feudal times it was an island of exile for political "outs" and today, though by no means remote or undeveloped, it is a goal for those traveling escapists who deplore beaten paths and tourist atmosphere. There are Western-type hotels in Takamatsu and the good-sized city of Matsuyama, but the exploratory traveler will have to seek lodging in most towns only in Japanese inns.

Shikoku is "beautiful by axiom," for you can hardly find un-beautiful scenery anywhere in Japan, and this island's relative seclusion has its own appeal, but there are odd and special attractions too. The people of Tokushima, a city on the eastern rim of the island, make some of Japan's most elaborate and ingenious puppets for the Bunraku and the people of Kochi, a city on the southern rim, breeds sturdy and bellicose "sumo dogs" of the *Tosa Inu* breed. These powerful dogs are actually accoutered as sumo wrestlers, complete with "topknot" hairdo and loin cloth (!), and they compete in sumo bouts. Several rural communities in Shikoku, concerning themselves with bigger beasts of battle, breed bulls, which fight in arenas as they really should, bull against bull, not stupid brute against sharp-brained *torero*. And the village of Oshino, not far from Kochi, boasts the oddest specialty of all, the breeding of *naga-o-dori*, which must surely be the most peculiar domesticated birds in the world. They are the size of ordinary barnyard hens and roosters and they are, in fact, just that, but the rooster of the species grows a long white tail which often trails for ten feet after him and may reach a length of *twenty* feet. One is reminded of a little girl masquerading in her mother's wedding gown, but with a fantastically long white train.

Whether or not you take time out to visit Shikoku, with needed aid from the JTB to plan your tour, you will surely enjoy your steamer ride through the lovely Inland Sea aboard the "Yellow Gold" or one of her sister ships.

Railway to Hiroshima, Center of Tragedy and Hope

The railway from Kobe to Hiroshima, running due west along the shore of the Inland Sea for 190 miles by way of Himeji and Okayama, passes through lush rice-clover-rapeflower stretches alternating with industrial towns and providing frequent glimpses of the sea on the left and the mountain backdrop on the right. On all this long run there is perhaps just one "must" sight, namely *Himeji Castle*, seen on the right just before reaching Himeji's station. I have mentioned this earlier as the one castle whose striking appearance rivals the one in Osaka, but perhaps, in view of its location on an isolated hill, it should be given the first prize for "dramatic excellence." It was built by Sadanori Akamatsu in the 14th century and brought to its present state of perfection by Ikeda Terumara, who spent nine years on it, employing thousands of laborers. The seven-story keep is the heart of it, soaring in many-gabled splendor like the Castle of Osaka. The castle's sobriquet, as I have said, is "The White Heron," or "The Egret," because of its gleaming white-plastered walls.

Hiroshima was done to death on August 6 (U.S. time August 5), 1945, at 8:15 A.M. by an atomic bomb of one megaton, having the blasting power of 20,000 tons of TNT, dropped from a B-29 Superfortress bomber prettily named *Enola Gay*. The deadly bomb was dropped from a height of 37,800 feet and the swift *Enola Gay* had time to fly for safety ten miles before the bomb exploded at a height of 1800 feet, creating a miniature sun, or fireball, 66 feet in diameter with a temperature of 540,000 degrees Fahrenheit. This bomb was a piffling little toy compared with the infinitely more powerful hydrogen bombs of today, packing a punch of 30 megatons (600,000 tons of TNT) or more, yet it killed 80,000 persons outright and 160,000 more, in the total to date, from the deadly effects of radiation. About 163,000 were injured but have survived. Six thousand buildings and homes in the city, being 89 per cent of the total, were destroyed outright or damaged beyond hope of repair. A highly educated English-speaking guide who showed me the city told me that he, at that time a young conscript soldier stationed in a camp just outside Hiroshima, was one of a squad detailed to "clean up" only three days after the explosion. Said he, in a calm, dispassionate tone, "It was some job, for we had only two trucks and a few pushcarts and the bodies were everywhere. Just over there across the river there was a school where nine hundred children had been doing calisthenics when the bomb fell. Their charred bodies, all of them, lay around like dead fish on a beach. There was no place to put them so we shoveled them into the river, but it's a tidal river and for days most of them washed in and out with each tide's flow and ebb. We couldn't do anything about it."

Hiroshima was selected as the first target because it was an important military center and leading symbol of Japan's saber-rattling militarism of the period—two divisions of the Japanese Army were caught here and largely annihilated, along with the civilians. The city had been given a warning by the dropping of thousands of printed leaflets urging civilian evacuation, but this was considered by the Japanese authorities to be a mere "scare" and indeed the inhabitants were sternly forbidden to pick up or read the leaflets. The next day, August 7, our airmen flew over Nagasaki dropping thousands of similar printed leaflets warning the inhabitants to avoid experiencing Hiroshima's fate. The clear, grim story of what had happened to Hiroshima was set forth, but the people of Nagasaki just wouldn't, couldn't, didn't, believe it, for the thing seemed preposterous, an obvious trick intended to scare them, so, on August 9th, 73,800 people of the southern port city were killed by Bomb Number 2 and 76,500 more were to die later from the effects of radiation. Many of those in both cities who were burned but not killed outright spread flour on their blackened and bleeding bodies, thinking thus to gain some measure of relief and maybe save their lives, but the flour quickly hardened into a sort of cement and they died anyway, in terrible agony.

The American bombing calendar called for the destruction of the following cities, after Nagasaki, in this order: *Omuta* (an important industrial and port city near Nagasaki), *Osaka, Yokohama, Tokyo, Hachioji* (a weaving center near Tokyo), and so on until surrender, but fortunately surrender came quickly, on August 15th by Japanese time, August 14th by our time. As we all know, Russia formally entered the war against Japan about a week before that date and the quaint Red propaganda has held ever since that it was only the growl of the Russian Bear that made Japan give up.

For a while after the war the Hiroshima area was called "the atomic desert," and it was generally believed that it might be 75 to 100 years before it would become habitable again. This belief was strengthened by the fact that "radiation ghost shadows" of objects and of persons were "printed" by the blast even on granite and solid concrete—the city's Memorial Museum exhibits some gruesome photos of these ghosts—but happily the public and even many scientists were proved wrong and within two years the city began to come to life. As if symbolizing this renascence, the ghost shadows faded out. Today Hiroshima has 400,000 inhabitants and is flourishing as much as it ever did before the blast, but no trace of its traditional militarism is left. It devotes itself with urgent enthusiasm to its self-selected role as the Peace City of Japan. It has its Peace Park, in which stands the leading and first-rate hotel, the *New Hiroshima;* its Peace Boulevard crossing the river on Peace Bridge; its Peace Memorial Museum and Peace Tower; its modernistic Peace Memorial Cathedral (Roman Catholic); and its Memorial Cenotaph, before which, on August 6th, the anniversary of the disaster, it holds an annual Peace Festival. The Hiroshima Peace City Construction Committee, strongly backed and supported by the Japanese government, pushes steadily ahead on a program for the rebuilding of the city, a program that is expected ultimately to cost thirty billion yen (nearly ten million dollars). Only one pre-bomb structure is being left untouched, namely the former industrial Promotion Hall, in the heart of the city. It is a weird, gaunt, steel-and-concrete ghost of its former self, but will remain always as a marker, for it was exactly above this building that the bomb exploded.

I have not had the opportunity to witness the annual Peace Festival, but the ceremony at the Memorial Cenotaph must be a solemn and moving affair. Under a cement arch that looks to Americans something like the roof of a covered wagon but is supposed to resemble the roof of an old home of feudal times is a stone box and on it these words are carved in Japanese and English: *Repose Thou In Peace. We Shall Never Make That Mistake Again.* Mistake or not, it is the heartfelt wish of every beholder that "we," the human race, shall never again be led into inflicting such mass agony on any city.

The stone box of the cenotaph contains a record, for posterity, of the names of *all* the 240,000 victims of the bomb. The box is opened only once a year, on August 6th, and any relative or friend of any victim may find the name of his or her loved one there. Buddhist, Shinto, Catholic and Protestant mourners join in worship according to their respective faiths.

I have saved the best news, the news of Hiroshima's hope, for the last. By this I mean the development of a great research center, on the city's Hiyajima Hill, by the *Atomic Bomb Casualty Commission,* which is not a U.S. government commission but an agency of the United States National Academy of Sciences. The ABCC buildings are in the style of quonset huts but they are equipped with every modern device and implement for studying and offsetting the effects of radiation. Here a staff of some 50 Americans and 700 Japanese, including doctors, nurses, technicians and skilled scientists, work side by side in utmost harmony, former enemies become friends. In the first ten years of the Center's existence 200,000 persons were examined and even now every victim, young or old, who may still suffer in any manner or degree from atomic radiation is given free, compulsory, periodic examinations.

Trained guides show visitors through the Research Center on the hill and some ten or twelve thousand American tourists take advantage of this service annually. The tour, which requires about half an hour, is a very heartening thing, leading all who take it to believe that after all there is some hope for the survival of the human race.

To Miyajima, Great Shrine in the Sea

Miyajima, meaning literally Shrine Island, must certainly be one of the most photographed sights in Japan after Fuji because of its "seagoing," or perhaps I should say "seacoming," shrine. This is built over the edge of the sea, with a huge camphor-wood torii rising from the water 530 feet from shore, and when the tide is in one gains the impression that the whole shrine is afloat. When the tide is out the glamour recedes with it, for the crinkling blue water is replaced by stagnant flats, but even at its worst Miyajima—this name is loosely applied to the shrine as well as the whole island—is a marvelous spectacle.

The whole island, 19 miles in circumference, is sacred to all Japanese and by sacred I do not necessarily mean holy, for there is a real distinction. Every Japanese venerates Miyajima and tries to visit it at least once during his life for patriotic reasons if not for religious, and dedicated believers in Shinto approach it from the mainland by a sacred boat that is actually propelled through the big vermilion torii in the sea. Ordinary people, and that's where you and I come in, approach it by a JNR-operated ferry that leaves on a frequent and regular schedule from Miyajima-guchi, which is a halt on the main rail line about 200 miles from Kobe and 20 or so from Hiroshima.

The entire island, culminating in Mount Misen, is clad in virgin forest and this forest is a "venerable virgin," for no Japanese would dare fell a single tree. It has the distinction of being almost, if not quite, the only remaining large stand of virgin forest in all Japan.

The shrine itself is a three-fold one dedicated to the three daughters of a Shinto god bearing the eight-syllable name, if you care, of Susano-o-no-Mikoto and it consists of a main shrine connected with subsidiary shrines by wooden corridors that stretch over the sea, or the flats, on both sides. The whole affair is of very ancient origin, having been mentioned in records as far back as the beginning of the 9th century, but it has been rebuilt several times. So replete is it with beautiful or odd features that I think I should list some of them seriatim, following the order of a tour on which I was conducted by one of the most intelligent and knowledgeable guides I have had in Japan.

1. An enclosed camphor-wood floor of extremely wide boards is said to be the only part of the shrine that actually dates from the original construction of it. On this floor Shinto priests perform their *Kagura* sacred dance. If this isn't going on when you arrive, a performance can, I understand, be arranged through the payment of a fixed fee—to the impersonal shrine of course.

2. An outdoor ceremonial dance floor is for the performance of the vigorous and fantastic *Bugaku*, a ritualistic dance that is done in elaborate costume with the faces hidden by grotesque masks of a type formerly worn by warriors to terrify their opponents. It was originally done only for the nobility, whereas the Kagura was done for the common run of people. Only one family, I am told, has been empowered, for the past 800 years, to perform this strange, posturing dance at Miyajima.

3. A noh stage also exists in this shrine and it too is built over the tidal water or flats.

4. The National Museum of Miyajima, to enter which you must leave your shoes at the door, contains many interesting curiosities such as ancient samurai swords and still more ancient Bugako masks. It also contains models of gaily decorated festival ships such as are still used by fishermen in summer festivals here.

5. Two pagodas loom up as we make our rounds, one very old one of two stories, the other, still older, of five stories. The five stories represent "the five necessary elements of life," according to Buddhist theology, namely: 1st (ground) floor—earth; 2nd floor—wood; 3rd floor—water; 4th floor—fire; 5th floor—heaven.

6. LUNCH may be had at the charming *Iwaso Inn* in "Maple Park," in a room that looks out on a lovely glen threaded by a cheerfully noisy brook. The meal, unless specially arranged otherwise, will be of the tempura type and you will be expected to squat on your heels, or sprawl any way you can on the tatami matting while you eat it. You'll find this lunch break very welcome after your trudging, no matter how you are able to dispose of your legs.

7. After lunch you may see, on the edge of a ledge, a dwarf pine tree called "The Dragon's Beard" that is unique even in Japan. It is two feet high and runs along the ground at this same height for *eighty-five feet*. I know because I paced it off.

8. The *Senjo-kaku*, or *Hall of a Thousand Mats*, actually contains only about 450 mats. It was built of camphor-wood (by legend from a single super-tree) at the order of Hideyoshi Toyotomi and dedicated to the shrine. Its unique curiosity is the display of thousands of rice scoops of all sizes hung up before and around a small shrine within the big hall, each scoop inscribed with the donor's name and with a good-luck message to some friend or relative. The person at whom this good-luck wish is aimed normally does not know about the gift, but the sanctity of the shrine is supposed to be of such power that it will reach and aid him anyway. This queer custom, originating from a play on words—*meshi-toru* meaning "rice-taking" and also "to conquer"—dates only from 1894, at a time when troops engaged in

the Sino-Japanese War were quartered here. They offered these meshi-toru as a sort of prayer for the victory and safety of loved ones. Finally, a rice scoop, in case you're puzzled by the term, is the wooden implement with which rice is scooped from kettle to bowl.

Miyajima is wonderfully beautiful at any season but most beautiful in the cherry-blossom season of early April when thousands of cherry trees add their luminous pink glow to the scene.

I have mentioned the *Iwaso Inn* and in case you wish to spend a night on the island this is a good place to find lodging, Japanese style, but a still better place, indeed much better, is to be found on the "mainland" shore of Honshu, near the ferry wharf, namely *Issaen Inn*. This is considered one of the outstanding Japanese inns of the country and it is always ready to serve U.S.-style food. Its lawn, running to the sea, is one of the finest I have seen in Japan, being decorated with stone lanterns, fanciful topiaries, lovely flowering shrubs and, in the center, a giant azalea that is trimmed to the shape of a sea urchin and when in bloom gives forth a veritable flood of floral radiance.

And So, by Tunnel, to Kyushu

The *Straits of Shimonoseki*, between Honshu and Kyushu, are "underpassed" by trains of the coastal line, continuing the main railway route from Tokyo–Kyoto–Osaka–Kobe–Hiroshima by means of a tunnel 2.3 miles long. (This is now being paralleled by a highway tunnel.) The train emerges at Moji, on Kyushu, and continues thence 108 miles to Fukuoka-Hakata, the largest city of Kyushu, and another 160 miles to Nagasaki.

The hyphenated city, a big industrial one of 400,000 inhabitants having two distinct and equally important parts separated by the Naka River, is graced by fine parks, a double-moated castle and other pleasant features but perhaps its chief interest to hurrying tourists lies in its name. Back in 1885, a popular vote was taken as to whether it should be called Fukuoka or Hakata. Fukuoka won by *one vote*, but the dismayed Hakatans have continued ever since to call it Hakata and the railway station, lying in their part of the city, is also officially called Hakata. The city's best hotel, and very good, too, straddles the issue nicely by calling itself the *Hakata Imperial Hotel of Fukuoka*.

Nagasaki, now recovered from its atom-bombing and having as much tourist allure as ever, will be covered hereinafter, in Chapter 11, as the climax of a circular tour of Kyushu starting at Beppu.

CHAPTER 11

SELECTED CRESCENT IN KYUSHU

The Belching "Hells" of Beppu

THE Japanese always designate as "hells" (in Japanese *jigoku*) all such volcanic phenomena as fumaroles, *solfataras,* boiling pools and spouting geysers and when you see the hells of Beppu, a port city on the eastern coast of Kyushu, you'll think the word well chosen, for they are weird and satanic and chock full of devilishly ingenious variety. Beppu is by far the most important and popular hotspring resort in Kyushu, with no less than three hundred hotels and inns, according to the *Official Guide.* The best for Western visitors is the centrally located *Hotel Kamenoi,* with 12 rooms of Western style and 23 of Japanese style. Other good places for your consideration, all located in the hillside portion of Beppu, are the *Beppu,* the *Haku Un Zan,* meaning "White Cloud Mountain," and the *Kanko,* which, as you now know, means "Tourist," though this is a Japanese-style inn catering chiefly to Japanese tourists. Beppu is a crowded, noisy, even brassy, resort, where bold girls clutch at passers-by and where geishas, by common report, are not above turning a fast dollar by extracurricular services, but you'll find the Kamenoi, if you are able to book there, a very pleasant retreat from the busy bustle surrounding it.

The tour of "the hells in the hills" just above and beyond Beppu proved an experience unique in my life of travel. I've seen, first and last, a lot of hells in a lot of countries but even those of Iceland and the Azores aren't a patch on those of Beppu for fascinating variety. Without attempting to list them all I'll report briefly on half a dozen that fixed themselves indelibly in my memory.

1. *Tsurumi* (named for a near-by mountain) is a *roaring* hell, of boiling-bubbling type, within a popular and well-landscaped park.

2. *Bozu* (Monk's Hell) is a pool of boiling mud that continuously gargles and gurgles and belches and burps as if its particular Satan—or is it a monk that went wrong?—were experiencing a severe case of dyspepsia. Oddly enough there's a cool pool immediately adjacent to old Bozu and in it a squadron of goldfishes maneuvers here and there, although jets of steam emerge from poolside rocks within inches of where the fishes swim.

3. *Umi* (Sea Hell) is of a deep green color and although its temperature is 195 degrees Fahrenheit it merely steams contemplatively all the time and is never so rude as to burp in public. Perhaps its relative calmness is due to its depth, for it is over 400 feet deep.

4. *Wani* (Crocodile Hell) is a series of cool pools filled with crocodiles of all ages, from babies a foot or two long to ugly, full-grown hellions who would doubtless be happy to snap off an arm or leg if you have one to spare. These ugly reptiles are, of course, a tourist attraction and they do attract crowds, stealing attention from a boiling mud pool close by.

5. *Chinoike* (Bloody Hell) is bloody indeed, for its waters are of a sanguinary crimson color, shading off in parts of the pool to rich, rusty orange. Chinoike is not so hot as Umi, its temperature being a mere 169, and it is the deepest hell of all, the soundings showing 540 feet.

6. *Tatsumaki* (Tornado Hell) is by all odds the most thrilling of them all. Every six minutes, exactly, it sends up a tornado geyser that is like a solid pillar of boiling water a foot thick and it *would* be about thirty feet tall had not a heavy stone roof been placed over it at a height of about twenty feet to prevent the scalding water from being blown upon the admir-

ing customers. For a period of some ten years, just after the war, the tornado was effectively blocked by a heavy fall of rocks and could only grumble and sputter discontentedly, but in 1956 the rocks were dug out and the tornado blew again. So exactly regular are its "gusts" that an attendant announces over a public address system "In just one minute Tatsumaki will spout again." Crowds gather at the protecting rail and the seconds tick by. At the 59th second you hear subterranean sounds and at the 60th second behold "There she blows!" In a boiling pool just above and behind the geyser, girl attendants are continuously on duty to boil eggs and these they sell, along with other snacks, to the throngs of watchers.

The whole area of Beppu and its environs is said to be nothing but a thin crust over a stewing ocean of hot water. Dig *anywhere*, they say, and after you've gone down five to ten feet you'll find hot earth and then hot water. In front of Beppu's railway station a fountain of natural hot water gushes copiously day and night. A beach of coarse sand fringes the bay and at several places, even within Beppu itself, the subterranean hot ocean is so near the surface that the sand is hot, at and above the high tide line. A favorite relaxation of visitors is to bury themselves in the sand, the head and arms protruding, prop up the head with a pillow and spend an hour or so reading a favorite magazine or whodunit. Others may feel in the mood simply to go to sleep in the arms of the comforting warm sand. Such relaxation is supposed to benefit arthritis, but if you haven't that excuse for a sand cure try one anyway.

A Land-and-Sea Design

A natural and most interesting approach from Beppu to Nagasaki, the obvious climax of any visit to Kyushu, is as follows:

Train from Beppu to *Oita* and thence, still by train, clear across Kyushu, passing through *Mount Aso National Park* to

Kumamoto, near the island's western coast, with an overnight halt in that interesting city. Mount Aso National Park is far from incidental to this passage, for it is actually the world's largest crater basin, nearly 80 miles in circumference, with five volcanic peaks, one of which, Naka-dake, is ever active.

Train from Kumamoto to *Misumi*, a small port at the tip of a peninsula.

Steamer across Ariake Bay to *Shimabara*, famous as the place where the Christians, holing up in Shimabara Castle, made their last stand (1641) against the purge of the Tokugawa Shogunate (see Chapters 2 and 5). A luncheon halt should, if possible, be made at the very attractive inn called Nampuro.

Private auto to and through Unzen Park and on to Nagasaki. Now for some details.

Kumamoto, although the largest city in central Kyushu, is little known by tourists, but it is worth knowing and seeing and it has a pleasant Japanese inn called *Hotel Tsukasa Honten*, whose cheery chambermaids like to fill the air with song while they make up the rooms. There are two outstanding sights of this city, the exceptionally lovely *Suizenji Park*, with a lake fed by underground rivers from Mount Aso, and the remains of *Kumamoto Castle*.

The castle was built by Kiyomasa Kato, a retainer of Hideyoshi Toyotomi, and after the latter's death became a far-western stronghold of the Tokugawa Shogunate. In 1877, during the Satsuma Rebellion, its beleaguered forces had to endure, and *did* endure, without surrender, a terrible fifty-day siege that destroyed much of the castle. What is left, rising from an eminence in the western part of the city, gives impressive evidence of what it must have been, for there is a vast and intricate system of turreted walls and protecting moats. Among its special charms are the approaching avenue of cherry trees, planted to do honor to Emperor Meiji, who paid a visit here in 1900, and a gingko tree of gigantic proportions in the upper courtyard. This tree has earned for the whole fortress the nickname "Gingko Tree Castle."

Shimabara is worth a halt if only to visit the charming beach-side Japanese inn, referred to above, officially named *Hotel Nampuro* ("South Wind") and partake of a Japanese luncheon in it. In its setting, its landscaped sea-lawn and its general air of quality it is quite as appealing as the Issaen Inn on the shore opposite Miyajima. *Shimabara Castle*, mentioned above in the Land-and-Sea Design, is now only a site, recalling the famous incident of Christian heroism.

In the public playground near the hotel I was treated quite unexpectedly to the excitement of a community athletic meet, if one could call it that. The chief event, following a girls' relay race in which most of the girls ran barefoot, was a tug of war between a team of women and the men of the Town Council. Of course the women won, for on such an occasion a sense of gallantry is bound to crop up even in a land where women still play a subservient role to their menfolk.

The auto trip from Shimabara up and through *Unzen National Park*—Unzen means literally "Paradise in the Clouds"—and along the shores of Chijiwa Bay to Nagasaki is a varied and stimulating one that should rate high in any travel calendar with room for mountain scenery. This National Park, being 32,000 acres of beauty and grandeur in the center of the Shimabara Peninsula, is well seen by means of a lofty scenic road that circles the highest peak (crest, 4500 feet) and a new cable car that ascends from this road to the peak itself. Beyond this mountain, in the direction of Nagasaki, is the very popular Unzen Spa, at the 2400-foot level.

The Park (we'll capitalize it to distinguish it from the local park of Unzen Spa) is particularly famous for its glories of azaleas in the spring, maples in the fall, when the leaves turn, and tens of thousands of hero-sized cedars at all seasons. In winter these forests often take on a dazzling coating of what has been called "silverdown," a powder frost that crystallizes into weird and wondrous shapes, as of otherworldly flowers.

Unzen Spa is really three neighboring hamlets whose names may be translated as Old Spring, New Spring and Little Hell.

The leading hostelry of many good ones, by name the *Unzen Kanko Hotel*, has sixty-four rooms, all of Western style, and is proud to announce to us Westerners that it is one of only two hotels in the whole of Nagasaki Prefecture where you don't have to remove your shoes upon entering. The other one is Nagasaki City's own *Nagasaki Kanko Hotel*, and there's that word again, Kanko (Tourist), the most heavily worked word in Japanese hotel nomenclature. It goes without saying that all the hotels in the threefold spa have abundant hot mineral water piped into them and the leading ones have hotspring pools. As an added attraction to spagoers there is a handsomely located 9-hole golf course in the neighborhood.

Parts of the road connecting Unzen and Nagasaki are, or recently were, in a deplorable state but valiant and expensive efforts are now being made to provide an early link of paved highway worthy of two such glamorous terminal points, so perhaps all will be completed by the time your car negotiates this stretch.

Nagasaki, the Port of Madame Butterfly

Nagasaki, with but 300,000 inhabitants, rates a modest 14th among Japanese cities yet to many foreigners it symbolizes Japan far more than Tokyo does and rather more even than Kyoto and Nara.

Yoritomo Minamoto, founder of the Kamakura Shogunate, gave Nagasaki its name, but in his day the place was hardly more than a fishing port and not until the middle of the 16th century did it become an important gateway to foreign trade. Then, however, it quickly developed as the principal gateway and later the *only* gateway, to world trade during the centuries-long period of Japan's seclusion, the period that Commodore Perry finally brought to an end in 1853. During the peak of Nagasaki's era of importance in foreign trade, before the Tokugawa Shogunate expelled the Spanish and Portuguese and restricted the Dutch traders to one small island called Dejima in Nagasaki Bay, there was extensive trade with China, the Philippines, Siam (Thailand) and, of immense cultural as well as commercial significance, Portugal, Spain and Holland. The European traders introduced Western books, Western methods of business, Western science, medicine, chemistry, geology and astronomy and even Western military science. In the field of religion St. Francis Xavier, the dedicated Spanish missionary who came here to preach Christianity, won, as we have seen, an impressive measure of success in Kyushu, a success that was destined to endure even through and after the blood bath inflicted upon the converts by Ieyasu Tokugawa. That Christianity has endured in Kyushu even through World War II is a measure of its power, for the chief stronghold of this faith, Nagasaki (hardly matched even by Kobe), was atom-bombed by Japan's Christian enemy and the Urakami Church (Roman Catholic), the largest Christian church in the Orient, seating 6000 worshipers, was reduced to ruins. The same fate also overtook, though in less total fashion, the Oura Church (since rebuilt), which was the oldest one in Japan, built by a French missionary in 1864. Japanese religionists and others hostile to Christianity were quick to notice, and proclaim, the incongruity of this destruction, in which thousands of civilian Christians in Nagasaki also lost their lives, but the flames of passion have largely died down and Christian churches, new ones, again flourish in Nagasaki and its neighborhood.

The situation of this port, surrounded as it is by steep heights, is of rare beauty and every visitor should make sure to ascend the Kazagashira Hill at dusk, to watch the lights come on, for this is one of the stirrings sights of Japan. A pleasant restaurant, the *Yataro*, perches on a ledge near the crest and a jutting platform provides a perfect belvedere. At present one must ascend by private car or bus, but a cable car line is planned for the immediate future.

The view from the Yataro belvedere embraces both the city

and its striking harbor. At the harbor's edge, for instance, on the far side, stretching along for two miles or so, is the huge Mitsubishi shipbuilding yard and we learn that this immense company—or has it once again become, in effect, a cartel, despite the postwar ban on such combines?—currently builds more ship tonnage than any other one company in the world. Shipbuilding is only one of many elements in the Mitsubishi business empire—a vast department store chain is another—and it sometimes seems, as Japanese have more than once said to me, that "Mitsubishi owns everything." That, however, is Japan's problem, not ours.

Nagasaki is an alluring town for shoppers, its tortoise-shell ware and delicate porcelains being specially prized. Another item of commerce, and you would never guess this one, is a delectable kind of layer cake called *kasutera,* and thereby hangs a tale of trade. It seems that centuries ago a Spanish importer brought to this port a shipment of layer cakes on each box of which appeared the word *Castillo.* This was the name of the Spanish bakery that made it, but the Japanese took it to be the product, and how they loved it! Soon they applied their "adapters' technique" to the matter and several baking establishments began producing it, but since Castillo can't be easily pronounced by the Japanese they Japanized it to kasutera, and that name still holds. Today's customers love kasutera quite as much as their forebears did in the 1600's and when you sample it I think you will see why.

The sights of Nagasaki can be fairly well seen, with the aid of a guide and a car, in half a day, starting perhaps with a bit of footwork to see the central shopping area and what was once *Dejima Island,* the restricted quarter of Dutch traders, but has long since been absorbed by the mainland, due to earth fill and the construction of a large quay. Today it has little of its old character but there are some touches of Holland in the old buildings. A convenient order for seeing the sights that call for transportation by car may be as follows:

1. The rebuilt *Oura Church*, as mentioned above, memorializes twenty-six Christians who were martyred here in 1597 rather than renounce their faith.

2. A *Memorial Monument* of green marble marks the grim spot where the second atomic bomb struck at 11:02 on the morning of August 9, 1945. One need not here recount the details of this horror, as was done earlier in discussing Hiroshima.

3. The *International Cultural Center* is housed in a new and dignified white building standing on a hill very close to the Memorial Monument and in front of it, in a garden, is a marble statue of a mother and child. This building is the nucleus of a developing idea dedicated to peace and it is surrounded by an area that is being cleared and landscaped to serve as Nagasaki's *Peace Park*, vying in hopeful symbolism with that of Hiroshima.

4. A colossal *Peace Statue* 66 feet high by a widely known sculptor named Seibo Kitamura stands in this same developing Peace Park. It is cast in bronze but covered with material that makes it look like stone. Strongly reminiscent of Ossip Zadkine's famous memorial statue in Rotterdam eloquently named *Mei 1940*, yet of quite a different artistic conception, Kitamura's giant of peace holds his right arm straight up and his left stretched out horizontally, palm downward, in a soothing gesture of peace. He squats on his folded right leg in a manner that would strain an American limb but would be easy for any Japanese. You may not like this statue—some do and some don't—but you will readily agree that it is extremely dramatic in delivering its message.

5. The ruins of the big *Urakami Church*, mentioned earlier as a victim of the bomb, should be included on every sightseer's itinerary. It was built over a period of 33 years through the contributions of 20,000 Nagasaki Christians and was opened only in 1941. Four years later it died. Today, services are held in a makeshift wooden structure.

6. Finally, the *Home of Madame Butterfly* draws all who have in their systems the least sense of romance. It is about as synthetic

as Juliet's Balcony in Verona or Ophelia's Grave in Elsinore, having once been the mansion of an English resident named Thomas Glover and being now a Mitsubishi property (!), but for all that, it *is* romantic. The structure is of most unusual design, with a sort of hexagonal front and porch, and it rises from a gardened knoll that commands a splendid close-up view of the bay. Just forget Mr. Glover and the Messrs. Mitsubishi and think instead of poor Butterfly, waiting hopefully for Lieutenant Pinkerton.

*   *   *

Nagasaki, though a rather small city in population, is rich in pleasures of the flesh, for it has good restaurants of many types. Of its Japanese restaurants the two best, in expert local opinion, are the *Suuaso Inn* and the *Kagetsu* (Flower Moon), this latter with a superb garden. Of the many Chinese restaurants in the city's Chinese Quarter, which vies in importance with that of Yokohama, the best is probably the *Shikai Ro*. With a group of Japanese friends I once attacked a 10-course meal here of such excellence and lavishness that it had me "hanging on the ropes" after the sixth or seventh round. Of Western restaurants perhaps the best is the *Ginrei*.

The city is by no means lacking in pleasures of the night for it has the usual array of cabarets and dance halls and one of these establishments, the *Florida Nightclub*, is said to be the mother club of Tokyo's Queen Bee. Friends took me one night on a ride through the *Maruyama Quarter*, which is Nagasaki's "gay quarter," and gay it certainly was, both actually and in the euphemistic sense in which Japanese use that phrase. Before each of the many "gay" houses in several streets and squares young women, mostly clad in kimonos in this town of tradition, issued urgent personal invitations to all masculine passers-by. It remains to be seen whether Maruyama, along with the countless other gay quarters in other cities, will gradually exchange its red lights for blue now that the relentless calendar has reached and passed the fateful deadline.

CHAPTER 12

HOKKAIDO, A WORLD APART

How Far Apart, and Why?

HOKKAIDO, the northern island which comprises 21 per cent of Japan's total area but only 5 per cent of her population, is as different from the rest of Japan as Alaska is different from California, though I do not offer this as an analogy. In climate it is quite as cold as Maine, the snow sometimes being six feet deep even in the bustling streets of its capital city, Sapporo, whose January temperature average is 21 degrees, and attaining a depth of ten feet in some western sections, whereas Honshu's average temperature is more like that of Virginia, and Kyushu's more like that of North Carolina. In background it is as different from the rest of Japan as in climate, for its aboriginal inhabitants, now reduced to perhaps 10,000 of pure blood, were the mysterious Hairy Ainus, whose broad faces, pale eyes and luxuriant beards are as un-Japanese as anything could be. And in civic development, as well as in agricultural and industrial development, Hokkaido is brand-new, being born, so to speak, of American parentage in the 1870's, whereas the civilization and customs of the other islands are basically of Oriental extraction, with a new Western veneer, and as old as antiquity itself.

Hokkaido is a rugged island where thousands of brown bears roam the wilds and about five hundred are shot by hunters each year, and it has a sort of Texan bigness about it, though it is only Maine-sized in area. It has the biggest national park in Japan by name *Daisetsuzan*, with 573,000 acres, and the longest river, the Ishikari, with a course of 250 miles before it enters the Sea of

Japan, and it has big dairy farms, Wisconsin style, and big sheep farms with thousands of sheep grazing on wide plains. Only in one major respect, its intense volcanic activity, does it seem to match or surpass the other islands, for it has a great many hot springs and hells and among its volcanoes is one, by name *Showa Shinzan*, which burst from a vegetable field in 1944, exactly in the manner of Mexico's famous Paricutín, and built itself up in a single year to a height of 1300 feet and is still climbing, though far more slowly.

From a traveler's viewpoint most of Hokkaido is an escapist's island even more than balmy Shikoku, yet there are interesting places that can be very comfortably visited and whereas the train-and-ferry journey (to Sapporo) consumes a formidable and tiring twenty-six hours, JAL's efficient air services can fly us to them from Tokyo in a matter of three hours. So let's see what they are, maybe confining ourselves, for the purpose of this brief report, to the two or three most popular goals.

Sapporo, a Capital Born of America

Ninety years ago, Hokkaido's 30,000 square miles were a barren wilderness and its capital, now a flourishing city of 450,000 inhabitants, eighth in size in Japan, didn't exist at all except as a frontier village, but then Japan, awakening with a start from her isolation and then spurred by the progressive spirit of the Meiji Restoration, made a bold move. The Japanese government invited American engineers and agricultural experts to take over this wilderness and see what they could do with it. They accepted and they did big things, worthy of the challenge. The most conspicuous of these pioneers was Mr. Horace Capron, an agricultural technician selected and sent over by President Grant. He taught eager Japanese farmers the American methods of large-scale farming to convert waste land into fields and gardens, and he also laid out the plan of Sapporo, with its broad boulevards intersecting each other at right angles, a strange novelty in the Orient.

Another American pioneer was Professor W. G. Clark, who took up a teaching position—conducting his courses in English—in what has become the important *University of Hokkaido*, with 5000 students, 10 faculties and several research institutes, including a famous underground laboratory for the study, appropriately enough, of Low-Temperature Science, meaning COLD. I mention Professor Clark because we "encounter" him on the road that leads from Chitose Airport, where our plane from Tokyo has touched down, to Sapporo. At a point about halfway between the airport and the capital there is a fifteen-foot granite pillar with a greened bronze plaque affixed to it bearing his name, his face, wreathed in its 19th-century whiskers, the date, April 10, 1877, and the cryptic words BOYS, BE AMBITIOUS. It seems that when Clark made his final departure from Sapporo, hardly for Chitose Airport but for a port on the island's south coast, his admiring students accompanied him en masse. At this point of the road (now a splendid U.S.-built boulevard), 14 miles from Sapporo, Clark halted them, gave them a farewell pep talk and concluded with the three words that appear on the monument. To you and me this sculptured plea may not seem in the least original or stirring, but the point of this tale is that they have become a stimulating slogan. Clark's boys grew up and *were* ambitious, as their sons and grandsons are today. Many of the leading men adopted the Christian faith and to them and their progeny Professor Clark became almost an island saint, or at least an apostle of progress. Another statue to him, bearing the same three words, stands on the campus of the university.

Because Hokkaido is cold it prepares for its weather, as the Scandinavian lands do and as Italy-in-winter does not, so you need have no fear of being cold when you tie up to your tourist moorings, presumably in the topflight *Sapporo Grand Hotel*. In this hotel I have had some of the best Western-type meals that I have enjoyed in Japan, for not only is the beef excellent in Hokkaido but there are various northern specialties, notably giant crabs, that one doesn't often encounter in Honshu. There is the giant *wakkanai* crab, for instance, a Goliath of his race, who flourishes only in cold waters, but has flesh as tender as a gourmet's dream; and there are the equally delicious varieties of "hairy crab" known as *kegani*. Hokkaido grows a great deal of fine asparagus, but this may be hard to come by, since the island's ambitious boys export much of it to the United States.

The sights of Sapporo are few and not too demanding of our time, for this is a new city and it is the new American-influenced life of it that chiefly attracts us, but there are some things that need seeing. The *University* is one of them, its buildings surrounded by so many stately elms that it has won the nickname of Elms University. The *Okura Schanze* is another sight and this may surprise you, for it is the highest and best constructed ski jump (*Schanze* is German-Austrian-Swiss for ski jump) in the Orient. There are splendid parks such as *Maruyama* and *Naka-jima*—in the latter an annual skating carnival is held in February—there's a *baseball stadium*, where the Yankees and Dodgers have played, and, perhaps of more interest than anything else, there's a *Botanical Garden*, with a museum that features the life and habits of the Hairy Ainus and also of Hokkaido's shaggy brown bears, some real bears being on display in dens just outside the building.

In the evening you should certainly see the *Street of the Badgers* (*Tanukikoji*), which is Sapporo's entry in the national Evening Fun Street Competition. On a frigid late-May evening when the temperature was in the 40's and I was clad for the climate of Honshu I walked the full length of this street, a good half mile, and was so fascinated by its roaring life, its bright, wide-open shops, its noisy pachinko dens, its restaurants and bars and Americanesque girls, that I actually forgot to shiver.

A group of Sapporo businessmen, ambitious boys every one, took me into one of the numerous nightspots and thereby gave me a memorable evening. It was a pleasant little upstairs place called *Bar Gold* and no sooner had we seated ourselves than a bevy of pretty hostesses descended upon us. "Here they come," I said to myself, "the Yen-Diggers' Drinking Sorority," but I was in for the surprise of my tour, for these girls *didn't drink*.

That's what I said, they didn't drink—not even cokes. They merely sat beside us, looking demure and pretty, and talking—in Japanese. I learned that the management, eschewing for his girls the usual names ending in *ko*, had christened each one with an American name, so our hostesses were Alice, Betty, Nancy, Annie and—Scarlett. I asked my friends if the management wouldn't do me the high honor to name two of his girls for my two grand-daughters, Mardi and Laurie. They passed the message along to him and he to the girls and they were more than glad to accommodate, though they could not quite abandon the names by which they were already known to the bar's customers, so Scarlett became Scarlett-Mardi and Annie became Annie-Laurie. The former, who was the head girl of the quintet, posted herself at the door when she saw that we were about to leave and as I passed her she gave me a radiant smile, bowed from the waist, and declaimed: "My name Scarlett-Mardi." Following her lead, Annie said sweetly: "My name Annie-Laurie."

It must not be thought the Bar Gold is typical of Sapporo's nightspots, for the Great Ulterior Motive of quick gain is prevalent in this city's night as it is in all night cities of the world, but the management of this particular den conceived the unique and novel idea of *not* fleecing the customers. Moreover, all of his girls are of good family, most of them working at daytime jobs but wishing to supplement their meager earnings with extra evening wages. At 11:30 promptly, the Bar Gold closes and the manager sends his girls straight home in taxis. The amazing spirit of this pleasant retreat makes me proud to have my granddaughters represented in the night life of Sapporo!

A Halt at Shiraoi, for Its Aboriginal Ainus

Almost every Westerner who visits Hokkaido wants to see some if its mysterious aborigines, the Hairy Ainus, who are thought by most ethnologists to have entered Japan from the north, presumably from Siberia by the stepping stone of Sakhalin

Island. Of the 10,000 or so persons in Hokkaido with enough
aboriginal blood in them to be officially rated as Ainus a considerable number live in four villages, Shiraoi, Chikabumi, Otofuke
and Fushiko. Of these villages, the first-named is by far the
easiest to visit, since it is a halt on the railway line leading from
Sapporo to Noboribetsu, Hokkaido's leading spa, and is only 12
miles short of that spa's station.

Shiraoi Village is for the most part a Japanese fishing village,
with many long and narrow fishing boats always to be seen in
the water or drawn up on the beach, but about ten minutes walk
to the east is the *Ainu Settlement*, whose people also make their
living from fishing, though tourist trade is now a strong com-
petitor. One could wish it were possible for Westerners to visit
the Ainus naturally rather than touristwise, paying a fee—200 to
300 yen is the customary gratuity for a small group—yet one
cannot blame the Ainus for capitalizing themselves as curiosities
and actually they are very gentle and courteous about it rather
than "grabby" or venal.

The patriarch of Shiraoi, at least so far as tourism is concerned,
is one Ikashima Toku, who has adopted, for business purposes, the
easier name Miyamoto, and he lives with his wife in a substantial
though gloomy hut standing near the main highway. This patriarch once visited San Francisco and boasts of it with shining
pride.

In the interior of the hut we find "Mrs. Miyamoto" and we
discern, even in the dim light, that she wears the traditional
badge of a married Ainu woman, a *painted mustache*. Formerly,
the Ainu matrons had this proud badge of their connubial status
tattooed on the lip but some years ago the squeamish Japanese
government forbade this practice, so now the women have to
resort to make-up. Anyway, the mustachioed wife of Miyamoto
squats on her heels on the floor and explains, in Japanese, the
customs of Ainu life, at the same time displaying Ainu products
for sale. Yes, the visit is tourist-commercialized, of course, but it
is interesting, for all that. You'll enjoy seeing this mild, wide-

eyed, hirsute, Russianesque couple and their smiling daughters and after the visit you may stroll about the Settlement and along the boat-lined beach.

The Bodies of Noboribetsu, Clad in Steam

Noboribetsu, on Hokkaido's southern coast, has one of Japan's greatest displays of volcanic hells and also, beyond all competition, its greatest display of bodies. We'll come to the bodies presently, but first let's take a look at the spa itself, its hotels and inns and its tourist sights.

The spa, located 5 miles inland from the railway station and reached by bus or taxi, has surely the largest assemblage of hotels and inns in Hokkaido, for it lives solely on its transient visitors and even the surrounding communities consist largely of inns. The leading and impressive goal for Western tourists is the *Noboribetsu Grand Hotel,* with thirteen rooms of Western style and fifty-five of Japanese style, some very luxurious, and of course it has its own pool of ever-flowing hot mineral water and many private baths with the same abundant flow. But by far the largest hotel, with the largest pool, is the *Dai-ichi Takimoto,* a strictly Japanese inn where you may well prefer to stay. Other inns, myriads of them, are all over the place.

The *Grand Hell of Noboribetsu,* reached from the Grand Hotel by a 10-minute uphill stroll past the big inn, past a new public bathing hall and past the *Hotsprings Institute,* a branch of Hokkaido University, is a weird brown valley from which many columns and swirls of white steam are constantly ascending through vents of various sizes, but there are no real geysers here as in Beppu. Above the Grand Hell, at a point reached by a stiff climb, or more lazily by taxi, is a viewpoint pleasantly backed by a clump of white birches, from which you may look down, and very far down, to a pair of hot lakes, one large one, whose temperature is just at the boiling point, and a much smaller one, whose temperature is 230 degrees Fahrenheit. On the larger one you'll probably see a scow dredging up sulphur, its unfortunate crew being quite literally in hell, or on it. The smaller lake, which is immediately under the viewpoint, at the base of a sheer cliff, is said to be very alluring to would-be suicides, especially, for some reason unfathomable by Westerners, in spring. To despondent Japanese there seems to be something rather grand and praiseworthy in "ending it all" in so romantic and dashing a manner. A guide who accompanied me to this viewpoint said that only a fortnight previously he had *seen* a young woman, presumably lovelorn, hurl herself into this hottest of hells!

* * *

The best time to take a hotspring bath in one of the pools of Noboribetsu is late afternoon or early evening and the best place is certainly the outsize bathing hall of the Dai-ichi Takimoto, for this is called and must, I think, actually be the largest bathing hall in the world, since at least 200 persons can comfortably sog in its waters at one time. It is not a single large pool, as in the Grand Hotel and most other Japanese baths and spa hotels, but a series of lesser pools of varying mineral solutions and widely varying temperatures, some *very* hot.

In discussing Atami, in Chapter 9, I have presented a general picture of how mixed nude bathing works out in Japanese spas and I need not spin out this exotic topic here, but the bathing hall of Dai-ichi Takimoto is unique even in Japan and a few embellishing comments do seem in order. In the case of this vast establishment males and females disrobe at opposite ends of the bath, but then they enter the steamy hall and become one happy family. At various points there are small circular washing installations, around whose rims bathers meticulously soap and rinse themselves, for this is the cleanly and invariable Japanese custom, before entering any pool for a pleasant soak. The soapers and rinsers consist of individuals of both sexes, of mixed groups, of couples, especially honeymoon couples, for Noboribetsu rivals Atami as the Niagara Falls of Japan, and of whole families. Near

me, as I industriously soaped and rinsed, I noticed a group consisting obviously of mother, auntie and two teen-agers, a boy
and a girl. Mother and auntie were talking a mile a minute, while
brother and sister, or maybe they were cousins, chatted less
animatedly but in a friendly and utterly natural manner. They
just weren't interested in each other's nudity, not one bit.

The same thing was true of a group of teen-age schoolboys
and teen-age schoolgirls who entered while I was there. There
must have been thirty boys and at least twice as many girls and
it was plain that the boys tended to herd by themselves, indulg-
ing in lots of horseplay, and the girls also by themselves, racing
about with happy squeals from pool to pool. Neither camp
seemed able to give much of any attention to the other, and this,
I suppose, is the grand talking point of earnest nudists. What is
common, what you see every day, ceases to be provocative,
whereas a plunging neckline or a wind-blown skirt can have more
impact than an all-naked body.

After I emerged from the bath hall and had dressed and gone
up to the lobby of the Dai-ichi Takimoto I encountered three
uniformed schoolgirls of perhaps thirteen or fourteen years who
accosted me and were obviously quivering to try out on me their
choicest phrases of English. I asked them if they had been in the
pool and they nodded assent. I couldn't possibly have recognized
them from among so many, but for them it was easy to recognize
me, an obvious foreigner and presumably an American. We had
been bathing together and now we were chatting together, so
what? They were typically eager, smiling, pleasant-spoken children and I said within myself, "More power to you, for of such
is the future of Nippon."

YOURSELF IN THE PICTURE OF MANILA

CHAPTER 13

A SOJOURN WITH SOLID FRIENDS

The Pan Am Approach via Wake and Guam

THIS book, being chiefly about Japan, has discussed Japan first, but actually the course, all by Pan American Airways, that led me to that country was a roundabout one, shaped something like a fishhook, which proved to be well-advised and full of special rewards. After a halt in Hawaii it took me to *Wake, Guam* and *Manila,* then, by curving around, to *Hong Kong* and finally up to the fishhook's point, *Tokyo.*

Wake and Guam, on each of which islands the PAA planes halt for about an hour en route to Manila, may be only minor rewards of the course but each has its own historic interest and on each the passenger has time to stroll about, though not too far, for at least half an hour after enjoying cold fruit juices and light refreshments "on the house." Before landing on each island your PAA hostess will give you a company leaflet telling you something about it.

In the case of Wake, the leaflet gives a considerable story about what has happened there and who was associated with the happenings. Wake is named for Captain William Wake of the British schooner *Prince William Henry,* who is credited with discovering it, though actually it is known that a Spaniard named Alvara de Mendana had visited it in the 16th century and called it San Francisco. Wake's high point of drama prior to its involvement in World War II came in 1866, when the German barque *Libelle,* bound for Hong Kong with a cargo of gold bullion and quicksilver, ran aground on a reef and broke up. Twenty-one survivors set out in a small boat for Guam and finally reached that haven after a perilous journey of eighteen days, but another small boat containing Captain Tobias and seven members of his crew disappeared into the blue and its passengers were never heard of again. The fabulous treasure is supposed to have been cached "somewhere" on Wake, but if you're in transit you'll hardly have time to find it and in any case you'll be asked not to stroll too far from the snack bar building. Wake is an isolated island, not a part of any group, and quite without a native population. It became a formal possession of the United States in 1899, when Commander Taussig of the *U.S.S. Bennington* held a flag-raising ceremony here and gave the island a 21-gun salute. In World War II it played its hard and tragic role, which need not be dwelt on here.

The Pan American folder on Guam presents the needed travel pointers but, unlike the one on Wake, gives no account of island history and glamours. However, "I can reveal" (to borrow Drew Pearson's punch line) that Guam is the largest island of the Marianas; that it has an area of 225 square miles and, in sharp contrast to Wake, a population of some 25,000 Guamanians, who are an island people as distinct as Okinawans or Hawaiians; and that, by the Treaty of Paris, Spain ceded it to the United States in December, 1898. Like Wake it was a scene of gruesome carnage during World War II. The most interesting thing about it for those air travelers who make the short halt here en route to Manila is the opportunity to glimpse such Guamanians as happen to be at the airport. They are a sturdy-looking lot, with fine, light-chocolate skins.

The formalities of landing at Manila International Airport are set forth in yet another of Pan Am's "advance leaflets," which reveals a lot of important things, but fails to mention "Mabuhay." That interesting word, pronounced "Maboohigh," is the Filipino greeting, toast and farewell, being quite as comprehensive and quite as beautiful as Hawaii's more familiar Aloha. Philippine requirements may seem a bit formidable in print, but they are mild enough in practice. First you have to make a declaration of the currency and cash you carry, and this is important, since it will enable you, upon your departure, to change back into dollars any unspent Philippine pesos. Then you have, of course, to go to the immigration desk to present your passport, *with visa*, secured at a Philippine consulate, and finally through the customs formalities, but if your stay is to be less than two months you'll find the formalities cursory and you'll be exempted from the Philippine Head Tax. Once through the barriers, you may wish to relax for a few minutes with a cold drink in the air-conditioned coffee shop and take a peek at the busy airport itself, for busy it certainly is. This Far East crossroads of air travel is the major link uniting Europe and Asia on the west with the two American continents on the east and both with the South Pacific, Australia and New Zealand. There are nearly one hundred international flights a week to and from this airport, operated by some sixteen companies of nearly as many countries, and locally there are eighty flights a day to and from all parts of the Philippines by PAL (Philippine Air Lines). That system can be your travel "pal" indeed, for its services are quite as good, and as punctual as those of JAL, and in domestic travel more important, since Philippine rail service is limited in scope by its multitude of islands.

When you're ready to proceed into town you'll find limousine service to the chief hotels awaiting you, at a charge of a dollar a head, and after a ride of a mile to the edge of the bay and then four miles right along the shore on Dewey Boulevard there you are in the heart of the metropolis (population, 1,500,000), at the big, elliptical, four-part bayside park, around or near which all the chief hotels cluster, not to mention the American Embassy, which has a fine shorefront location.

The park's four parts, since I've mentioned them, are the big *United Nations Park*, with its Gateway-to-the-East Arch, beyond which is an impressive *"étoile"* of traffic; the *Old Luneta* (the park was originally shaped like a crescent moon, or luneta), with a monument to the national hero, José Rizal, who was executed on this spot by a Spanish firing squad in 1896; *Burnham Green,* on which faces the Manila Hotel; and the *New Luneta,* a sort of picnic area on made land stolen from the bay. In mentioning the swirl of traffic around the park's "star," which sends out five rays of traffic in as many directions, I should surely mention also the *jeepneys* that compose at least half of this traffic, for you've never, I'm sure, seen their like elsewhere, at least in such numbers. They are American military jeeps that outlived their usefulness for our Armed Forces and have been converted—others are still being converted—into public jitneys. They are all privately owned and each owner-driver attempts to outdo his competitors in fancifully painting and dolling up his "mount." These gaily caparisoned vehicles, each bearing its painted name—Roland, Juliet, Baby Rose, Marilynn, Dear Jesus, Happy Days, Strongheart—roam central and suburban Manila in thousands, adding impressive color and sparkle to what would otherwise be ordinary dull motor traffic. The jeepneys travel regular routes, selected by the various owner-drivers, and the chief destinations are soaped onto the windshields or otherwise indicated by painted signs.

Your Anchorage and Some First Facts

The *Manila Hotel,* handsomely situated with very broad frontage both on Burnham Green and on the bay itself, is the queen of Philippine hotels, and just between you and me a queen-*hôtelière* runs the vast place. I registered, secured an air-conditioned room facing the bay, washed up and then came down to the long, breeze-swept lobby, which is always chock full of social and business life, quite apart from guests and tourist life. As I was passing through the lobby I was greeted by a very lovely young lady seemingly about thirty years of age, who said, "Oh, Mr. Clark, how do you do? Welcome to Manila. You're one of my children now." I was pleasantly shocked, puzzled, nonplussed, dumbfounded, for I simply didn't know who this charming apparition was, but I managed to pull myself together and suggest, to cover my confusion, "Wouldn't it be more probable

that I'm one of your grandfathers?" We chatted for a minute
or two and as soon as I had left her I surreptitiously asked one
of the staff "Who *is* that young lady, please?" He answered
"Why that's our manager, sir, Mrs. Zamora." And so I became
one of the children—let's call me that—of Mrs. Cielito ("Little
Heaven") Zamora. I learned that her husband Mariano and she
together own the Bay View Hotel, a good one on Dewey Boulevard, and that they have a long-term lease on the Manila Hotel,
which she manages. He is the financier, she the astute practical
executive and dispenser of personality.

Well anyway—the Manila Hotel is a city in itself, quite in
the manner of Tokyo's Imperial. It has 265 rooms and baths
and an additional building, under construction, will contain 450
air-conditioned rooms, each with bath. Many of the present
rooms have air-conditioning and they all have a radio and music-
without-commercials, meaning Muzak. If your radio is like the
ones I've had on two stays you press Button E—there's no sign
to explain this—if you want good music without obstructing
plugs. The hotel has a post office, a travel agency, various airline
offices, various fine shops, these in a shopping center called
Plazita Zamora, an open-air swimming pool on the lawn beside
the bay, and dining rooms galore. Among these last are the main
dining room, called the Petal Room because of its murals of
Philippine flowers, serving American and European food; the
Winter Garden for dining-and-dancing; the Fiesta Pavilion (now
undergoing reconstruction); the Moongate Room, serving first-
rate Chinese food that is to be eaten with chopsticks, and the
Bamboo Room, serving Philippine food in fabulous variety; plus
a lot of luxuriously decorated smaller rooms (Candle Room,
Bell Room, Fan Room, Dao Room, Tindale Room, etc.) for
private parties.

The fare in the Bamboo Room is particularly intriguing, and
of course appropriate to the country, since each item on the à
la carte menu, the table d'hôte menu and the list of Daily Spe-
cials is printed in the Tagalog language as well as English. Here,

for instance, is a luncheon menu that I enjoyed: *Manok Sa Sotanghon* (Chicken with Rice Noodles); *Relyenong Talong* (Stuffed Eggplant); *Acharra* (Native Salad); *Leche Flan* (Egg Custard); *Kape o Tsa* (Coffee or Tea).

All sorts of events go on in this hotel, for it is one of Manila's principal centers of social life, and wedding dinners are frequent, while for the guests there are, of course, dances and fiestas; and just in case you'd like a "wee drappie" now and then you'll find the Jungle Bar as cool and dim, even on the hottest noon, as a shady mountain glen. There's a waterfall in its dim recesses to add to the illusion.

Other hotels in Manila are richly worthy of mention, including the Zamora-owned *Bay View*, with 135 rooms, many air-conditioned, and an air-conditioned lobby and dining room.

The newest hotel (until the Manila's Annex is completed) and certainly one of the very best of them all, is the *Filipinas*, an ultra-modern, completely air-conditioned establishment on Dewey Boulevard. With its patio swimming pool, its Golden Lotus Restaurant, its Blue Room, its Green Room, its Sampaguita Coffee Room, named for the Philippine national flower, its cool cocktail lounge and its Celebrity Nightclub, it has just about every luxury and refinement that an exigent tourist could wish.

Other recommendable places, all close together on Dewey Boulevard, are the *Swiss Inn*, small but good; the *Shellborne*, with its Rose Room for meals; and the old-fashioned *Luneta*, still popular as a place of family type. There are, of course, some lesser hotels, but I think this lengthening list is quite enough. Manila is warm-to-hot the year around and in such a climate few American visitors are willing to economize in their choice of lodgings.

* * *

Now for some first facts, set forth alphabetically, as in the case of Japan—but "before the first" you'll want to know about the tourist setup in Manila. Briefly this is the story:

The TRAVEL CENTER, with offices in the modern Shurdut Building in the historic center of Manila called Intramuros, three minutes by taxi from the hotels, is your wellspring of information about Manila and the provinces. Here you'll find the *Philippine Tourist and Travel Association* (PTTA), headed by two very able and experienced men, Modesto Farolan, who is Commissioner of Tourism and president of the PTTA (also he was the first elective president of the Pacific Area Travel Association), and Salvador Peña, who is the executive director of the PTTA. The doors of the Travel Center are wide open to welcome you and answer all questions. (I have mentioned in Chapter 1 the new *Philippine Travel Information Office* in San Francisco, at 153 Kearny Street and I should state here that a similar office has also been opened in Honolulu.)

A 300-page book called *Philippine Industry and Trade*, half of it devoted to "Travel and Tourism," is published by the Department of Commerce and Industry but unless you're making a real study of the Philippines you'll find this volume too bulky to tote around. Of more practical use is a pocket folder brought out and distributed by the PTTA called *Manila and The Philippines at a Glance*. Its glance covers a surprising range of pertinent facts well set forth, and on the back there's a clear map of Manila. You may pick up this handy guide—it is almost that despite its small size—before starting on your travels at all by contacting the Pacific Area Travel Association in San Francisco. (See the opening paragraphs of this book.)

And now our "alphabet."

Climate and Clothing. Manila is hot (average year-round temperature 80 degrees) and it is humid (65 to 98 per cent), so you should "act accordin'," but the almost constant sea breeze substantially tempers the heat in all the bayside hotel area and all along that artery of tourism, Dewey Boulevard. The dry season, when it's a little less hot and a good deal less humid, is from early November through March. April, May and June are the hottest months, and then the rains come, but only intermittently, not as in the play *Rain*.

You should, of course, dress as for hot weather at home, meaning *hot*, not warm. For men there's a wonderful Philippine garment called the *barong-tagalog*, which is a thin shirt worn outside the trousers. The barong-tagalog submits to very fancy frills and embroideries and it is equally suitable for daytime wear and—praised be common sense—for dressy evening functions, *without* any coat. I know of no garment anywhere of such "fashion catholicity." More and more American visitors, even short-stayers, are adopting this sensible and good-looking type of shirt. Shops everywhere, including those in Plazita Zamora, sell the barong-tagalog. Philippine women of fashion very often wear the charming *mestiza dress* (though it is now thought of almost as a national costume) at evening affairs and it's a lovely thing to behold, with interesting "butterfly wings" at the shoulders. One wishes American society would adopt it for summer wear. It flatters any wearer who is blessed with reasonably slender build, as most Filipinas are.

Electrical Appliances. Bring along your electric razor. The voltage is not the same as at home, but the leading hotels in Manila provide transformers as an expected part of their service. This, at any rate, I have found to be the case in the Manila Hotel.

Food and Drink. American food is served as a matter of course in all the leading hotels of Manila and the provinces. Rice is a staple of Philippine fare, but there are, of course, some fascinating meat dishes. *Lechon*, for instance, is roast suckling pig; and the popular *adobo* is mixed chicken, pork and beef. These two are the national dishes and you'll find them served at their best in such resort inns as the Taal Vista Lodge (see description hereinafter) at Tagaytay. Adobo is flavored with garlic so keep your distance for a while after eating it. *Sincamas* is a plant root something like the humble turnip and I have found it very good when garnished with a vinegar and sugar dressing. *Mangoes* (in spring and summer) and *lanzones* (September to Christmas) are favorite fruits and there's a thick breakfast jam, called *mangosteen* that you devour—crunch-crunch—large seeds and all. I balked when I first saw the formidable seeds in it, half an inch long, but a Filipino table mate said "Oh, go on. Sink your teeth in them, like peanuts. You'll love the stuff." I did—and I did.

The drinking water of Manila is good and perfectly safe. Philippine beer is wonderfully good, and how kind to your throat when served frost-cold. *San Miguel Pale Pilsen* is exported in quantity to many countries of the Orient and some of it even finds its way to the United States. Philippine rum is good, especially such favored brands as *Manila, Añejo* and *Tanduay*, though less famous than the rums of Cuba and Jamaica. A refreshing cold drink called *calamansi*, made from limes, can be as kind to your throat as San Miguel beer.

Language. The official national language of the Philippine Republic, as I've said in the Foreword, is English (spoken in the American manner), though most Manilans speak also both Spanish and the native Tagalog (accent on the penult). Interestingly enough, this makes the Philippine Republic, which consists of 22,000,000 inhabitants on 700 islands, the third most populous English-speaking country in the world, following the United States and the United Kingdom. "The coming of the English language [with the U.S. occupation after the Spanish-American War] was providential," said a Filipino educator to me. "It has been the cement to bind our nation together, for things were very difficult, language-wise, before that. Although Tagalog is called the national native language, it is not too widespread and actually our people spoke, and still speak, many different languages, up to seventy in all, in different areas on different islands, such languages as Sugbuanon, Hiligaynon, Pampangan and Iloko, to name a few, and without some common medium they couldn't understand each other. Spanish never was able to bridge these gaps, but English spread everywhere through the educational methods introduced by the American administration and it has been the exclusive medium of school and university education now for nearly six decades. We should be eternally grateful that we acquired this binding language." And we visitors *are* grateful that we can speak our own tongue everywhere in the Philippines instead of coping with Spanish or the local dialects.

The *name* of these islands was bequeathed to them by Magellan in 1521, when he landed on Cebu. He was a native of Portugal but had been engaged by Spain to make this voyage of discovery in Spain's name. He erected a cross—it is claimed that a cross now standing in the main plaza of Cebu City, enshrined within a larger cross, is the very one he set up—then planted a red and gold standard of the Royal House of Spain and named these newly found islands *Filipinas*, for Don Felipe, who was later to become King Philip II.

Money. Philippine money is at present entirely of the folding kind, even the unit of 5 centavos, which is 2½ cents U.S. The peso, or Philippine dollar, is pegged by stringent financial legislation at 50 cents U.S. In other words, you get an even two pesos in exchange for a dollar. This rate is artificial, and puts too high a value on the peso, at least in the view of dollar-visitors. The result is that the cost of almost everything concerned with travel is high, *too* high, and I would be doing the reader a disservice to say otherwise, but I suppose it's all a matter of comparison. Prices in general are no higher than in the States, so it's only if you've been spoiled by the very favorable exchange rate in certain foreign lands that those of the Philippines will seem unduly high.

Photography. Manila is photo-conscious and you'll find plenty of shops with both black-and-white and color films. Developing and printing can be about as quickly and well done as in the States.

Religion. Most Filipinos are of the Roman Catholic faith, but religious tolerance is a basic feature of the law and Protestant churches of various denominations are to be found, at least in Manila. There is also a Jewish synagogue.

Take Pride in Reflection

In this swiftly moving report I shall not attempt to present even a thumbnail history of the Philippines, but it does seem important that even the transient visitor should be aware of what the country means to us and, in frank pride, of what our country has meant and does mean to the Filipinos. Here is that story, in the smallest nutshell.

In 1896, General Emilio Aguinaldo led a formidable Filipino rebellion against Spanish rule. Eight provinces of Luzon were chiefly concerned in it and they are permanently memorialized in the present red-while-and-blue flag of the Philippine Republic, which has a red stripe below and a blue stripe above, the inner ends of these stripes opening to form two sides of an equilateral white triangle. The third side is against the flagpole or cord. At each angle of the triangle is a star, the three symbolizing the three geographic groups that comprise the Philippines, namely Luzon, the Visayas and Mindanao, while the center of the triangle is filled by a sun with eight rays, for the eight provinces that rebelled.

In April, 1898, the short Spanish-American War commenced and on May 1 of that year Commodore, later Admiral, George Dewey destroyed the main Spanish squadron under Admiral Montojo in Manila Bay. Manila, as we've seen, has named its fine shore boulevard for Dewey. Aguinaldo, who had been exiled to Hong Kong by the Spaniards, returned to the Philippines in an American vessel.

On August 13, 1898, Spain lost Manila to the United States and the war quickly came to an end, but, most unhappily, friction between the heroic Filipino rebels and their American allies soon led to a Filipino-American War, which finally ended with the capture of Aguinaldo in 1901 and the full surrender of the scattered rebel forces the following year.

On July 4, 1901, William Howard Taft was inaugurated Civil Governor of the Islands and a policy of constructive Filipino-

American collaboration was instituted. By this the Philippine government was to be "Filipinized" as rapidly as possible. In 1916, the U.S. Congress passed the Jones Law—a prominent traffic bridge in Manila now bears the name Jones—whose preamble promised ultimate independence to the Philippines, though no date was then fixed.

In 1933, the U.S. Congress voted full independence to the Philippines, this not to take effect, however, until ten years after the establishment of the Commonwealth of the Philippines.

On November 15, 1935, the Commonwealth *was* inaugurated, following approval by President Franklin D. Roosevelt of a newly drawn up Philippine Constitution and its ratification by the Philippine electorate.

On December 8, 1941 (December 7 by U.S. time), Japan's airmen invaded the Philippines as well as Hawaii and the Japanese-American part of World War II was on.

On April 9, 1942, Bataan fell, and on May 6, Corregidor. The horror of the Death March occurred.

On October 20, 1944, General MacArthur "returned," effecting a landing on Leyte Island. Three days later the Philippine Commonwealth Government was re-established under President Osmeña.

On February 3, 1945, the U.S. forces entered Manila and shortly after that the public administration of the city was turned over to the Commonwealth government.

On July 4, 1946, the present Republic of the Philippines was inaugurated, with Manuel A. Roxas as its first president. Roxas was succeeded by Elpidio Quirino and he by Ramon Magsaysay, in 1953.

The Magsaysay Era was a very great one for Philippine-American relations and for the whole of the Free World. Magsaysay was a tower of strength against Communism, brilliantly defeating the dangerous Communist-led Huk Rebellion and establishing a firm and progressive government notably

friendly to the West. The Philippines came to be thought of
everywhere as freedom's Far-Eastern Bastion.

On March 17, 1957, a few months before his term as president would have run out, Ramon Magsaysay died in a plane crash
on Mt. Manungal in Cebu and a wave of shocked consternation swept the Free World. But Philippine friendship and loyalty
to freedom proved not to be dependent on the prestige of one
man. These have continued and will unquestionably continue.
Magsaysay's elected successor, President Carlos P. Garcia, is an
avowed friend of the West, and Vice-President Diosdado Maca-
pagal is an equally strong and dependable friend. He was not
running on the same ticket with Garcia but was of an opposition
party and the fact that Philippine voters split the ticket to team
up two men of their choice is a most heartening proof of the
political maturity of the electorate.

So much for the steppingstones to the present, but why and
wherein should we take pride in reflection? Here are some reasons.
We *did*, if a bit haltingly, grant the Philippines genuine independence, which a Communist country, with its standard take-
all-and-hold-all policy would not conceivably have done, and
by and large we pioneered in administering the country to such
effect that Filipino life today reflects our life in many facets, and
no matter what fleeting clouds may pass over our mutual relationship our basic two-way friendship is as firm and fixed as
anything can be in this murky world. America pioneered in the
Philippines on a broad scale, in education, in science, in "budg-
etry" and in many other fields. Filipinos of standing sometimes
like to remind us that many of our great figures had their roots
in the Philippines. They call the Bureau of Science of the Philippines the "incubator," in which many ideas and theories were
hatched and then put into pioneering practice. Leonard Wood,
John Pershing, George Marshall, Douglas MacArthur and Dwight
Eisenhower (as a young man) developed roots, these Filipino
commentators tell us, in the Philippines, and William Cameron
Forbes, of Boston, built the highway system of the Islands. Fili-

pinos refer to him, with whimsical affection, as William *Caminero* Forbes, the middle nickname meaning road-builder. One more well-known personage with roots in the Philippines should be mentioned here, namely Dr. Victor G. Heiser, whose widely read book *An American Doctor's Odyssey* is a saga of American public health work throughout the world, but primarily in the Philippines. Starting in Manila as a young sanitary inspector he rose to be Director of the Philippine Health Service.

Let's take a closer look at *education* as it has developed in the Philippines following the American lead and the coming of independence, for there's much that is pleasingly phenomenal about it. Education is *not* compulsory, yet the desire to secure it has become so general and so burningly eager that it is often referred to as a "national obsession" and the school administration is strained to its limits to cope with it. In a population of somewhat over 21,000,000 about 5,000,000 are enrolled in the country's schools and colleges, which means nearly *20 per cent*, an almost incredible ratio. There are 1500 municipalities in the country, of which 26 are chartered cities. There are, in all, 30,000 schools, which means that the *average* number of schools is 20 to each municipality. In the economy of the Republic *one-third* of the national budget is allocated to the school department. For higher education there are 10 universities in Manila alone and others throughout the country. The Far Eastern University has an enrollment of 30,000; the University of the East, 24,000; Santo Tomas, which is 25 years older than Harvard, 22,000; the University of the Philippines, which is the state university, attended by more and more students from other Asian lands, 17,000.

Two of Manila's universities are exclusively for women and are run by women, namely the Philippine Women's University and the Centro Escolar University, and even in legal, medical and technological studies the Filipinas take a prominent part. I once attended the graduation exercises of the coeducational FEATI, which letters stand for Far Eastern Technological Institute, and was utterly amazed at the number of young women who were called up to the platform to receive their diplomas and move the tassel on their mortarboards from right to left. Ninety per cent of those majoring in pharmacy were women, 60 per cent of those majoring in medicine and 20 per cent of those majoring in law, and the president of the Institute, who gave out the diplomas, was a woman. All the proceedings were in English, as was the inspirational address delivered by the President of the Republic. As an indication of the hold that the English language now has on the Philippine people it should be noted that six of Manila's daily papers, four being published in the morning and two in the afternoon, use the English language as their medium, whereas only two use Spanish. Two also use Tagalog, and there are others in Chinese, for the Chinese element is very strong in this city. Supporting the diffusion of news and entertainment by the papers are twelve broadcasting stations, grouped in three networks, and two television stations, broadcasting chiefly in English.

The Sightseer's City—and Environs

Manila's Intramuros section, which is still literally within ancient walls, though pierced by numerous roads, was the scene of Japan's last, desperate stand when the turning tide of war drove her troops out of the Philippines, and as a result the whole city took a beating from bombs and artillery such as few cities have ever experienced. Central Manila was almost totally destroyed, necessitating the rebuilding of it practically from scratch, one result of this, for tourism, being that many old landmarks, former sightseer's items, have largely or wholly disappeared from sight.

Guided tours (for arrangements consult your hotel or the Travel Center) usually head, first of all, for Intramuros, the city's historic heart. In it, in addition to such new-blood intruders as the Travel Center, are at least two places of tourist importance. One is old *Fort Santiago,* with the cell, now a sort of shrine, where José Rizal languished before being taken to the Luneta for execution, and with the post-war Tomb of the Unknown

Soldier. The other is *San Agustin Church,* which is the oldest stone church (built in 1599) in the Philippines and even, it is claimed, in all Asia. It somehow survived four devastating earthquakes and even, unimaginably, the cataclysm of World War II. You'll admire its peaceful and lovely cloister garden and you'll want to linger in its cool interior, where you'll notice, among other things, confessionals that enable the faithful to confess in English, Spanish, Tagalog or one of the other major Philippine languages. More importantly, you'll notice and admire the beautifully carved doors and pulpit of this church and the even more admirable molave choir stalls. This church has seen a lot of history and has made some of it. In its vestry the Spanish commander signed the terms of capitulation to the American forces on August 13, 1898.

Santo Tomas University, run by Dominican Fathers, is a tour feature, partly because of its gruesome associations with World War II, when its venerable halls were used by the Japanese as a concentration camp, but these are soon offset by a visit to the lovely and well-gardened *Malacañang Palace,* on the east bank of the River Pasig, which flows through the center of the city. This palace, very little damaged during the war, is the official residence of the President of the Republic and it accommodates also the Executive Offices, yet visitors, accompanied by a soldier guide, are allowed to visit not only the grounds but the luxurious and spacious interior. They are shown the marble-floored Social Hall; the magnificent Reception Hall, with three huge chandeliers valued at $250,000; the Ceremonial Hall; the State Dining Room, with a hardwood table 48 feet long that's so shiny you could use it as a mirror for shaving; and, adjacent to the main palace, an all-bamboo building erected by the Japanese when their commanding general was "in residence" here. In the palace park is a nice garden of orchids and also a small zoo, one of whose attractions is a white monkey named Pinkie.

Of course various other public buildings and parks are shown on the standard City Tour, but they need hardly be recounted here. Of more interest are some of the things, shown on other tours, on the perimeter of the city and just outside it. The following are some of them.

1. *Forbes Park*, which is the city's most fashionable and expensive residential quarter, with some notable millionaire homes. It is, of course, named for William "Caminero" Forbes, the road-builder.

2. The *Church of the Redemptorist Fathers*, interesting because confessions may be *written* in a note to the priest, who will state the penance in a letter of reply.

3. The *Church of San Pasquale Bailon*, which childless couples approach with an odd *dancing walk* "to get a baby."

4. Two churches in Old Quezon, an extremely modernistic Protestant church directly facing an extremely modernistic Catholic church, as if the two were daring each other to see which could excel in boldness.

5. *Quezon City*, lying two or three miles outside the northeastern limits of Manila, is of obvious importance, since the government of the Republic is to be transferred there within a few years, when the new government buildings are completed.

6. The *Balara Filters*, where Manila's water supply is purified. An attractive picnic ground has been created here, with swimming pools, dance halls and other features that enable thousands of Manilans to make merry on weekends.

7. The *Bamboo Pipe Organ of Las Piñas* is one of Manila's more celebrated sights, for it actually does consist of 714 pipes of bamboo, the largest one being 8 feet tall and 5 inches in diameter. This remarkable instrument, sounding more muted than the ordinary organ, was built in 1794 by Father Diego Cerra, a member of the Order of the Augustinian Recollects, and the enterprising father built it of this unique material because he simply could not find in the Islands the materials of which organs are normally built. Records of the Order show that he built another organ of the same material and had it shipped as a present to the Queen of Spain, but that one has been lost from the horizon of

tourism, so the Las Piñas organ, in the old village church by the
side of the road, remains as the sole testimonial to Father Cerra's
ingenuity.

*   *   *

Far enough from Manila to be considered one of the city's
more distant environs, yet within one hour by car, is a resort of
extraordinary interest, for the place has a checkered past and a
very appealing present. It is *Tagaytay Ridge*, due south of the
city, and the ridge rises 2250 feet directly above a volcano in a
lake, both named Taal. A volcano in a lake may seem rather a
paradox, like hot snow or a river flowing uphill, but Lake Taal
and Taal Volcano *are*, in combination, one of the strangest tricks
that Vulcan has played with the earth. The volcano rises, though
only two or three hundred feet, from an island in the middle of
Lake Taal, which is itself the crater of a much larger extinct
volcano—Tagaytay Ridge is a portion of its old rim—and within
the crater of the present volcano is a smaller lake of hot water,
so we have a lake in a crater in a lake in a crater, which begins
to sound like a rose is a rose is a rose.

Taal Volcano has been a terrible-tempered Mister Bang, erupt-
ing no less than eighteen times since records have been kept. The
last time was in 1911, when it quite literally blew its top in one of
the most violent of all its eruptions. Early in the morning of January 30 it had an appalling paroxysm, suddenly hurling aloft such
vast quantities of boiling water and volcanic ashes that 90 square
miles of land about it were ruined and 2000 persons lost their
lives. Perhaps Taal repented of this murderous outburst, for it
has been pretty quiet since 1911, so much so in fact, that brand
new pleasure resorts are now springing up on the low-level shores
of Lake Taal and even on the Taal Volcano Crater Island in the
lake.

In 1945, Tagaytay Ridge played a part in World War II, for
here, on February 3rd, the first landings of our 511th Parachute
Infantry Regiment were successfully achieved. Today, Tagaytay
Ridge is graced with a first-rate resort inn of cabin type, by name

Taal Vista Lodge, and you would do yourself a memorable favor by spending a day and a night here, though *not* on a weekend, when it is always crowded to the eaves, for it has only 8 cabañas, one 3-room cottage and 9 rooms in the main building. The Lodge maintains an excellent cuisine and, to repeat this from an earlier ·mention, this is a good place to experience *lechon* (roast suckling pig) and *adobo* (beef-chicken-pork), the two chief national dishes. Another Lodge delicacy is *lopu lopu,* a Lake Taal fish of rare flavor, with, however, an unfortunate name, for Lopu Lopu was the Filipino who killed Magellan when that intrepid explorer reached the Islands in his journey around the world.

Another resort of interest in the more distant environs of Manila, this one some 90 minutes distant by car, is *Los Baños,* on the southern shore of a large body of water called Laguna de Bay, whose level is only three feet higher than that of Manila Bay. Los Baños has been known since Spanish times for its mineral hotsprings, whose pleasant and curative waters are piped into the pools and private bathrooms of the modest hotels that cluster along the lake shore. One of the best of the bathing establishments, where you may swim in a hot pool and follow it by a refreshing cold shower, is *Lake View Resort,* run by a couple named Mr. and Mrs. Conrado Santa Romana.

At a little distance back from the shore, on the rising slopes of Mount Makiling, is the *Makiling National Park,* really a botanical garden of quality and wide range, in whose bosky depths are the buildings of the State University's College of Forestry, College of Agriculture and Central Experiment Station.

Bataan and Corregidor

Tales of horror hardly belong in a book devoted largely to pleasure travel, yet the names above cannot be omitted from a chapter on Manila. *Bataan,* to be geographical for a moment, is a peninsula jutting so far out into the South China Sea that it almost encloses Manila Bay. The bay is further enclosed, though with wide channels on either side, by the island of *Corregidor*, which got its name in Spanish times from the "Corrector" stationed here to check (correct) the papers of all incoming ships. It was at these two places, to restate what everyone knows, that the Filipino-American forces made their gallant last-ditch stand against the Japanese invaders in the spring of 1942 and it was from Bataan that the ghastly Death March of the captured troops from the point of the peninsula to Manila, a distance of 105 miles, was made, thousands dying from exhaustion and semi-starvation along the route of march.

Bataan surrendered on April 9, Corregidor, whose fortification had cost the United States $50,000,000, on May 6. The long, heroic stand before surrender may have seemed futile, but it delayed Japan's program of conquest so long—five months from the initial air attack in December, 1941—that it is often credited with having saved Australia from conquest and thus aiding materially to effect the ultimate turn of the tide.

Since the autumn of 1957 a daily ferry service has been operating to and from Corregidor and simple overnight accommodations on the island have been established. Arrangements can be made through the Travel Center to fly from Manila International Airport to Corregidor, with a landing on that island, and then to continue, in a wide circle over Bataan and back across the bay to Manila. Corregidor is a grim wreck today, of no military use in this new age of atomic and hydrogen bombs, but Bataan looks green and peaceful. Both areas have been designated National Shrines dedicated to "those who died here that we might live."

Baguio, the Mile-High Summer Capital

Baguio, less than an hour distant from the capital by PAL, which operates several flights a day, and only four or five hours by automobile, is to Manila what Petropolis is to Rio and, coming closer to our field, what the shores of Lake Chuzenji are to Tokyo. It is the summer capital of the diplomatic set, of the social

set, of the "tourist set," of all who can by any means manage
to get there. It is *cool* and it is thrillingly beautiful. It is brilliant
with wild flowers and with carefully nurtured garden flowers.
It is fragrant from cultivated mint beds and from extensive pine
forests, this being one of the very few places in the tropics where
pines flourish so abundantly. It is gay with life, including that
on a golf course, and rich in tempting things to buy, especially
in its bustling Central Market. If one can sensibly say of any
place, "It has everything," then surely one can say it of Baguio.

Records show that a Spaniard named Guillermo Galvey "discovered" Baguio and in later decades the Spanish authorities made
considerable efforts to develop it, but with negligible results. It
was the Americans who succeeded in developing it early in this
century, when an American landscape architect named D. H.
Burnham, for whom Manila's Burnham Green is named, drew up
plans for the resort, and you'll find abundant outcroppings of
U.S. life in Baguio today. The *U.S. Embassy Compound,* where
the ambassador has his summer residence, is handsomely located
on its own hilltop, with a stunning view of Luzon's mountains
in range after range finally growing dim with distance, and the
residence itself is a thing of beauty, its white plaster walls brightly
"painted" with purple bougainvillea. On another height is *Camp
John Hay Whitney,* the Far East's largest Recuperation Center,
and this too is gloriously located, with its own grand prospect.

There are many hotels in Baguio's animated center, the
Filipinas being one of the good ones, but the resort's best one,
appropriately named *The Pines,* is on a separate small knoll, not
far from the center. Those who know Yosemite's Ahwanee Inn
will find The Pines somewhat like it, for its large lobby has a
sort of rustic luxury and its Bontac Bar is sheathed with pine
bark. Its pleasant tearoom is named Kankakui and, oh, yes, its
public lavatories are clearly labeled Adam and Eve. The hotel's
former manager, an energetic young man with the interesting
name Augusto D. Resurrección, developed the place very effi-
ciently and was rewarded by being appointed Deputy Commis-

sioner of Tourism, assistant to Commissioner Farolan.

I've mentioned Baguio's Central Market and I would emphasize that this is a sight no visitor should miss, for it has tempting things typical of the region, things such as carved objects and implements in hardwoods and various items woven in "Ilocano cloth." The Market's most curious product is "everlasting flowers" in red, yellow and purple hues, a strange product of nature that grows in the Philippines *only* in these hills around Baguio. The flowers are supposed to last, without drooping, "forever," which seems rather a long time. The Market's most curious spectacle is that of the shoeshine boys, a dozen or more of them, shaking off the cares of life to *bury* themselves in a newly arrived batch of comic strips. If such a feast of entertainment comes to the boys while you are in the Market don't, for heaven's sake, request a shine. The chances are that they wouldn't hear you anyway.

Outside the Market and all around it are shops whose signs, some of them with Indonesian and East Indian names, reveal the cosmopolitan character of this resort and now and then, though more often on the open roads than in the crowded center, you'll encounter primitive Igorots, for the mountains of northern Luzon are Igorot country. The men of the tribe wear *nothing* but the slimsiest loincloth.

Among the sights and viewpoints of Baguio don't miss the conspicuous *Mansion House*, with its handsome crescent of terraced gardens; the *Dominican Hill*, with a Dominican monastery on it; and, above all, the belvedere called *Mines View Point*. From here you look far, far down at the gold mines, which are still worked to some extent, and out and over to endless miles of forested hills. Of all the viewpoints in and around Baguio, Mines View Point is, I think, the undebatable best.

*   *   *

Philippine Air Lines can take you to a lot of interesting and exotic places in this country of many islands if you have the time for explorations farther afield. *Mayon Volcano,* just for instance, rising 8000 feet from near Legaspi, in the province of Albay, must surely be the world's most perfect volcanic cone, for it is absolutely without flaw, no matter from what angle it is viewed, and in this respect it outranks even Fujiyama. From Mayon's flanks and base, as from the areas around Fuji, gush many hotsprings. Legaspi is near the southern tip of Luzon, which island is to the Philippines what Honshu is to Japan, but there are many large islands, with exotic travel goals, south of Luzon, culminating in Mindanao, which is exceeded in area only by Luzon.

Some goals for you to inquire about at the Travel Center and from PAL are *Tacloban City,* on Leyte, to whose Red Beach MacArthur "returned" in 1944, a memorial now marking the spot; *Calapan,* on Mindoro, with a look at the marine gardens of *Puerta Galera; Cebu City,* with a launch trip to nearby *Mactan Island,* where Magellan met his death; and certainly *Zamboanga,* the very colorful home of the Moros, on a southwestern peninsula of Mindanao. But this chapter is supposed to limit itself to Manila and points near it, so I will call a halt to these rambling suggestions.

Back to Manila, Its Shops, Its Restaurants, Its Sports, Its Nights

I've been straying a good bit yet haven't shown you in detail the pleasure facets of Manila, so let's take a plunge into the four-ply subject of pleasure in shopping, eating around, sport and night gaieties.

Most American visitors to this tropical city tend to do their shopping the easy way, in such hotel centers as Plazita Zamora, but at least two shopping streets are worthy of considerable exploration. One is *The Escolta* reached by crossing the Pasig River by Jones Bridge, and the other is *Mabini Street,* which runs parallel to Dewey Boulevard two blocks in. Escolta means Escort and we are told that in the old days the Governor-General, always preceded by escorts, was accustomed to pass on his rounds of inspection through this street, so when his escorts were sighted people would cry out, *Escolta! Escolta!*—which cry became, in time, the street's name. The Escolta is today the "downtown" center of shops, department stores, business houses, banks and theaters. Its animation is fascinating though some shoppers might find it forbiddingly crowded and hectic. Mabini Street, on the other hand, is a newer one, more "uptown," with smaller, more exclusive shops. *Aurelia's* is one interesting shop on this street, with a lot of tempting gift items. It calls itself "The Emporium of Things Philippine." A rival shop of the same type, on the same street, is *Tesoro's,* which has other shops on the Escolta, in Plazita Zamora and at the airport. Among the city's department stores are *Esquire Bingham,* on the Escolta, and *Aguinaldo's* on Echaque Street; and finally, there are the *neighborhood* "catch-all" emporiums called *sari-sari stores.*

* * *

Restaurants are numerous in Manila and many of them are good, but I doubt that the average short-time visitor devotes much time to exploring them, the meals being so good in the air-conditioned dining rooms of the hotels. Nevertheless, just in case you feel in the mood to eat around I will name some of the good places that have come within my ken.

The *New Europa,* an air-conditioned, German-run place on Isaac Peral Street, two blocks back of the Bay View Hotel, is perhaps the leader of the standard restaurants of conservative, international type. Its steaks are as expensive as they are excellent.

Town's Tavern is a folksy restaurant on Mabini Street, a good place for lunch.

Max's, in Quezon City, is a character restaurant in a garden that seems nearly always to be swept by cooling breezes. Max started, right after the war, serving Southern fried chicken to American G.I.'s, but the Filipinos soon developed a liking for it and he has been doing a roaring business ever since. His fried chicken dinner, locally famous, starts off with an iced rum drink called Forever Amber and here is Max's startling recipe for the drink: 1 dash Angostura bitters; 1 jigger of Southern Comfort; 2 jiggers of champagne; a cherry and a slice of orange; stir gently, but don't shake; then "serve with confidence." Max is a character, no doubt of that, but he's much more than that term usually suggests, for he reorganized the whole restaurant industry in Manila and instituted seminars for the teaching of good cooking and service. He had a hand too in the founding of Manila's semiannual *Philippine Food Festival*, which takes place in some glamorous setting, often in Hotel Manila. Sometimes this event becomes a still gayer Food and Cocktail Fair. In this festival any comer, by merely paying a general admission fee of 5 pesos ($2.50) has the privilege of knocking around from table to table sampling anything and everything that looks good to him.

Aristocrat, on Dewey Boulevard, serves both foreign and Filipino fare.

Bulakeña, also on Dewey Boulevard, specializes in Filipino delicacies.

Alba's, on Florida Street, serves Spanish dishes.

Casa Marco is a simple but good place of Spanish style and food far out on Dewey Boulevard, a favorite haunt of jai alai players. Here you may eat in the open air in a shaded patio.

Café Indonesia, on Dewey Boulevard opposite the U.S. Embassy, serves hot Indonesian food of the rijsttafel order.

Minamoto, on Dewey Boulevard Extension, serves Japanese sukiyaki, but Japanese dishes don't seem too appropriate in the Philippines.

D & E is a highly progressive and recommendable restaurant and catering establishment out in Quezon City.

A French restaurant called *Au Gourmet* is worth looking up; as are two places for Italian *pasta* dishes, namely *Di Marks Restaurant* and *Cucina Italiana*.

Of course there are bars galore, mostly air-conditioned, but the best ones are in the big hotels and have been already mentioned.

*   *   *

Sports of almost every type you can think of are practiced in Manila, from golf to baseball and from boxing to polo, this last splendidly played by competing teams, on the grounds of the Manila Polo Club, but the two most characteristic sports are cockfighting and jai alai.

Early one Sunday afternoon I witnessed the former sport in the fancy *Grace Park Cockpit* in the suburb of Rizal. It was called the *Pintakasi* [Cockfight Tourney] *Festival of Champions*, the best cocks from all over the Philippines being entered, and a gory spectacle it was. I confess that it made me cringe to see these splendid birds, with three-inch steel spurs spliced onto their natural spurs, do each other to death in a spatter of blood and swirling feathers, while hectic betting cries filled the air. I just did not, *could* not like this slaughter and I was relieved when respite came and I could regale myself with a picnic lunch of a *lumpia*, washed down with a bottle of cold San Miguel. What is lumpia? It is a pastry cylinder containing bits of pork, shrimps, vegetables, potato and very young coconut shoots, seasoned with a sauce of soya and cornstarch, the whole securely wrapped in a cylinder fashioned of dough. However this may sound to you, it was, I can assure you, very good indeed.

Jai alai is played in a truly magnificent, all-air-conditioned temple of sport, the *Manila Jai Alai Frontón*, which accommodates 3000 persons. An evening spent here, preferably on Saturday, provides an event that should not be missed, for it is far more of a spectacle, all things considered, than any such frontón evening in Spain, Cuba or Mexico. As a matter of course top-flight Basque stars are imported to play the game and on the program you are sure to read such names as Belaustegui, Mintegui and Zarauz. The play itself is quite terrific, for this is the fastest game in the world, but so it is in Havana and Madrid. The thing that distinguishes this huge frontón from others in other large cities is its luxurious quality, along with its social eminence. I'll try to describe it.

The ground floor has the *Keg Room,* a quiet and cheerful public restaurant—it could well have been included in our list above—where American, Spanish and Filipino dishes are served every day except Sunday, from 8 A.M. to midnight. The second floor has the *Bamboo Room.* The third floor is the one for general admission to the stands, for watching the play down below. Here bets are accepted on the winner alone, but on the more exclusive floor above bets are accepted only for win *and* place. The fourth floor is the de luxe one of this temple of sport and pleasure. One pays extra to reserve a seat here and is expected to be pretty free with bets. On this same floor is the *Sky Room Restaurant,* which, be assured, is the one international nightclub in all Manila where "the best people" are happy to be seen. A first-rate orchestra dispenses smooth dance music, special entertainers alternating with it, while well-trained waiters dispense the best of foods and wines. So I would say, even if you have but one free evening in the city brush aside other possibilities and devote it all to the Manila Jai Alai Frontón.

Mention of the Sky Room's orchestra leads me to make a further comment on the subject of Filipino dance bands for they are in urgent demand all over the Far East and you encounter them everywhere. Filipinos have been called "the troubadours of the Orient" and the tag is really apt, for wherever you go in smart hotels or nightclubs, emphatically including those of Japan and Hong Kong, you're likely to find the establishment advertising with pride its "Filipino Orchestra." This brings in the customers.

In Manila itself music "busts out all over" during the semi-annual (October and March) *Philippine Folk Dance and Music Festivals.* In the terpsichorean side of the festivals there are often more than one thousand participating pairs of dancers. The *Christmas festivities* commence at 4 A.M. on December 16 with the *Missa de Gallo* (Cock Crow Mass) and continue, with carol singing in the streets every night, right up to Christmas Day. Even after the big day various gaieties go one, without any appreciable letup, until Epiphany, on January 6th.

* * *

Manila's *nights* have plenty of earthy dance halls, mostly on Dewey Boulevard, where socialites are *not* eager to be seen, though I believe the men don't mind too much. In nearly all of them there are multitudes of lovely young hostesses. One prominent establishment of this type, located in Pasay City, just beyond Manila's limits, is the *Kapit Bahay*, where the charge for the company of a hostess is 5 pesos an hour, plus 2.50 pesos for a shot of whisky or 1.50 pesos for beer. Two other such pleasure palaces in the same vicinity are the Bayside Club and the Sportsman's Club. This indoor sport comes high, especially in an expensive city such as Manila, for it is axiomatic that the girls are thirsty creatures. I will say this for Manila's hostesses-of-the-night. Very many of them are lovely to look at, dainty young girls with flawless light-chocolate complexion and glistening black hair, clad in light, frilly dresses, usually with a neckline that plunges generously, but from any of these nightspots the customer will find it a simple matter to emerge about $30 poorer than when he went in so short a time before.

A Sunday afternoon-into-evening of real glamour, costing nothing at all, may be spent on the sward of the harborside New Luneta, listening to a first-rate band concert by the Philippine Constabulary Band and then watching the sunset. Manila's sunsets, seen over the harbor, are deservedly world-famous and it will be an unlucky day if Old Sol lets you down. As he disappears for the night you may wave him down with a Philippine "Mabuhay!" which, as I've said, is a Tagalog word used by all Filipinos and which means almost anything generous that you want it to mean. If you say it in farewell as the sun sinks you may say it in welcome as it rises to light you through another day. Mabuhay is a fortunate and versatile word that can add spirit and good cheer to all the contacts you make in your Philippine travels.

YOURSELF IN THE PICTURE OF HONG KONG

CHAPTER 14

TWO PRONGS OF AN ORIENT MAGNET

The Peninsula Lounge, Nucleus of the East

THE lounge of the *Peninsula Hotel,* which is in Kowloon, on the mainland portion of the Crown Colony of Hong Kong, reminds me, in one respect, of the Café de la Paix in Paris. If you sit there long enough everybody you ever knew will pass your chair. But in appearance it resembles the lobby of any huge British hotel anywhere in the world. At scores of small tables sit groups of tourists, businessmen and assorted local residents, British and Chinese, sipping Scotch and soda, gin and tonic or tea. By the time you've been in the hotel a day you'll find that it takes fifteen minutes to pass through this lobby. Those nice folks you met in Manila have just turned up here and they hail you and propose to buy you a drink—"Oh, *come* on! Just a quick one anyway." And—"Well, for heaven's sake, if it isn't Jock! What on earth brought *you* here?" A local airline executive said to me, "I make it a fixed policy never to enter that merry madhouse at all unless I have at least a good half hour that I can devote to it."

For the tourist-far-from-home there's a sure thrill in the many-faceted, cosmopolitan folksiness of the place, for the faces and races are a grand mixture of East and West. The twain have met right here, making Kipling a false prophet. Gushing girl tourists have been known to say, before they've been out on the streets at all, "Isn't Hong Kong di*vine!*" and convivial male tourists have been known to spend virtually all their time in the club-like lounge, begrudging any hours "wasted" elsewhere.

The Peninsula is a little city unto itself, like the Imperial in

Tokyo and the Manila in Manila, with airline offices, fine shops, a bank (The Hong Kong and Shanghai Banking Corporation), a glamorous restaurant (Gaddi's) and a leading travel agency. This last, whose services you may need right off, is *Hong Kong Tours and Travel Service*, run by Fred Clemo, probably the best-known travel agent in the Far East, with a powerful assist from his son-in-law, George Hamilton-Dick. In 1957, a government-sponsored *Hong Kong Tourist Association* was organized with office in Victoria, on the colony's island portion, and this is of great value for those engaged in special research, but for most travelers the services of the regular travel agencies are fully adequate and more convenient.

Let's take a look, now, at the hotel itself before discussing its special shops and services. It is a big place, air-conditioned throughout, with 296 bedrooms and baths (plus 76 more in a new Annex), a delightful dining room and various private rooms for business luncheons and parties. The bedrooms are equipped with radios that pour out good music, good British commentaries, good and bad news of the day and not too many commercials. There are no chambermaids to serve you but only "China-men" and they're a smiling lot of men. You'll have a "Numba One Boy" at your beck and call all the time and in his pleasant pidgin talk he'll respond to any request, from mending torn pajamas to doing a one-day laundering job to supplying a transformer so that your electric razor can be used. (The H.K. voltage is 220 A.C.) The regular hotel dining room, as distinguished from Gaddi's Restaurant in the same building, is called the "Playpen" because it somehow suggests one. It is on the mezzanine floor and enjoys a superb outlook over Salisbury Road and the railway terminal to the animated roadstead and beyond that to mountainous Hong Kong Island, with the shorefront skyscrapers of Victoria, the colony's capital. The food served in this Playpen is international, but the big, hearty breakfasts are like those in Britain.

The other restaurant referred to above, by name *Gaddi's*—Leo

Gaddi, manager of the hotel, is its proprietor—is Hong Kong's most famous and elegant eating place and one of the very best in cuisine, serving superb meals of Continental, American or Chinese food, according to your mood of the moment. Gaddi's is primarily a dine-and-dance restaurant with a first-rate Filipino orchestra, but it also serves lavish luncheons. It does not serve breakfasts.

The *Hong Kong Tours and Travel Service* is one of the colony's most dependable travel agencies for bookings of every sort, for guided sightseeing tours, both within the colony and to Portuguese Macao, only 40 miles distant by sea, and, not least in importance, for *shopping tours* in the shoppers' heaven that is Hong Kong. I'll have more to say about the sightseeing tours and of course about the shopping centers, but first a bit more about the "geography" of the Peninsula Hotel and its numerous offices and shops. The building, fronting on busy Salisbury Road, faces approximately south. On the southeast side of the vast lounge you'll find the entrance to the travel agency just named, and also some airline offices, and directly on the eastern side the entrance to Gaddi's Restaurant. On the west side, in a sort of arcade, are other airline offices, notably that of Pan American Airways, for this is the city terminal point of the Pan Am busses serving the colony's Kai Tak Airport, some 4 miles distant. On the hotel's mezzanine floor are some of the smartest luxury shops, including the world-famous Dynasty Salon, which offers silks and brocades in great variety, and Betty Clemo's Shop, which offers fine dresses, embroidered blouses, piece goods (including Thai silk), furs and Chinese costume jewelry. Betty Clemo is the wife of Fred Clemo, mentioned above as heading the Hong Kong Tours and Travel Service.

Hong Kong Close-up; Essential Practicalia

Hong Kong as a British crown colony has a history of less than 12 decades but during that period, a very brief one as the Orient views time, wonders have been accomplished and since World War II (see below) the colony has become a house of refuge for at least a million and a half hard-pressed Chinese who fled from the rigors of their homeland, especially since the Communists fastened their grip on it. In 1839, the so-called "Opium War" broke out in southern China, at which time the Chinese Imperial High Commissioner sought to drive all foreigners from the China coast. The attempt soon backfired, for Britain sent out a fleet under Captain Charles Elliot, R.N., who met in battle and decisively defeated the Chinese forces on January 7, 1841. As a result of this defeat China ceded to the British Crown in perpetuity the 32-square-mile Island of Hong Kong, which cession was ratified by the Treaty of Nanking in August, 1842. The selection of this island as a stronghold that should serve to protect British traders proved wonderfully fortunate, though it was widely ridiculed at the time by certain political leaders and newspapers in London. The roadstead between the island and the mainland offers one of the finest harbors in the world, as well as one of the most scenically beautiful, for it provides no less than 17 square miles of landlocked anchorage, a special boon in a region threatened by fierce typhoons.

In 1860, China ceded in perpetuity 3¼ square miles of mainland territory where Kowloon now is, along with Stonecutter's Island, and in 1898 it greatly enlarged the mainland holdings of the British by granting a 99-year lease of the district called The New Territories, together with a large island called Lan Tao, bringing the total land area of the colony to 391 square miles.

When Captain Elliot first reached Hong Kong its population consisted of a few score humble families eking out a living by fishing. In the course of its first century under British rule it grew to be a solidly prosperous colony with a population of about 850,000 but the flood of refugees after World War II tripled this population. Valiant efforts have been made, are still being made, to cope with the flood but this is far from easy, and there are still some 300,000 squatters existing by government dole in rudest shacks and tumble-down shelters. They constitute one of the sights of the colony, a slummer's sight of pitiable squalor, but gradually these unfortunates, who nevertheless feel themselves lucky not to be in Red China, are being rehabilitated through various government measures. Another strange sight of poverty, though much less pitiable, is that of the floating population, to use that term in its most literal sense. In other words, there are at least 120,000 persons living in boats, chiefly junks and small sampans, several hundreds of these latter being jammed close together in a floating slum in the harbor of Aberdeen, on Hong Kong Island. The water people are born on boats, die on boats and spend their lives on these small craft, whole families being packed into them like human herring.

Of the colony's 2,550,000 inhabitants more than 99 per cent are Chinese, there being fewer than 20,000 British and other European residents and perhaps 3000 Americans. The density of population in the island city of Victoria and the mainland city of Kowloon reaches *2000 to the acre* in many parts and still the colony grows, for the annual excess of births over deaths is at least 70,000, not to mention some refugees that still seep in.

Hong Kong is a colony of color and contrast, of a thousand strange sights, of lovely, peaceful beaches, of rickshaw rides and walla walla rides—they're native motorboats—of smart cosmopolitan nightspots and hectic Chinese dance halls, of British garden parties and the surf-like roar of clicking mahjong tiles from the Chinese clubs and restaurants along Queen's Road, of the fashions of Mayfair and the Hong Kong split skirt, sometimes hip-high, worn by Chinese women and girls. Experienced travelers generally agree that no more vivid plot of earth exists than this crown colony straddling its salty roadstead.

Before plunging into the subject of Hong Kong practicalia I should, perhaps, say a bit more about that fashion of the Hong Kong split skirt, sometimes called the Shanghai split skirt. It consists of two panels of cloth, front and back, offering generous revelations of the legs on both sides, and the style is quite as common for middle-aged society women as for schoolgirls. The bolder girls reveal an astonishing expanse of legs, often well above the stocking hems, and even the conservative older women don't hesitate at all to reveal their knees and a good six inches above. When the wind blows, or when they sit down, "the split rides up." Fortunately nearly *all* Chinese women are trim and petite of physique, so the leg scenery is by no means distressing, especially to males, but one shudders to think how it would "unbecome" our portlier Western women. Long-time residents of Hong Kong tell us, "We never even notice it any more," but the first-time visitor decidedly does notice it, and since this fashion is traditional and normal, without provocative intent, he notices it with pleasure—unless he happens to be a prude. Anyway, an offsetting feature of the Hong Kong (or Shanghai) style is that a plunging neckline is *never* seen. Always there is a neat round "choker" collar to cover even the Celestial neck, clear to the chin.

*   *   *

Airline Services to and from Hong Kong's Kai Tak Airport are impressively numerous and to meet the ever-expanding traffic the airport is now being greatly enlarged and modernized. Pan American Airways, Canadian Pacific Airlines and Japan Air Lines are but three of the dozen or more systems using this airport and I mention them because they all have *direct* overseas services to the colony, usually involving no change of plane at Tokyo. Northwest Orient Airlines has an interesting overseas service to Taiwan (Formosa), connecting there with the colony's own Hong Kong Airways, a company which now serves also Okinawa, Manila, Seoul and Tokyo.

My own recent approach to Hong Kong was by the "fishhook" route of Pan American that I have already mentioned, meaning San Francisco—Honolulu—Wake—Guam—Manila—Hong Kong (—Tokyo), and I shall always remember the grandeur of the approach as the plane came within sight of the Chinese mainland and then lost altitude as it slid past the Peak of Hong Kong

Island and drifted down to Kai Tak Airport. And since I'm on the subject of this fishhook design I may state that the Pan Am flight from Hong Kong to Tokyo, or vice versa, passes directly over Taiwan, and at such a moderate altitude that passengers can clearly see the physical contours of the Nationalist Chinese island as if gazing at a maquette. They can easily distinguish roads, villages and even individual homes, inducing inevitable speculation as to the future of this island country, now seemingly marooned from the currents of world life.

Climate is mildly warm in Hong Kong but not tropically hot except in summer. The best season for a visit is from mid-autumn to early spring. April, May and June are wet months and when the rains let up the heat comes on.

Entering Hong Kong is easy for transient travelers, though American passport holders must first have secured a visa from some British consulate and a form must be filled in on the approaching plane or steamer and two passport photographs supplied. At the airport or wharf where you land you'll find, I'm sure, that the British customs officers maintain the traditions of their homeland for fairness and courtesy. I should state, however, a point that the PAA leaflet on Hong Kong brings out, namely that "The United Nations forbids the taking of many articles into Hong Kong without license and customs may direct you to leave such articles in custom bond until your departure." Customs *may* do so, but I doubt very much that it *will* bother you in any way, since you don't have that dangerous and subversive look. Certainly in my case entering the colony proved to be quite as painless as entering any country of Europe or Latin America. As for tobacco, each passenger is allowed to bring in, duty free, 200 cigarettes, or 20 cigars or 8 ounces of pipe tobacco. One quart of liquor may also be imported without duty. But *Hong Kong is a free port anyway*, though there is a small duty on tobacco and spirits, and for that reason British and American cigarettes can be bought at prices little above those at home and liquors are pleasantly low in cost. Many articles in the shops are priced *far* lower than in U.S. shops.

Hotels are considerably more numerous on mainland Hong Kong than on the island. Among mainland hotels, following the Peninsula, the air-conditioned *Miramar*, in the heart of Kowloon, deserves high rating. Following this, the *Grand* and the *Shamrock* are fairly good. On hilly ground above and behind Kowloon is *Hotel Carlton*, a first-class place of modern design opened in the spring of 1957. This is some distance from the central shopping area and the ferries to Victoria, but the hotel maintains an hourly bus service to and from town. Because of its commanding location it has a marvelous outlook over the double city and the roadstead. Another first-class place, this one well out in the countryside of the New Territories, is *Shatin Heights Hotel*, in a superb location high over Shatin Valley and its lush rice paddies.

Among *island* hotels, the only one of high quality in downtown Victoria, amid the business offices and skyscraping banks, is the *Gloucester*, on the upper floors of the massive Gloucester Building. About 20 minutes distant from the center by car is a lovely beach resort called *Repulse Bay*, with two recommendable hotels. One, the *Repulse Bay Hotel*, is a place of considerable luxury under the same ownership as the Peninsula. The other, *Seaview Hotel*, is much less pretentious but it has a perfect location directly on the beach.

Money and costs constitute the one most elemental consideration in planning any trip abroad, so I'm happy to report that in the case of Hong Kong its currency is simple and its costs are very moderate. The currency is the Hong Kong dollar (with subsidiary cents) and the official exchange rate is now HK$5.80 for one U.S. dollar, making the colony's dollar worth a little over 17 cents. *But* the colony has a completely free money market, so you exchange your dollars at the free market rate, paying no attention to the official rate. In doing so you are not dealing in the black market, or even the gray market, but in the wide-open market, as government pamphlets explain. You may obtain the free market rate at the Hong Kong branch of the *National City Bank of New York* or at any money-changer's office or even at the counters of leading travel agencies, such as the one mentioned above, which has connections with an exchange office. This open market rate fluctuates, of course, but of late it has been at least HK$6.15 to the American dollar and thus more favorable to the visitor. If you think of your Hong Kong dollar as 16 cents U.S. your arithmetic will work out with reasonable accuracy. At first you'll have many a shock, turning quickly into many a pleasant glow, when you see prices marked with our dollar sign but no HK before it, and think the figure zenith-high until you snap to and realize that it is *16-cent dollars* the sign means.

Costs are indeed moderate and will seem even more so if you have just come from Manila. The rate for a single room and bath, European style, ranges from about $5 to $7.50 U.S., and for a double room $9 to $12.50. Meals are in proportion, averaging, I'd say, at least a third less than in America. And shopping costs are thrillingly low on very many articles, not only of local manufacture, but imported. As Pan Am's *New Horizons* crisply puts it "Because the port of Hong Kong is free of import duty on everything except liquor, tobacco and bullets, it is much cheaper to buy things here." This goes for French perfumes and British woolens quite as much as for the exotic things that are made in the colony. (See below for shopping details.)

Photography is of the essence of Hong Kong, since *everything*, to exaggerate only a little, is worth shooting. Shutterbugs find the colony the realization of their dreams, for not only is it photogenic-plus but films of every type may be bought duty-free and therefore at low cost.

Tipping is geared to British custom, there being no such thing as a service charge. You tip individually those who serve you in any way and the scale usually suggested is 10 to 15 per cent, but I think you'll find that in practice 15 per cent is about the irreducible minimum.

Transportation in Kowloon and on the island may be by hum-drum taxi, by streetcar or bus, by romantic rickshaw or even, on some of the steeply climbing streets of Victoria, above Queen's Road, by sedan chair! Rickshaw riding is absurdly cheap, one Hong Kong dollar (16 cents) being actually on the generous side for an average short haul of half a mile or so. It is wonderful fun to roll along in the open air on big, rubber-padded wheels, and yet the average visitor finds it difficult, at first, to reconcile himself to being drawn by a man. You see the rickshaw runner's buttocks wimbling in front of you like those of a small horse and it seems "inhuman" that this custom should still prevail, yet the men clamor ardently for your trade and seem to feel no sense of degradation. They can pad along endlessly on their tough bare feet without tiring or even puffing.

Weekly Information, along with all needed practicalia about Hong Kong, may be had in convenient and dependable form from a periodical called *Where To Go And How To Get There.* This publication, in the form of a tall-and-narrow pocket-sized pamphlet, is distributed free in the hotels.

Quick—the Shops

Shopping dominates the tourist scene of Hong Kong as it dominates no other scene or city, including Paris. If convivial men sometimes feel that hours spent elsewhere than in the Peninsula lounge are wasted their womenfolk *usually* feel that hours not spent in shopping are wasted, for the fame of the colony's shops has gone out through all the world. This urgency is not much lessened, nor the enthusiasm dampened, by the fact that the Foreign Assets Control of the U.S. Treasury Department requires that "certain types of Chinese manufactured goods" may be brought back to America "only if a Comprehensive Certificate of Origin is obtained to prove that they were made in Hong Kong." Such articles include items of bamboo, hardwood, ivory, embroidered linens and cottons, silk garments and piecegoods

and—lots of other things which may look to the Foreign Assets
Control as though they might have originated in Red China or
North Korea. Jade items arouse special suspicion in the Foreign
Assets breast since most of the best jade does originate in China,
though some good things are now made in Hong Kong. An official pamphlet on the subject, attempting to mollify visitors, explains that, "Many things can be imported without a certificate."
I looked over the pamphlet's list and discovered that I could indeed buy freely such items as putty, fish oil, gas mantles, cement,
brassières ("other than cotton or silk and if not embroidered or
with lace"), coathangers, gramophone needles and printer's ink.
I have been told—but please don't hold me strictly to this—that
certain more desirable items such as watches, cameras, cosmetics,
leather goods, rattan ware and first-rate British woolen suiting
materials are also as freely purchasable as fish oil and cement.

To report my personal experience, I may state that I went
through the business of securing and filling in the forms of the
Certificate of Origin—each Certificate costs HK$5 but may in-
clude items up to a total of HK$1000—and having these treasured
documents right in my pocket when I eventually went through
the American customs, but the genial customs officer just couldn't
have cared less where I bought the things listed on my declaration.
The Certificates stayed right in my pocket and are now "among
my souvenirs"—which isn't to say that you'll have the same easy
time. It's certainly "worth the pain" to conform to the requirements, which aren't, after all, severe, so you'll have no worries
on returning home. Any reputable shop can furnish the needed
forms and help you fill them out, but if you plan to do extensive
buying you would do well, I think, to engage the services of a
shopping counselor through Hong Kong Tours and Travel Service or some other reputable agency, especially since the chief
shopping areas are widely separated. In Kowloon the better shops
are pretty well bunched at the south end of *Nathan Road* and its
offshoots, with the tempting *Miramar Arcade* of specialty shops
on Nathan Road opposite Whitfield Barracks. On the island they

are more scattered, though the main center is in the heart of Victoria.

For me to name and recommend individual shops from among the multitude of them in Kowloon and Victoria seems almost like pulling names out of a hat, but I will mention a few outstanding places to which I was directed by knowledgeable Hong Kong residents and which I know from my own shopping experience to be recommendable. I have already mentioned two shops in the Peninsula Hotel, Betty Clemo's and the Dynasty Salon. The latter represents Mandarin Textiles, Ltd., a manufacturing concern of international repute, with representatives in many lands, including America. I went through its main factory on Castle Peak Road and was fascinated by the variety and richness of the Dynasty fabrics. I saw something of the processes of manufacture of mandarin coats, silk and brocade housecoats, hostess gowns, cocktail dresses, cocktail suits of bolero type, men's silk bathrobes and silk shirts, children's dresses and I don't know what else. Although a house-supreme of silks, Mandarin Textiles goes in also for articles in Swiss organdie, Irish linen and even humbler rayon.

Old Mary Sing Shun Co., with factory on Castle Peak Road and shop at Number 27 Nathan Road, close beside the Peninsula Hotel, makes beautiful chests and other furniture of teakwood lined with camphor-wood grown in the New Territories, many of the articles being surfaced in shiny black lacquer. Some fine rosewood chests are also in evidence, along with many smaller gift items. "And who is Old Mary?" you're asking. Well, she *was* a hawker who originally sold souvenirs to incoming visitors at the steamer docks, but that was a long, long time ago. Mary *is* a wealthy and respected merchant now in her 90th year, and she is still to be seen in the factory and the shop for she still bosses the business, though a nephew is the active director. I once saw Old Mary lurking in the back of the Nathan Street shop and was amazed by the spectacle for she is a tiny little old wisp of a woman, full of years and wrinkles, about 4 feet 9 inches tall and weighing, I would estimate, a maximum of 80 pounds. Old Mary was written up in an article in the *Saturday Evening Post* long years ago (issue of November 18, 1944) and she was an old woman then. Now she is merely an older woman but her brain, they say, is still clear and sharp, for she heads, in spirit at least, a big and important house.

As a side note I may mention here that I saw in Old Mary's factory, as in several others, portraits of Sun Yat Sen, the Christian founder of the Chinese Republic, who, I am told, has attained the unique distinction of being revered by *both camps* in China, the Nationalists and the Reds.

Lien E. Ivory Factory has its factory on Mody Road and an upstairs shop at 31 Nathan Road on the corner of Peking Road. The range of offerings in carved ivory is a treat to the eye, but, as I said in connection with buying ivory in Japan, you need to know the product or else to have full confidence in the dealer from whom you buy, for bone articles are often foisted upon innocent customers as ivory, though bone doesn't have so fine a grain nor take so smooth and glistening a polish.

Men's suitings are a great specialty in the colony and first-rate tailoring establishments are almost the rule rather than the exception. They are found both in Kowloon and Hong Kong, which name is used both for the island and for the whole colony. A widely known house in Kowloon is *Harilela's Emporium*, with a shop at 1 Middle Road and another at 34 Nathan Road, and these are emporiums indeed, for they offer saris, fine silks and novelties from India as well as tailoring goods and services. Two well-known importers of British woolens with shops in the island city are *James S. Lee and Co.* and *Whiteaway, Laidlaw and Co.*, the latter being actually a full-fledged, British-operated department store located at 20 Des Voeux Road in the heart of Victoria. Several other department stores are in the same section of Victoria and at least one is in Kowloon, namely *Mohan's, Ltd.*, at 14 Hankow Road.

Polyglot bookstores are of great interest and one of the best of them, called the *Swindon Book Shop*, run by an erudite Chinese named Rupert Lee, is at 25 Nathan Road, only a few steps from the Peninsula. Its stock of books in English, French, German, Chinese and other languages constitutes a browser's heaven and browsers turn into buyers often enough to make this a prosperous shop. Among the bookstores in Victoria are two, the *Challenge Book Shop* and the *Harris Bookstore*, both on Ice House Street, the oddly named street that leads from the Star Ferry wharf directly to the heart of the city.

The Tourist Sees Double

Hong Kong is, as we've abundantly seen, a double city, each portion of it, like the two prongs of a magnet, having approximately the same drawing power upon visitors, so those who take local tours are prepared, as it were, to see double. The administrative, diplomatic and business centers are on the island—Victoria could be called the colony's "downtown"—whereas the chief hotels are on the mainland, with very many of the most famous shops and with large industrial areas in the remoter stretches. Both parts have high hills and splendid scenic drives. The names of the two parts, by the way, are as interesting as themselves, for Hong Kong means "Fragrant Harbor" (though just between you and me it isn't) and Kowloon means "Nine Dragons," from the nine-peaked rampart of hills rising in the background.

The Hong Kong Tours and Travel Servic offers two standard daylight tours, one of the island of Hong Kong, the other a 56-mile run through the more scenic and luxuriant portions of the New Territories, commencing with the "Corniche" road to Castle Peak, and in addition to these, a Hong Kong-by-night tour, a harbor tour and special factory and industrial tours. The most popular of the two standard offerings first mentioned is the Island Tour and that I will outline point by point.

1. The *ferry trip* across the roadstead to the island gets you off to a wonderful start, for there is no more exciting harbor crossing anywhere. The *Star Ferry* to Victoria, for pedestrians

only, leaves at very frequent intervals from Kowloon, at the end of Salisbury Road, two minutes walk from the Peninsula, but if you take the standard tour you'll be driven aboard the *Yaumati Car Ferry* at the foot of Jordan Road. (A second car ferry service is to open shortly.) By whichever means you make the crossing the ferry will thread its way through a maze of assorted craft ranging from tiny sampans, often sailless and propelled with a scull, through walla wallas and small fishing boats to the big photogenic junks and finally to ocean-going steamers. Among the latter I have been interested to note, and jot down the names of, the *Hermelin*, out of Drammen, Norway, the *Effie Maersk*, out of "Kjøbenhavn," the *Tjilwan*, out of Amsterdam, the *Heemkerk*, out of 'sGravenhage (The Hague) and the *Patroclus* from I could not read where, possibly the Piraeus.

2. The *Peak Tram*, to whose lower station, just off Queen's Road, your driver takes you, is a funicular that lifts you, by an extremely steep gradient, nearly 1800 feet to the Peak. You climb a further short stretch to the highest point of the Peak, and of the island, for a memorable view of the double city with the animated harbor between. Your guide will point out two ship shelters where junks and other craft run for shelter when typhoons threaten them late in the summer and early in the fall.

3. *Tiger Balm Garden* is an invariable halt of all tours and a strange curiosity it is. It is the garden of a private mansion of the late Aw Boon Haw, a Chinese multi-millionaire philanthropist who built up his first fortune, as the garden's own booklet says, "by producing a kind of medicine named 'Tiger Balm' and three other remedies: the 'Headache Cure Powder,' the 'Balashin Sai,' and the 'Chinkawite Wind Mixture,' . . . effective to cure cough." The crowning show piece of the Garden is a gleaming white 9-story pagoda, surrounded by blue grottoes, trick temples and all sorts of fantastic monsters in porcelain and other materials, such as dragons, monkeys, elephants and, of course, ferocious tigers, all calculated to suggest sermons. We learn that "in the hope of purifying our sins, the founder of this garden specially

selected these statues and erected them," but I confess that in my case his hope was vain, for I felt no sense of purification. On the contrary, I felt a vast boredom at all these heavy fripperies. I am told, however, that the interior of the Aw Boon Haw mansion, still in private use by members of the rich man's family, is in quieter taste, with many *objets d'art* of fabulous worth.

4. *Repulse Bay*, visited on all the trips, has already been mentioned as a smart bathing resort. It got its name from *H.M.S. Repulse*, which took a major part in driving away the pirates and bandits who plagued the colony in its early days. One of the sights of the resort is a baronial mansion named Eucliff, supposed to have been designed by its rich and eccentric builder as a sort of miniature Château de Versailles.

5. *Deepwater Bay* is usually the tour's next "port of call." It boasts a beautiful 9-hole golf course, of the Royal Hong Kong Golf Club, and your guide is sure to point out a house that made movie history. It is a shore-front mansion that played a prominent part, if I'm right, in "Love Is a Many-Splendored Thing," with Jennifer Jones and William Holden.

6. *Aberdeen* has been mentioned for its bay, where thousands of "water people" live and die in the floating slums of sampans. It will be mentioned again later, and more cheerfully, when this chapter discusses restaurants, for two large and popular floating restaurants dominate one side of the bay. The village is a fishermen's village and along its hectic shore you'll see live crabs, lobsters, prawns and various types of fishes held captive in baskets moored in the water. If you're in a marketing mood you may select whatever you like from this rich motley and buy it on the spot—but I don't think you're likely to do so. A big date in the calendar of Aberdeen Bay is May 5, for then occurs a colorful annual event called the "Dragon Boat Race."

7. And so back to Victoria and its ferries by one of several alternate routes either across the island or around it by Island Road, which skirts the shore along its whole perimeter. If the return is made along the eastern shore you'll pass the hamlet of

Stanley, with its own "squadron" of fishing junks, and later lovely Shek-O, with the British Country Club and a superb beach, ultimately reaching the city through the congested Wanchai District.

In a street of one such crowded area I happened to pass a Chinese funeral procession and noted that the sons of the deceased (as the guide identified them) walked first behind the hearse, wearing long white robes and queer yellow headdresses. Behind them came the wives, led by the first wife, who bosses her colleague-wives, and then some other women of the family. This was but one of an almost unceasing chain of odd, sometimes pathetic, exotic sights sure to be witnessed on this or any tour of the colony, whether on the island or the mainland.

In Victoria itself, you should by no means fail to climb some of the steep stairway-streets that ascend the lower flanks of the Peak from Queen's Road, for there you'll see Oriental city life at its most huddled and strident levels. *Wyndham Street* is a good one to climb, and so is the parallel *D'Aguilar Street*, which is brightened by a lovely little flower market and a fruit market. You'll also see vegetable stalls by the dozen, especially on the side lanes, and if you're *very* unparticular, which I can't imagine, you can buy assorted "eats," mostly fried things, from any one of a score of tiny stalls.

I have scarcely mentioned the *scenery* of the more open portions of this town, but you know without my telling you that it is all beautiful and frequently dramatic.

Restaurants on Land and Sea

Good restaurants abound, both in Kowloon and on the island. There are, in fact, so many recommendable places, of widely varying types and appeal, that selection becomes a problem. I will, however, attempt a listing in the full knowledge that any such attempt is an open invitation to argument from fellow-listers. So, without further ado, let's plunge into this succulent subject, considering, in turn, Kowloon, Victoria, Out-of-Town and On-the-Water restaurants.

IN KOWLOON

Gaddi's has been already mentioned with glowing words, for this is generally considered the dean of them all, invariably excellent and sure of itself—and therefore on the expensive side.

The *Champagne Restaurant,* a *Cantonese* place on Kimberley Road that opened in 1957, has met with deserved success, for its food is varied and excellent and its décor exceptionally cheerful. A meal I enjoyed here commenced with shark's fin garnished with shredded chicken, continuing through a chicken-and-walnut dish to sour-sweet pork and sautéed shrimps concluding with fried rice, yong chow style. Perhaps this last item seems like returning to start all over again, but it should be borne in mind that fried rice is a standard finale of many a Chinese meal. In time you get to like this system. When I had finished my meal I saw the guests at another table receive a boiled live lobster whose eyes had been fitted with tiny electric light bulbs connected with a battery inside him. His eyes fairly *glowed* in thinking of the pleasure he was about to provide.

Princess Garden Restaurant, in the Princess Theater Building on Nathan Road, is another high-class Chinese restaurant, but this one specializes in *Pekingese* food, which differs somewhat from Cantonese. A typical meal that I enjoyed here started out, as in the Champagne Restaurant, with shark's fin, this time in chicken soup, and was followed by fried shrimps and rice in tomato sauce, fried chicken legs, fried bamboo shoots and salted cabbage, sliced chicken and Peking mushrooms in soup and assorted fried rice. In this case the fried rice did not quite conclude the feast for there was a final and tasty item called toffee apples. The featured beverage in the Princess Garden is a Chinese rice wine called *shiao shing,* which Chinese gourmets insist is the *original* rice wine, imitated by Japanese sake. From mid-evening on, this restaurant turns into a quasi-nightclub with dancing.

The music is by a first-rate orchestra composed of "troubadours of the Orient," meaning, of course, Filipinos.

The *Winter Garden,* at 221 Nathan Road, a little beyond the Whitfield Barracks, specializes in *Shanghai* food, whereas its near neighbor, the *Kowloon Restaurant,* at 221 D Nathan Road, specializes on the food of the province of *Szechuan.* By trying each of the above four restaurants in turn you may "eat around China." In all of them, as in every Chinese restaurant in the Orient, you must be prepared to use only chopsticks as your table implements.

Princess Restaurant, in the Shaw Building on Nathan Road, is still another very good Chinese restaurant, included here because it is often one of the goals of Hong Kong-by-night tours.

Rikki's, on the corner of Cameron and Carnarvon Roads, is a *Russian* restaurant of the very highest quality, inviting us to switch the appeal of our taste buds from China to Moscow. It provides all the established delicacies of Russia plus superb cakes and pastries from its own bakery.

And finally, in case "kitchen nostalgia" overtakes you, a couple of Kowloon restaurants offering honest-to-goodness *American* food are *Gingle's,* at 70 Nathan Road, a thrift restaurant for hard-pressed budgets, and the far more pretentious *Roundup Room* of the Miramar Hotel.

IN VICTORIA

Parisian Grill, at 10 Queen's Road, known to its devotees by the affectionate tag P.G., is a very superior French restaurant directed by a widely known restaurateur named Émile. This top-flight establishment is a haunt of Society with a big S and is always crowded to capacity at meal times, so it is essential to book a table in advance. The P.G. has an upstairs and a downstairs section, the upper floor being preferred by knowing patrons.

Café de Paris, almost adjacent to the P.G., is a ritzy, *intime* French restaurant, much smaller than its neighbor but with its own devoted clientele.

Maxim's, in the Telephone House on Des Voeux Road, is a dine-

and-dance restaurant, maintaining the plushy continental traditions suggested by its name.

Jimmy's Kitchen, on Theater Lane just off Queen's Road, is a Jimmy-of-All-Kitchens (except Chinese), offering American, French and Russian food, but it would be ever so wrong to call its proprietor "master of none," for his multi-national food is always good. Jimmy looks like a cross between King Farouk and a Dutch burgher, but he is a master chef and takes personal and loving charge of his patrons.

Chinese restaurants abound in Victoria and its purlieus, as in Kowloon. Among them are the *Sky Restaurant and Nightclub,* on the top floor of the Great China House at 8 Queen's Road; the *Mandarin,* in the Winner House at 310 King's Road, one of the best of the colony's restaurants for Peking duck; the *Tai Tung,* a specialist in Cantonese food; and two other Cantonese restaurants known for their enormous size, namely the *Golden City,* at 122 Queen's Road, and *Kam Ling,* in the West Point section of the city. The latter is indeed a colossus and calls itself unhesitatingly, "the largest restaurant in the world," but I can't help wondering if Kam Ling has compared his floor space with that of Tokyo's Restaurant Tokyo Kaikan (Chapter 7).

OUT-OF-TOWN

Most of the colony's out-of-town restaurants are of the dine-and-dance order, some offering special entertainment that puts them more in the nightclub category. On the mainland, the two most popular places of this type have already been mentioned under the hotel heading, namely the *Carlton Hotel* and the *Shatin Heights Hotel.* Both have good dance orchestras. On the island, four out-of-town places seem especially worthy of mention for their glamour as well as for their good food and good dance orchestras, Filipino of course.

The *Champagne Room,* in the Sunning House on Hysan Avenue, is an air-conditioned restaurant of real charm, with atmosphere on the intimate side, where you'll be well fed and well entertained, though the orchestra is a small one. The entertainment feature of the moment is a vocal quartet.

The *Repulse Bay Hotel* has been mentioned in the hotel listings, but it needs further emphatic mention here as perhaps *the* outstanding goal for a pleasant day-and-evening far from the crowded centers. On Sunday noons an opulent Swedish smörgasbord is offered, this being a most unusual touch in the Orient. Afternoon hours may be pleasurably spent in the sun and surf of the beach and the evening hours in the hotel's luxurious restaurant, which is enlivened by first-rate dance music.

The *Ritz Garden Nightclub*, at North Point, is one of Hong Kong's most desirable goals for a gay evening, with good food, good dancing and an interesting floor show.

The *Lido*, on Repulse Bay, is an out-and-out nightclub, with an orchestra that purveys its contagious rhythms until 1 A.M. For inner refreshment the Lido features both European and Chinese food.

ON-THE-WATER

The floating restaurants of Aberdeen Bay are the most unusual and distinctive ones in the colony and perhaps the most appropriate to a community that was established for maritime commerce. Well out in the bay you'll see two big restaurant ships bearing the names *Tai Pak Fong* and *Yue Lee Tai,* and the business of reaching either one of them is "half the game," as you'll certainly see. From the moment your car reaches the village of Aberdeen it will be surrounded and all but blocked by a shrilly clamorous mob of white-clad sampan girls, each pleading for the privilege of sculling you out to one of the ships. I have mentioned that hundreds of sampans anchored in Aberdeen Bay serve as the lifelong homes for as many poor families and one's first impression, at least upon coming here of an evening, is that *all* of these water families must be engaged in ferrying diners out to the brightly lighted ships. Anyway, you manage to indicate to one of the screaming girls that she may be your ferrywoman

and presently you embark and are sculled across the water, presumably to the Tai Pak Fong, considered the better of the two,
whose rows and constellations of bright lights are reflected in the
crinkling water.

The last word of the ship's three-part name is said to mean
"Showboat" and it certainly is more than a mere restaurant-on-
the-water. It has two decks, the lower one being for games and
the upper one being a fine and dignified dining room. For your
dinner (or lunch) you may pick out your swimming or crawling
food from large baskets floating beside the ship. Among the
swimmers you'll see groupers, white snappers and green perch
the color of good jade, and among the crawlers you'll see lobsters, crabs, prawns and huge sea snails, as well as some giant
horseshoe crabs, which last are *not* edible.

The principal game on the lower deck is mahjong and you
hear it even from shore—when the sampan girls aren't clamoring too loudly. I have spoken of the surf-like roar of clicking
mahjong tiles along Queen's Road in Victoria, and here in Aberdeen Bay the same roar of clicking ivory tiles emanates from this
showboat and its rival, though perhaps I should say chirping instead of clicking, since the word mahjong in Cantonese means
house sparrow. All of 144 tiles are used to make up a set for four
players and if, let's say, ten games are going on in the same room
it means that 1440 tiles are in action, which, as the man said, are
a lot of tiles.

Hong Kong in Neon

The spectacle of Hong Kong Island when dusk turns into darkness is a marvel of the Orient. Along the waterfront for two or
three miles are scores of large neon business signs and advertisements, some in Chinese characters and some in English and of
course each one is faithfully reflected in the bay—upside down.
It is no strain on the truth to say that from the distance of Kowloon, about one mile, they actually *adorn* the night scene. Above
the neon stratum are myriads of ordinary electric lights in homes

and streets and certain public buildings. They rise in tiers, in whorls and coils, in long pendants and in intricate geometrical patterns clear to the crest of the Peak in such vivid and fantastic designs that you'd think a special fiesta was in progress such as the New Year's illuminations of Funchal and its hills, on Madeira Island.

The Hong Kong-by-night tours, starting from Kowloon, usually include, first off, a ferry trip across the roadstead and an ascent of the Peak to look down on all this mass of varicolored lights and across to the lights of Kowloon. This is a wonderful curtain-raiser for more intimate close-up scenes to follow, scenes that include the reeking labyrinth of hillside streets in some Chinese quarter of Victoria and then a seafood dinner in one of the floating restaurants of Aberdeen. After this the tour usually returns to Kowloon to top off the evening by an hour or so of Chinese opera at the new big *Po Hing Opera House* opposite the Alhambra Theater. Chinese opera differs from Western opera as radically as jazz differs from a Haydn symphony and even if you've seen one of these weird Oriental shows in San Francisco's Chinatown or in Havana you still should see the real thing, on a great and lavish scale, as done here in Hong Kong. An individual visit can be arranged for you, if desired, by any travel agency.

Many Western visitors are too timid or too conservative to explore Hong Kong's night on their own, but couples or groups or male individuals can "have themselves a time" if they want to, and with no more danger than in New York or Chicago. There are dozens of dance halls both in Kowloon and Hong Kong, ranging from the smart and elegant *Metropole Ballroom* (in Hong Kong), where Western tourist couples may feel quite at ease, to little garret dives where a few Chinese girls in cotton pajamas are eager to dance with visiting males for one Hong Kong dollar.

With Chinese friends from one of the airline offices I went one evening to the Metropole Ballroom and had a most gay hour dancing with two demure Chinese hostesses named Leung Chun and Lam Tung. They were well-behaved young ladies who spoke a little English and did their best to earn the established fee of HK$8.80 apiece ($1.50 U.S.) for an hour of their really pleasant company. Tea is served free in this as in most dance halls of standing, but all other beverages, including coffee, must be paid for. Hong Kong dance halls can be good, clean, exotic fun, but I doubt that you'll give them much time, for the street life of the crowded quarters, especially in the upper reaches of central Victoria, is the sort of thing you came to the Orient to see.

YOURSELF IN THE PICTURE OF MACAO

CHAPTER 15

PORTUGAL IN CHINA

The Tai Yip Ship Approach

THERE is, at the moment, no airplane service from anywhere to Macao, Portugal's tiny enclave of Western freedom amid the probing tentacles of Red China, though a service of twin-motored Beechcrafts from and to Hong Kong is under earnest discussion. The slower sea approach in three or four hours instead of 20 minutes, does, however, have its compensations, for this journey by one of the ships of *Tai Yip Company*, spins out the pleasures of anticipation and provides, in itself, a very pleasant trip of 40 miles along the China coast and across the estuary of the Pearl River, on which Canton lies. Three ships of this company, built since the war in the Cheoy Lee Shipyards of Hong Kong, are now in the Macao service and their names are as interesting as themselves, *Takshing, Tailoy* and *Fatshan.* The day journey is made in 3 hours but the overnight services deliberately dawdle, leaving Hong Kong (from the island) at midnight and tying up to the wharf at Macao at 4 A.M. First-class passengers may continue to sleep in their comfortably furnished cabins until 8 o'clock and when they emerge they'll be greeted by the sights and sounds—and a few smells too—of a Chinese port, with some business signs in Portuguese to indicate the colony's national ownership. Along the wharves they'll see a jumble of oddly mixed traffic, including many pedicabs, whose operators are clamoring for customers. In the river around the ship they'll see scores of junks and sampans, and with luck they may see, at a neighboring wharf, a big green steamer of fantastic, junk-like appearance taking on passengers and cargo for Canton and other ports of Red China. This steamer appears to be straight out of a Gilbert and Sullivan operetta.

The standard guided tour arranged by the Hong Kong Tours and Travel Service condenses the whole journey into 18 hours, the guests leaving Hong Kong at midnight, visiting Macao from 8 A.M. to 3 P.M. the following day, and returning on the 3 o'clock ship from Macao. The touring in Macao is handled in co-operation with *H. Nolasco and Company*, whose able young Portuguese director, Antonio Nolasco, could almost be labeled "Mister Macao" so far as tourism is concerned. The firm's headquarters may be easily found at Number 20 Avenida Almeida Ribeiro, which is the city's "main drag," and there is also a branch office in Hong Kong, at Number 10 Ice House Street, Victoria, where advance information may be had. Breakfast and lunch are usually had at the charming *Pousada de Macau*, a small seaside inn owned by the Nolasco firm, and English-speaking guides handle all details of transportation and sightseeing. The whole tour, done at this tempo, which is *not* a rush, for the total area of tiny Macao is but a fraction of 1 per cent of that of Hong Kong, is now priced at less than $25 in American currency and that includes a first-class stateroom on the midnight ship. It goes without saying that if you can spend a night at the Pousada, or at one of the larger but rather less desirable hotels such as the *Riviera*, the *Grand* or the *Bela Vista*, you'll find plenty to interest you for an extra 24 hours.

The midnight ship that I took from Hong Kong was the *Takshing* and it got me off to a nice start from the moment that the hostess announced over the public address system, "Ladies and Gentlemen, attention! The ship is about to sail. Visitors are invited to step ashore." She spoke these courteous words with the most liquid Chinese accent imaginable and then repeated them in Portuguese, "*Senhores e Senhoras, attençao!* . . ." following the Portuguese announcement with a longer talk in Cantonese, her musical syllables falling in a silvery cascade more beautiful by far than the practiced laughter of a geisha girl. If you think Swedes "sing" when they speak their native language you should compare it with the lovely lilting sound of good Cantonese as spoken, for instance, by an educated damsel such as our *Takshing* hostess.

So the visitors accepted the "invitation" to step ashore and we passengers accepted the invitation to remain on board. Through the galaxy of roadstead lights our vessel made its leisurely way to the open sea and after we had enjoyed a convivial half hour in the lounge-bar we invited ourselves to turn in.

Some Facts and Impacts

Macao, spelled by residents of the territory in the Portuguese manner, *Macau*, is a fascinating politico-geographic curiosity whose population, like that of Hong Kong, is nearly 99 per cent Chinese but whose life has a veneer, in this case, of Portugal, its venerable foster mother. The territory's reputation as a citadel of all the assorted vices of the East has been sedulously culti- vated by fiction writers and film producers, and in former times with plenty of basis in fact, but Macao's present character, though far from Puritanical, is also far from vice-ridden. The energies of its present dynamic governor, Comandante Pedro Correia de Barros, are directed toward building up a normal industrial and commercial life to replace what remains of the old com- mercialized vices.

Macao had its 400th birthday in 1957, which makes it incon- testably the Orient's oldest foreign settlement. It has barely 3000 persons of Portuguese blood out of a population of approximately 180,000, but the Portuguese have had overseas experience since the days of Henry the Navigator and Vasco da Gama and they are still able to cope with problems that must seem, in this case, fairly overwhelming. The territory has, for instance, no hinter- land at all, such as Hong Kong's New Territories, and it is con- sequently "cabin'd, cribb'd, confined, bound in" by its vast Red neighbor. At the Barrier Gate, on the neck of the Macao Peninsula, which is but a short walk from the city's very center, the territory actually touches Red China and across the Pearl River, some 200 yards distant, loom the frowning Communist fortifications, toward which Macaoans may not even point their cameras, yet these resourceful people have learned to live at peace with their Marxist neighbors and there has not been even a border incident of any significance since 1952. Of course the Reds could gobble up Macao in one gulp, as they could, for that matter, Hong Kong, but there are powerful reasons of self-interest that deter them from doing so and it seems probable that these reasons will prevail until and unless a new world conflict breaks out, so you're as safe in Macao as in New York or Washington and maybe safer—from atomic bombs at any rate, which wouldn't be wasted on so tiny a fragment of the world.

Macao has no room whatever to expand and it seems remarkable that 180,000 persons squeezed into a small peninsula 2½ miles long by 1 mile wide, plus two little outlying islands, Taipa and Coloane, can live and move and have their being. These little islands, which are not included in the standard tour, support 10,000 persons and most of them make their living from the manufacture of firecrackers! Tightly rolled paper spills are made in humble homes by the tens of millions and taken to a dozen or so large factories to be filled with powder and ultimately exported in volume, about a million dollars' worth annually, to the United States, Canada and other lands. The manufacture of incense sticks, matches and matchboxes adds up to another business of considerable volume, but since these less hazardous items are mostly made on the peninsula the factories producing them have become sightseer's sights and we shall have a look, at least at the incense factory, later in this chapter.

Your *passport visa for Macao*, to mention this matter belatedly, costs about $2.00 U.S. and will be secured for you, quite without effort on your part, by the travel agency in Hong Kong that makes your bookings.

Macao currency, its dollar being called a *pataco* and its cent an *avo*, has exactly the same exchange value as the Hong Kong dollar and is, in fact, interchangeable with it, either currency being welcomed by Macao's hotels and shops, so you should simply use your Hong Kong money for all expenditures. However, in paying for anything with Hong Kong banknotes you will do well to ask for your change also in Hong Kong money, so you won't be left, at the end of your visit, with any considerable sum in patacas, which you would have to reconvert to HK dollars.

A *city map*, of pocket size yet with ample and well-organized tourist notes on the sides and back, is printed and distributed (through the hotels) by Macao's progressive *Office of Economic Services*.

Restaurants in Macao are neither very notable nor very numerous (except for scores of very unpretentious Cantonese places), but there are some that deserve at least "honorable mention," especially the one called *Fa Siu Lau* (Laughing Buddha), on Rua Felicidad, whose roast pigeon specialty is more than locally famous. A newer place called the *Helena*, on the wharf front, is also recommendable and a restaurant named *Belo*, conspicuously located on Avenida Almeida Ribeiro, is at least fair. Two restaurants in the *Central Hotel*, Macao's amazing 10-story gambling casino, have their talking points, but these shall be covered later in a night-life report.

I should not wander from the subject of Macao's restaurants without some mention of Portuguese dishes, which you'll find at their best in the Pousada de Macau. In general, they are on the rich and oily side, with plenty of spices, and they are greatly favored by many tourists, though not by all. The Pousada's manager-chef, named Americo Angelo, prepares certain specialties-of-the-house that are sure to tickle the palate, notably his "chicken African," which is a barbecued half chicken spiced with a mysterious sauce of many ingredients. If you try this savory dish, accompanied by one or two of Senhor Angelo's *casqueiros,* which are crusted rolls served so hot you can hardly touch them, you'll have a memorable meal. Other Portuguese specialties served in Macao's restaurants are *frango a bom bocado,* which is baked chicken, usually lubricated by a glass or two of port; pork sausages roasted in cognac; curried pork steaks in the manner of Goa, Portugal's colony in India; and Macao's own offerings of seafood, with emphasis on crab and grouper dishes. The last-named fish seems especially appropriate, since our word grouper is a corruption of that fish's original Portuguese name *garoupa.* And one thing more: Portugal's table wines, including the delicious port that is a part of the country's very name, are brought in duty-free and are therefore to be had at far less than what the same wines would cost in America.

Shopping is not of very strong appeal in Macao, since it is quite overshadowed by the shopping possibilities of Hong Kong, but one should remember that this, like Hong Kong, is a free port and that the gift articles for which Portugal is famous are obtainable at about the same prices as in Lisbon. On Avenida Almeida Ribeiro you will find plenty of things to attract you, the best-known tourist gift shop being *Rosita's,* opposite the hulking Central Hotel, where you'll find ceramics and pottery, fine filigree silver jewelry from Portugal and delicate laces and embroideries from Madeira. Postage stamps of Macao, I might add, will be of unusual interest to home-folk philatelists, for they are varied and beautiful. The 1-pataca stamp pictures a lovely white flower called Flôr de Lótus Lin Chi Fa on a deep blue background; and the 30-avos stamp shows us a busy street scene on Avenida Marginal.

Strange Sights and Scenes

The Macao map distributed by the Office of Economic Services lists no less than *ninety-four* "Points of Interest," but I think you'll be glad to settle for about 10 per cent of that formidable total, so let's get rolling, with a Nolasco guide to steer us.

First of all, we should be aware that Macao, like many another city throughout the world, has its Seven Hills. Rome set the fashion in hills and other cities have felt bound to follow. Three of Macao's seven certainly deserve our delighted attention, first *Penha*, filling the peninsula's southern tip, this hill being graced by the sumptuous summer residence of the bishop; second *Guia Hill* (with lighthouse), which provides the perfect view of the *ensemble* of Macao in its river setting; and third the eminence called *Forte do Monte*, which rises from the very *center* of the city, so precipitously and so close that no soaring seagull could gaze more intimately than you at the tangled street life below your lofty perch. Directly at the base of this "Fortress of the Mountain" you'll see, as the most conspicuous feature, the rich façade of the former *Church of St. Paul*, rising quite alone, like a vast screen of carved stone, the rest of the church having been destroyed by a fire and a typhoon in 1835. This elaborate façade, standing at the top of a great broad flight of stone steps, is considered quite comparable in its effect to the west fronts of many a cathedral in Europe. It was designed in the early 17th century by an artist-priest of Portugal named Father Spinola and was built by a band of Japanese Christians. One of the more prominent figures sculptured on the façade is that of Saint Francis Xavier, who made such valiant and partially successful efforts to convert the people of Nagasaki and its environs.

For your possible convenience I will list (omitting now the Seven Hills) some outstanding sights in the order in which a guide showed them to me, though you may, of course, see them in some quite different order.

1. The *Leal Senado*, meeting place of the Municipal Council, is a dignified building on a central *largo* (square) named for it. The adjective Leal (Loyal) refers to the unswerving loyalty of this colony during the sixty years of Portugal's humiliation (1581 to 1640) when Portugal was under Spanish rule. Macao alone never acknowledged Spain and a long inscription in Portuguese over the building's door commemorates "the exceeding loyalty

of the inhabitants." There is a small but very lovely public library in the Leal Senado which is a replica in miniature of the famous library of Mafra Monastery in Portugal.

2. The *Ma Kok Miu Chinese Buddhist Temple*, at the base of Penha Hill, is dedicated to the goddess A-Ma, for whom *A-mangau*, hence Macao, was named. It reveals the superstitions of the shoddier sects of Buddhism at their rackety worst, for here the hopes and worries of the most destitute people are exploited for gain. I saw a creaky old crone in rags kneeling in tearful prayer before a lurid shrine while at the same time holding, and continuously shaking, a cylinder filled with numbered bamboo sticks. For this privilege she had, of course, paid with her widow's mite. At what she must have hoped was the propitious moment she removed one of the sticks and took it to a seated priest, who was clad in a soiled undershirt. The priest matched the stick's number with a corresponding number on a yellow slip, one of many in a pile in front of him. He then made some markings on the yellow slip and handed it to the woman, who trembled with eagerness to clutch it, for this would tell her fortune for the ensuing year. While this little drama was in progress another priest kept up an interminable droning, in a low, dull singsong, reading from a book of prayers, or perhaps incantations. This he accompanied with a ceaseless beating upon a hollow drum of wood in the general shape, as it seemed to me, of a human head. It goes without saying that Buddhists of the higher sort, who cultivate philosophical peace and a striving for perfection, deplore such rackets quite as much as you and I do.

3. *Junk chandlery* and then *junk building* may be seen close-up by driving, south to north, along the entire length of the inner port, from the Ma Kok Miu Temple by a thoroughfare that changes its name from point to point, starting out as Rua Almirante Sergio and concluding as Avenida Almirante Lacerda. Here you will see dozens of shops purveying everything that junks and junk folk could possibly need, and at the northern end of the drive you'll see more junks being built and maybe even being

launched. One such launching I was lucky enough to witness, the ceremony being accompanied by a deafening uproar from Macao's most characteristic product—firecrackers.

4. *Kun Iam Tong* is another Chinese temple of Buddhism, but this one, far more extensive and dignified than the name-giving Ma Kok Miu, has three distinct courts. In the first we see large figures of Buddha and two of his disciples; in the second a figure of the Goddess of Purity seated on a lotus flower; and in the third the Goddess of Mercy, to whom the temple is dedicated. In support of this goddess there are no less than 18 golden "saints," one of them being *Marco Polo*, no less, who was astute enough to become a "temporary Buddhist" during his long sojourn in the Orient.

Connected with this inner court is an article of great historic interest, being the stone table, in a garden, upon which Viceroy Yi, representing China and Caleb Cushing, representing the United States, signed, on July 3, 1844, the first treaty ever concluded between America and China. On a large marble plaque on the wall a portion of the treaty is set forth in English, in Chinese and in Portuguese, the Chinese version being carved in red letters. For a lighter touch in this temple I enjoyed watching some 15 or 20 Buddhist monks engaged in a hot tournament of ping-pong, which was a refreshingly better activity than vending charms and fortune-telling papers.

5. A mansion of *Sun Yat Sen*, the universally revered founder of the Chinese Republic, is to be seen on Avenida Sidonia Pais, at the base of Guia Hill. It is a strange looking house of Moorish inspiration, with green spiral pillars. The great man who often dwelt here died in Peking in 1925, but members of his family still occupy his Macao mansion.

One may cross the peninsula from the base of Guia Hill by Avenida Conselheiro Horto e Casta and then turn south to reach what is perhaps the climatic cluster of Macao's established sights, three in number, namely the Old Protestant Cemetery, the Macao Museum, and the Camoëns Grotto and Garden.

6. The *Old Protestant Cemetery*, which encloses a small Presbyterian chapel, was laid out by England's East India Company in 1821 and has a wonderful story to tell to any visitor who can read between the lines of tombstone inscriptions. The stones tell of the pioneer courage that buoyed men and women of many nationalities and they reveal too that some of them died young, of typhoons, of fevers, of raids by Chinese pirates. Among typical names and inscriptions a few that caught my eye may be recorded here. Benjamin R. Leach of Salem, Massachusetts, died in Macao in 1838, at the age of 36. Christian Boeck of Denmark died in 1826 at the age of 23. Jacques Pierrot, a Frenchman born in Leiden, Holland, died in 1841 at the age of 29. Other interesting stones record the passing of Thomas Waldron, America's first consul to Hong Kong; of Hiram Tabbox, Ordinary Seaman Aboard the U.S. Frigate *Brandywine;* and of a Mrs. Dishkoon Seth, whose stone bears a long inscription in Syrian. Among stones of more celebrated persons are those of The Right Honorable Lord John Spencer Churchill (who was the fourth son of the fifth Duke of Marlborough, one of Sir Winston's ancestors), Captain of His Britannic Majesty's Ship *Druid;* George Chinnery, a British painter of considerable fame; and, perhaps the most to be admired of all, a British pioneer missionary named Robert' Morrison, who undertook and completed the stupendous task of translating the Old and New Testaments into Chinese characters and followed this by compiling a Chinese-English Dictionary. Morrison came to Macao in 1807, at a time when China was so isolated that the Chinese were forbidden to teach foreigners their language, yet by taking shelter in this Portuguese territory, which then as now was an enclave of freedom, he was able to master the incredibly difficult character writing and carry on his chosen life work.

7. The *Macao Museum* is even now being established in the East India Company's former headquarters building, which adjoins the cemetery.

8. The *Camoëns Grotto and Garden* occupy an adjacent hill-

side area that was once included in this same property of the East India Company. Today, this hillside commemorates Luis Vaz de Camoëns (or Camões), the greatest figure in Portuguese literature. This celebrated poet, who was also something of an explorer, is known to have taken part in the 1557 occupation of Macao and he may have written a part of his epic *The Lusiads* in a grotto of this garden, though that is hardly more than a strongly cherished tradition. In the grotto, which is a curious freak of geology, is a statue honoring the poet, together with various tributes and a carved excerpt of three stanzas from Canto 1 of *Os Lusiadas*, as the epic is called in Portuguese. The tributes to him are in Latin, English, Portuguese, Spanish, French, Italian and Chinese. This genius, born in 1524, was a kinsman of Vasco da Gama, and his classic is devoted chiefly to honoring da Gama's exploits and discoveries. Camoëns is credited with firmly establishing the Portuguese language, in much the same fashion that Chaucer established English and that Dante and Boccaccio established Italian.

* * *

The *factories* of Macao are quite as interesting as any of the regular tourist sights. We may visit a factory where teakwood and camphor-wood boxes are being made, almost on the street, and a factory where jams, preserves and sauces are made from peaches, lemons, beans, pecans, lichee nuts, etc., and of special interest, the factories devoted to Macao's most characteristic products. Among these are a small firecracker factory where we may see the spills being made, though the powder is put into them on the little isle of Taipa; a match and matchbox factory; and, perhaps the most interesting of all, a *joss stick factory*.

In the yard of this latter we see, first of all, a half acre or so of long strands and big coils of incense paste, some of it colored red and some yellow, drying in the sun. Upon entering the factory we are shown the whole process of converting the paste into these strands and coils and finally into joss sticks. The paste is made in a large gooey mess and placed in a big barrel, or more properly a tun, which has two small holes a few inches from the bottom. A wooden plank sticks out at an angle from the inside of the tun and by depressing this plank, which is about six feet long, clear to the floor a press within the tun is operated, forcing from the two small holes a couple of long, thin, brown "ropes" of what looks like unpalatable macaroni. In a fashion typical of China the pressure on the plank is exerted by an operative jumping on it. The brown strings that then squirt forth are deftly gathered up by another operative and arranged for the coloring, drying and hardening processes. I asked the foreman of a group operating one of these presses if I might jump on the plank-lever to squirt out the paste and he readily gave me permission, but alas, both he and I forgot about the *weight differential*. His men weighed about 90 pounds apiece and I weigh nearly twice that. Well, I jumped on the plank and two brown ropes then *spurted* from the holes in the tun and squirted in a splendid parabola the full six feet of the plank. Only by a nimble leap did I escape having my shoes and trouser cuffs inundated by the sticky paste. The Chinese may often look solemn but they have a child-like appreciation of the ridiculous and those incense workers burst into a vertible "typhoon" of laughter.

Chance on Four Levels

Vice is definitely in retreat in Macao, though furtive street touts still appeal to passing males to see "velly nice exhibition" or to meet "velly nice missy, only fifteen." Only that lofty temple of chance, the *Central Hotel*, still tries to carry on its old traditions, even against odds. The universal gambling instinct of the little Chinese people, not the wealthy international playboy set, now keeps this amazing place functioning and a palliative to the dark side of it is the fact that much of the profit from the gambling goes to poor relief and social welfare.

It's a real monstrosity, this towering Central Hotel, the only tall building in Macao, a hangover from a lurid past. It makes good on its name by being an actual hotel on some floors, though few American tourists ever register here. Four floors of the building are devoted to gambling, the favorite games being fan-tan (tombola), bingo and high-low dice, which is called *grande picino* in Portuguese, *sec pou* in Chinese. There are also certain concomitant attractions of the night, such as a Chinese opera and two restaurants, the *Golden City* on the 5th floor, this one on the pretentious side, and the *Golden Gate* on the 2nd floor. In this latter you may actually play fan-tan *from your table as you eat*. By means of a basket on a string your money is lowered through a "well" to one of the specially contrived gaming tables, and your winnings, if any, are raised to you by the same means.

The lower reaches of the Central Hotel are for poor gamblers, who ought not to be gambling at all, and here, any evening, you'll see the tables crowded three-deep with coolies, rickshaw runners, hucksters, pathetic old women hoping to win a few patacas and a general mélange of those unfortunates who are least able to lose *anything* in this seductive sport. I suppose the best that can be said for it is that *hope* springs eternal in the gambler's breast and perhaps hope is more important to these folk than the retention of their few patacas.

Fan-tan is by far the most popular of the games and as played in Macao it is the simplest. Let's take the elevator to the top floor, which is the smart one, for tourists and well-heeled residents, and see what happens. A presiding croupier invites the players grouped around the fan-tan table to bet on a number of their choice from one to four and when the betting is closed and the stakes collected he signals to a colleague, whom we may call the dealer. This man then plunges an inverted metal bowl into a big pile of white buttons that are all alike. Then he shoves the bowl out from the big pile and lifts it up, revealing a reduced pile of perhaps 60 to 100 buttons that his cup has captured. At this point he takes a sort of baton and with it deftly removes from this reduced pile four buttons at a time. The number of them left in the "kitty" at the end of this "operation baton" will obviously be one, two, three or four and that will be the winning number. Winners are paid off and a new game starts.

An amazing corollary to this game is that *as soon as the reduced pile is revealed* the croupier predicts what the winning number will be and not once in twenty times is his estimate wrong. This seems utterly impossible, a feat of magic, but the explanation is simply that the croupier's practiced eye and brain can judge, at the first glance, how many buttons are in that reduced pile and by simple arithmetic he can tell what the winning number will be. The present croupier at this top-floor table is a famous Chinese veteran named Ah Fong and the visitor can only say "Long may he preside."

On my first and only fling at Ah Fong's fan-tan table I tried out my luck in two successive games, choosing the figure three the first time and four the second, and by all that's incredible I *won* both times. With a seamy old smile Ah Fong passed me my winnings, but I was so embarrassed and confounded by my unexpected luck that I tossed a couple of patacas on the table to appease him and the Goddess of Chance. "Thus endeth the first lesson" in fan-tan à la Macao.

CHAPTER 16

ORIENT AFTERGLOW

ANY trip to unfamiliar lands with unfamiliar customs proves too full of sudden impacts and surprises to permit the mind to absorb and organize them quickly. Only on the way home and *at* home, in the ensuing months, do we begin to sense the full wonder of what we've seen. And often it is the *little* things that leave the most vivid and enduring impressions. We suddenly recall an extraordinary street scene in Nikko, that "travel trouble" in Kyoto that turned out so well in the end, a friend's wisecrack in Kobe that caught us amidships, a moment of pathos in a kabuki play, a moment of hilarity at an airport, an outsized American tourist lady dickering with a tiny little old Chinawoman in a Hong Kong market, a lurid jeepney in Manila named "Ike-and-Mamie."

A game that can enliven many a fireside hour back home is to let these small soldiers of memory parade through the mind, not in military formation but any old way, like the awkward squad on the first day of drill. The pleasures of recollection, spurred by this passing parade, will double the pleasures of realization experienced during the trip itself, and will leave in the mind an afterglow that never fades.

To illustrate what I mean I will let some of my own small memories of the Orient troop through my mind, just as they may happen to come, taking form here in black and white.

The cultivated seaweed beds of Tokyo Bay seen from the air. These extensive "marine meadows" furnish much of the food that sustains Japanese life.

My first three-point landing on Tokyo's Haneda Airport. The name means Feather Field and that's what it felt like as the plane touched down on the runway.

The superb painted screens, four centuries old and more, filling a large hall in Tokyo's National Gallery. In most of the scenes, gold predominates, and surely no softer, richer gold was ever achieved by any school of painting.

Tokyo Hall, visited in a western section of Tokyo. This eight-story building of pleasure and instruction includes four (4) big movie theaters and, on the top floor, a well-appointed planetarium.

The National Library of the Japanese Diet, in the Prince Arisugawa Memorial Park of Tokyo. The vast building looks rather like the Trocadero, straying far from Paris.

The sport of *browsing*, enjoyed in Tokyo's bookshops. Always these friendly, wide-open shops are full of browsers, and the clerks seem never to be concerned with how long they look or how much they buy, if anything.

The log rafts on Tokyo's Sumida River as seen from the elevated railway trains that cross it. Sometimes a tug draws three or four great rafts, recalling the old days when rafts were important features of Rhine traffic.

The skating rinks of Tokyo, artificially iced. In this Oriental setting they may seem strange, but the Japanese people are keen on Western sports of many types.

A game of *shogi*, or open-air chess, enjoyed, as a spectator, on Tokyo's Z Avenue. The chess board, of huge proportions, was set up against the wall of a building and the opponents' plays were indicated one by one, while a big crowd of "kibitzers" watched with rapt attention. Another well-liked game is *go*, a form of Japanese checkers.

The *doodle boards* seen in many Tokyo coffee shops. If you get restless you may step to this blackboard and doodle. Or you may leave a note dating your best girl, in the expectation that she will drop by to see if you've left a message.

A betrothed couple seen meeting for the first time in Tokyo's Kabukiza (Kabuki Theater). A very common custom is for the parents to agree on a marriage of their youngsters and to betroth them officially. Later, perhaps *much* later, the bride and groom meet, by tradition, in this theater, to see what fate has brought them and to judge of the future.

The "eye surgery" offices of Japan. Here fashion-conscious Japanese damsels not infrequently have their eyes *widened*, preferring to abandon the attractive Oriental slit in favor of the "Western Look."

The very humble and *un*fashionable "two-and-four women" of Japanese cities. They are streetcleaners receiving a daily wage of 240 yen (63 cents). Hence, by a little juggling of the figures, their accepted nickname.

The pickaback babies of Japan carried by their mothers, to whose sturdy backs they are secured by a broad sash. The mothers "wear" them, like knapsacks, as they go about their daily chores.

The large kerchief, called *furoshiki*, in which humble Japanese seem able to stow "everything but the kitchen sink," reminding one of the ample bag of green cloth which old-line Bostonians used to carry as a catchall.

A physical problem that threatens Japan. Very gradually the race is growing taller, so that it becomes less and less easy for people to squat on their heels.

A Philippine importation seen as one of the numbers in a show in Tokyo's lively variety theater, the Nichigeki Music Hall. The number was a Philippine Bamboo Pole Dance, requiring super-agility by the dancers to keep from getting their feet banged up.

A travel broadcast which I had the pleasure of making through the Japan Broadcasting Corporation (Nippon Hoso Kyokai). It was beamed, I later learned, to 25 foreign cities, including Moscow. Had I known it, I might have "expressed certain views" to the Muscovite listeners.

A "flower arrangement" seen in the lavatory of a Japanese train. One iris, one pink carnation and one white carnation were wired together and placed in a vase on the wall. Such decorations are standard in the lavatories of the limited expresses.

The famous "Sleeping Cat," a decoration over a gateway in Nikko's Toshogu Shrine. This cat is almost as famous as her neighbors the three monkeys, who Hear No Evil, Speak No Evil, See No Evil.

A curious statue of the Thousand-Handed Kannon, Goddess of Mercy, in a temple on the edge of Lake Chuzenji, above Nikko. It is all carved, from a *single standing tree* except for forty extending arms and hands, which are stuck on to symbolize a thousand.

The meticulous non-tipping honesty of Japanese hotel servants. In the fashionable Fujiya Hotel in Fuji-Hakone National Park, I ordered a bottle of beer, priced at 132 yen. I gave the waitress 135 yen and she promptly gave me 3 yen (less than a cent) in change *as a matter of course*. You don't tip in Japanese hotels—not even 3 yen.

Kyoto as Japan's Hollywood. In this venerable city, untouched by bombs, very many of Japan's finest movie scenes are shot.

The Shrine of the Genji Family in Nara, approached by a path lined with hundreds of stone lanterns. This recalls Japan's most famous classic novel of court life, *The Tale of Genji*, written early in the 11th century by a noble matron named Lady Mura-saki, who was in the service of Empress Akiko.

The subway of Osaka, veteran of Japan's increasing number of metropolitan subways. The one in Osaka started the trend.

The lovely rock gardens enhancing the lobbies of various tourist hotels in Japan. The finest one, brightened with azaleas, lilies and irises, is in the New Osaka Hotel of Osaka.

Lily, a famous lingerie shop in Kobe. Here you may buy the finest handmade silk nightdresses and pajamas, priced at $15 to $35.

A touch of Britain in Kobe—The King's Arms Steak House.

An itinerant "basket priest," encountered in Gifu, on the bank of the Nagara River—"where cormorants fish for fun" (Chapter 9). These Buddhist mendicants, seen all over Japan, wear inverted baskets over their heads but play a beseeching flute through a mouth hole in the basket.

The husky "pearl girls" of Mikimoto's Pearl Island. These fine plump divers, athletes of the sea, can easily remain underwater for two full minutes.

The Peace Memorial Cathedral of Hiroshima, a striking architectural, as well as spiritual, achievement. A huge gold cross decorates the façade and the simple gray plaster interior is illumined by small but bright stained glass windows back of the altar. A separate belfry is topped by an impressive cross of stone and brick.

A bronze statue to Emperor Kameyama in a park in Fukuoka. His Imperial hat is surmounted by a bronze plume one yard tall!

The Kin Sui En Garden of Beppu, a place that is all things to all men. In the daytime it is a lovely botanical garden with an old armory as a special attraction. In the evening a geisha restaurant flourishes here. At night, by common report, the geishas, unlike their dedicated sisters in Kyoto, are eager to be "companionable" with paying customers.

A house in the city of Kumamoto that was the home of Lafcadio Hearn. This remarkable Irish-Greek wanderer came to Japan in 1891, married a Japanese woman, was naturalized under the name Yakumo Koizumi, adopted the Buddhist religion and wrote a dozen or more books on Japan, some of them classics of their type. He taught English in what is now the University of Kumamoto.

A surprising matins tune heard in Nagasaki. It was *Home Sweet Home,* played fortissimo over a department store's rooftop loudspeaker system and must have been audible over half the city. Very welcome it was to this traveler.

The baby bears of Hokkaido. When they get "awful hungry" they sometimes invade the busy streets of Sapporo itself, searching or begging for food.

A Rotary Club luncheon enjoyed in Sapporo. Scrolls were awarded, along with congratulatory speeches, to the city's Model Postman, Model Fireman, Model Policeman, Model Tram Conductor and Model Street Cleaner. This last was one of the two-and-four women.

The "holiday hotsprings" of Noboribetsu, whose rising steam serves to clothe—sort of—the bathing multitudes. No Westerner who witnesses this climactic scene of Hokkaido ever forgets it.

The thousands of fish ponds and prawn ponds of Luzon, seen from the air as my plane approached Manila. The prospective seafood in these ponds is intensively cultivated by the Philippine government and the pools themselves are soon to become a tourist sight, close up.

The nighttime fishermen of Parañaque, near Manila. Every night they go out en masse in their boats, attracting fish by means of bright flambeaux and then lowering nets to scoop them in. At dawn they return to their home beach.

The amazing traffic of Manila, the "torrents of jeepneys" being interspersed with lesser streams of private motor cars and occasional *calesas* (two-wheeled, horse-drawn beachwagons) and *carretelas* (two-wheeled, two-passenger affairs).

The glorious "coolth" of Baguio-in-the-pines, where Manilans, foreign diplomats and tourists bask in mountain air, well away from the shimmering heat of the Philippine lowlands.

The animated roadstead of Hong Kong, bursting at the seams with widely assorted sea traffic. I recall, for instance, seeing a tiny motor launch towing a string of six or eight junks, each many times larger than the valiant towboat.

The rooftop squatters of Hong Kong. Thousands of unfortunates must still be allowed to camp out in the rudest of shelters on the flat roofs of the city's buildings. The roof squatters pay no rent at all, but those lucky refugees who secure quarters in the new resettlement areas pay all of 65 cents U.S. per month.

The greenest green in the world, being the rice fields of Shatin Valley seen from the terrace of Shatin Heights Hotel in Hong Kong's New Territories.

The imposing British bank buildings of Victoria, higher than any in London and just as solidly built.

The 77-lap Grand Prix Motor Race held every November in Macao. The dwellers in this Portuguese colony assert that this is the only such race held in the Orient.

Firecrackers! These are of the essence of Macao. They are made here in their millions and some of them are exploded here in welcoming ceremonies, in junk launchings and in holiday celebrations. More power to them, for they are *firecrackers of freedom* set off in the Reds' "front yard"!

INDEX

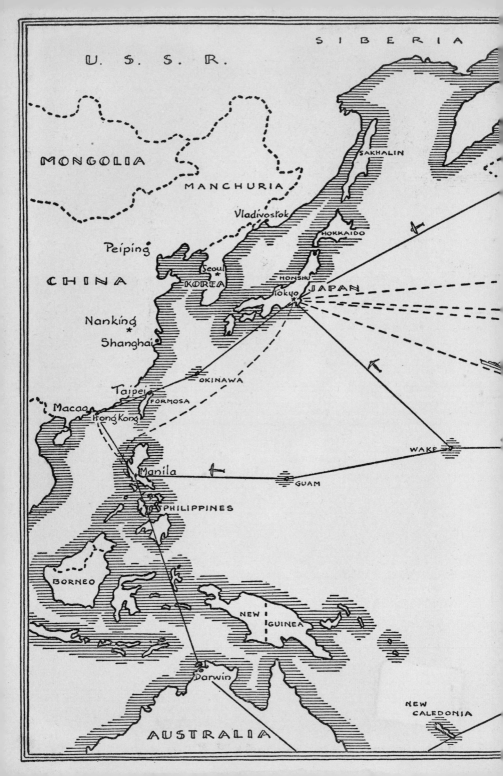